THIRTEENTH CENTURY ENGLAND II

PROCEEDINGS OF
THE NEWCASTLE UPON TYNE CONFERENCE
1987

THIRTEENTH CENTURY ENGLAND
II

PROCEEDINGS OF
THE NEWCASTLE UPON TYNE CONFERENCE
1987

Edited by P. R. Coss and S. D. Lloyd

THE BOYDELL PRESS

First published 1988 by The Boydell Press
an imprint of Boydell & Brewer Ltd
PO Box 9, Woodbridge, Suffolk IP12 3DF
and of Boydell & Brewer Inc.
Wolfeboro, New Hampshire 03894-2069, USA

ISBN 0 85115 513 8

ISSN 0269-6967

British Library Cataloguing in Publication Data
Thirteenth century England. — 2-
1. England ; 1200-1300
942.03′4
ISBN 0-85115-513-8

Library of Congress Cataloguing-in-Publication Data applied for

☉ Printed on long life paper
made to the full American Standard

Printed in Great Britain by
St Edmundsbury Press, Bury St Edmunds, Suffolk

CONTENTS

PREFACE

The second conference on thirteenth-century England took place in early September 1987. Like its predecessor, it was held in Newcastle upon Tyne at the University's Henderson Hall of Residence and the Polytechnic's adjacent campus in Coach Lane. We are, once again, immensely grateful for the hard work and unstinting support on the part of all those who helped make the conference an enjoyable, congenial and fruitful occasion, acknowledging especially the labours of the staff of Henderson Hall and of Coach Lane Campus, the generosity of the Vice-Chancellor of the University (which again made possible our opening reception), and the support of the two Departments of History in subsidizing this venture in co-operation across the institutional divide in higher education establishments. Without that support these would be considerably more expensive conferences for those attending them.

Special thanks, of a different complexion, are due to those who gave papers, as well as to those who animatedly discussed them, in conference session and informally. Regrettably, it has not proved possible to print four of the papers which were delivered, those by Professor Guy Bois, 'Contradictions in the Economic Growth of the Thirteenth Century', Miss Sally Dormer, 'Matthew Paris and the Revival of Tinted Drawing', Dr Clive Knowles, 'The Government of Simon de Montfort', and Miss Susan Reynolds, 'Magna Carta, 1297: Some Problems with the Text'. The twelve papers comprising this second volume of our *Proceedings* are printed here substantially as read, although some have been notably expanded from their original versions.

It is a pleasure to record the following debts of gratitude: to Professor Michael Prestwich for arranging the conference excursion to Durham and acting as guide, and to the staff of the Prior's Kitchen, Durham, for mounting a special exhibition of manuscripts; to the British Academy and the University's Academic Visitors' Fund for grants towards the expenses of Professor Guy Bois; and to our publishers for once again expediting the passage from typescript to print with speed and efficiency.

An index to volumes I – V of the *Proceedings* will appear with volume V. The third conference will be held in Newcastle between 4 and 7 September 1989.

Newcastle upon Tyne, March 1988

Simon Lloyd
Peter Coss

ABBREVIATIONS

Ann. Mon.	*Annales Monastici*, ed. H. R. Luard (RS, 1864 – 9)
BIHR	*Bulletin of the Institute of Historical Research*
BL	British Library
BN	Bibliothèque Nationale
CChR	*Calendar of the Charter Rolls Preserved in the Public Record Office, 1226 – 1516* (London, 1903 – 27)
CCR	*Calendar of the Close Rolls Preserved in the Public Record Office, 1272 – 1307* (London, 1900 – 8)
CDI	*Calendar of Documents Relating to Ireland Preserved in Her Majesty's Record Office, 1171 – 1307*, ed. H. S. Sweetman and G. F. Handcock (London, 1877 – 86)
CDS	*Calendar of Documents Relating to Scotland Preserved in the Public Record Office*, ed. J. Bain (Edinburgh, 1881 – 8)
CFR	*Calendar of the Fine Rolls Preserved in the Public Record Office, 1272 – 1307* (London, 1911)
CIMisc.	*Calendar of Inquisitions Miscellaneous (Chancery) Preserved in the PRO, 1219 – 1349* (London, 1916)
CIPM	*Calendar of Inquisitions Post Mortem in the Public Record Office (Henry III – Edward II)* (London, 1904 – 10)
CLR	*Calendar of Liberate Rolls Preserved in the Public Record Office, 1226 – 1272* (London, 1917 – 64)
CPR	*Calendar of the Patent Rolls Preserved in the Public Record Office, 1232 – 1307* (London, 1898 – 1908)
CR	*Close Rolls of the Reign of Henry III Preserved in the Public Record Office, 1227 – 72* (London, 1902 – 38)
CRR	*Curia Regis Rolls Preserved in the Public Record Office, Richard I-1242* (London, 1922 –)
DBM	*Documents of the Baronial Movement of Reform and Rebellion, 1258 – 1267*, selected R. F. Treharne, ed. I. J. Sanders (Oxford, 1973)
DNB	*Dictionary of National Biography*, ed. L. Stephen and S. Lee (London, 1885 – 1900; repr. 1921 – 7)
EHR	*English Historical Review*
Fees	*Liber Feudorum: The Book of Fees Commonly Called Testa de Nevill, 1198 – 1293* (London, 1920 – 31)
Foedera	*Foedera, conventiones, litterae et cuiuscunque generis acta publica inter reges Angliae et alios quosvis imperatores, reges, pontifices, principes vel communitates, 1101 – 1654*, ed. T. Rymer; new edn., ed. A. Clarke *et al.* (London, 1816 – 69)

GEC	*The Complete Peerage of England, Scotland, Ireland, Great Britain and the United Kingdom by G.E.C.*, ed. V. Gibbs *et al.* (London, 1910 – 59)
HMC	Historical Manuscripts Commission
Journ.	*Journal*
Paris, *CM*	Matthew Paris, *Chronica majora*, ed. H. R. Luard (RS, 1872 – 83)
Powicke, *Henry III*	F. M. Powicke, *King Henry III and the Lord Edward: The Community of the Realm in the Thirteenth Century* (Oxford, 1947)
PR	*Patent Rolls of the Reign of Henry III Preserved in the Public Record Office, 1216 – 32* (London, 1901 – 3)
Procs.	*Proceedings*
PRO	Public Record Office
Rec. Comm.	Record Commission
Rec. ser.	Record series
Rec. soc.	Record society
RF	*Excerpta e Rotulis Finium in Turri Londinensi asservatis, 1216 – 72*, ed. C. Roberts (London, 1835 – 6)
RH	*Rotuli Hundredorum temp. Hen. III et Edw. I in turr. Lond. et in curia receptae scaccarii West. asservati* (London, 1812 – 18)
RLC	*Rotuli Litterarum Clausarum in Turri Londinensi asservati, 1204 – 27*, ed. T. D. Hardy (London, 1833 – 44)
RLP	*Rotuli Litterarum Patentium in Turri Londinensi asservati, 1201 – 16*, ed. T. D. Hardy (London, 1835)
Rot. Parl.	*Rotuli Parliamentorum* (London, 1783 – 1832)
Royal Letters	*Royal and Other Historical Letters Illustrative of the Reign of Henry III*, ed. W. W. Shirley (RS, 1862 – 6)
RS	(Rolls Series) *Rerum Brittanicarum Medii Aevi Scriptores* (London, 1858 – 96)
ser.	series
Soc.	Society
Trans.	*Transactions*
TRHS	*Transactions of the Royal Historical Society*
VCH	*Victoria History of the Counties of England*, ed. H. A. Doubleday *et al.* (London, 1900 –)

War and Chivalry in the *History of William the Marshal*

John Gillingham

Ever since the *History of William the Marshal* was discovered in the late nineteenth century it has been universally recognized as a document of the very greatest importance: the earliest vernacular life of a layman in European history.[1] In Antonia Gransden's words, 'just as Jocelin of Brakelond gives a unique account of the life in the cloister', so the *History* offers 'a unique picture of the chivalric society'.[2] Thanks to the work of Paul Meyer, Sidney Painter, Jessie Crosland and now Georges Duby, there can be little doubt that, leaving aside kings and clerics, William the Marshal is better known than any other figure of the twelfth or thirteenth centuries. Yet, despite its fame, the *History* remains in some ways a curiously neglected source. This is because historians have come to the *History* knowing what they were looking for and confident that they would find it. For Painter it was the portrait of a 'typical feudal baron', the knight-errant who after years on the tournament-circuit finally settled down with his heiress wife to the life of the great landowner and, ultimately, elder statesman.[3] For Crosland it offered a literary atmosphere reminiscent of the *chansons de geste*, 'when physical courage and loyalty were the two qualities most to be admired in a knight, and romantic adventure and the cult of the woman had no place'.[4] For Duby it provided welcome confirmation of his views on the patterns of inheritance and marriage, and on the role of the *juvenes* in the shaping of aristocratic society.[5] In Duby's case, indeed,

---

[1] *L'Histoire de Guillaume le Maréchal*, ed. P. Meyer (Société de l'Histoire de France, 1891 – 1901). Quotations from the text, and references to this edition will be given as *HGM* hereafter. I would like to thank Maurice Keen and Malcolm Vale for their kindness and generosity in reading and commenting on this paper. Although *The Poem of the Cid* is earlier, it contains far too many fictional elements to be regarded as a genuine biography.

[2] A. Gransden, *Historical Writing in England c. 550 to c. 1307* (London, 1974), 345.

[3] S. Painter, *William Marshal* (Baltimore, 1933), viii.

[4] J. Crosland, *William the Marshal* (London, 1962), 13 – 14. While it is true there is no 'cult of the woman' in the *History*, nonetheless William did go out of his way to help, not a damsel, but an old woman in distress during the fire at Le Mans which threatened to engulf her and her property: *HGM* 8753 – 72. Indeed it is worth noting that, as the *History* tells the story, conspicuous gallantry in the service of great ladies was crucial to the social ascent of both William and his father, John Marshal — William as escort to Eleanor of Aquitaine in 1168, and his father as escort to the Empress Matilda in 1141. William may not have performed prodigies of prowess 'for love of a fair lady'; nonetheless, the chief reward for his good service was the hand of a great heiress, 'la pucelle' who, in the words of the poem, 'fu bone et bele': *HGM* 8303 – 4.

[5] G. Duby, *Guillaume le Maréchal ou le meilleur chevalier du monde* (Paris, 1984). An English translation with the sub-title, *The Flower of Chivalry*, was published in the USA in 1985 and in the UK in 1986, but since the translation is a particularly poor one, I shall refer only to the French edition.

1

there is one occasion when, on reading the *History* and not finding what he expected to find, he simply invented it.

He expected to find that the day when William was made a knight was given its due prominence, and so he argues that the poet decided to make his narrative of a real battle — the fight at Drincourt — do service as a description of the chivalric exercise which must have been held to celebrate so great a day in the young warrior's life. The fact, Duby tells us, that the poet wrenched an engagement which really occurred in 1173 out of its proper place in the sequence of events, and put it instead in 1167, at about the time of the knighting, reveals very clearly just how determined the poet was to provide the proper setting for, and so emphasize the crucial importance of, the young man's entry into knighthood.[6] Unfortunately, however, Duby got it wrong. The fight at Drincourt, as the poet describes it in 360 lines of verse, was between, on the one side, a party of Normans led by William de Mandeville and the young William's own lord, the chamberlain of Tancarville (who were defending the town of Drincourt), and, on the other, an invading force led by the counts of Flanders, Boulogne and Ponthieu.[7] Now, if this fight really had taken place in 1173, as Duby asserts, then William the Marshal, by that time in the service of the Young King (Henry II's eldest surviving son), should have been fighting on the side of Philip of Flanders, the Young King's ally in the revolt against his father. In 1173 William would have been attacking the town, not defending it.[8] The fact is that Duby's date, 1173, is the one year in which this particular fight could *not* have occurred. The evidence, such as there is, suggests that it actually happened in 1167, a minor incident — minor in the sense of not being noticed by any surviving chronicle — in a campaign noticed only by Gervase of Canterbury.[9] In that case, of course, it occurred precisely at the point in time at which the poet's narrative suggests it occurred. In other words there was no deliberate chronological dislocation on the part of the poet, and equally, therefore, no peculiarly revealing insight into the chivalrous mentality.

There is, however, a revealing insight into the mentality of modern historians. Few of us, I hope, go quite as far as Duby, but we all tend to see in the *History* what we want to see. Quite rightly, we see William as a model of chivalry: that, after all, is how he is presented. He had been, said the archbishop of Canterbury, at his funeral, 'the best knight in the world', and, says his thirteenth-century biographer, 'the story of his life ought to encourage all good men who hear it'.[10] Knowing perfectly well what a model of chivalry should be like, that is what we read into the *History of William the Marshal*, and in consequence we leave a great deal out. As an example of what I mean, let me cite the treatment of the work by one of the finest

---

[6] Duby, 86 – 8. Here Duby re-interprets Meyer's view that at this point the poet's narrative had simply become hopelessly confused: *HGM* iii. 16, n. 2, and 34, n. 2. Also following Meyer, yet moving in a different direction, G. H. White dated William's knighting to 1173: *GEC* x. 358. On the other hand, Duby's suggestion that William may have been knighted 'anonymously', as just one of a group, is a very reasonable speculation.

[7] *HGM* 805 – 1166.

[8] As pointed out long ago by Kate Norgate, *The Minority of Henry III* (London, 1912), 64, n. 2; and then, following her, by Painter, 20, n. 19. For Duby's own assessment of his use of Painter, Duby, 47.

[9] *The Historical Works of Gervase of Canterbury*, ed. W. Stubbs (RS, 1879 – 80), i. 203.

[10] *HGM* 19,072, 19,162 – 4. And whatever Henry III, that fine judge of men, may have thought, this is how he continued to be perceived. But, as Richard Marshal may have discovered to his cost, it is not always an advantage to have a father who is a hero-figure. See Paris, *CM* iii. 43, 273 – 6; iv. 157.

historians of chivalry, Maurice Keen. After summarizing William's early career, his tournaments, his role as the Young King's 'tutor' in chivalry, and his journey to the Holy Land — all of this brings us to 1187 when William was about forty years old — Keen goes on to write that 'the details of William's subsequent career need not detain us'.[11] Why need they not detain us? After all, in one of Keen's favourite texts, the *Livre de Chevalerie* of Geoffrey de Charny, we are explicitly and emphatically told that those who distinguish themselves in 'the great business of war' deserve higher praise than those who shine in jousts and tournaments, for 'war passes all other manner of arms'.[12] So why do we not hear of William's subsequent career in the highest arena of chivalry, of his role in the Angevin-Capetian struggle — 'the great war', as the poet calls it (*HGM* 7365), which started in 1188 —, of his role as *rector regis et regni* in the civil war of 1216 – 17?[13]

Reading modern authors, one might be forgiven for believing that the *History* has little to say about war, so little attention do they pay to it. Thus Gransden describes the *History* as a work which 'belongs to the artificial world of the knights errant', 'less concerned with heroism in real battles aimed at actual military advantage than with displays of bravery at tournaments'.[14] But this is not so. On my count, in a poem of 19,214 lines there are about 3150 lines dealing with tournaments, compared with some 8350 dealing with war — of which about 6800 describe the warfare of 1188 and after; they therefore belong to the details of William's subsequent career. Of course, it is true that those verses on tournaments possess rarity value. Other vernacular works describe warfare — Jordan Fantosme's *Chronique*, for example, or Ambroise's *Estoire de la Guerre Sainte*, or the *Histoire des ducs de Normandie* — but none contains anything remotely approaching the *History*'s detailed account of tournament after tournament. So it is perhaps only natural that historians should have been bowled over by the passages concerning tournaments and in consequence think of William chiefly as a bachelor knight, a tournament champion.[15] But they should not have forgotten to count what can be

---

[11] M. Keen, *Chivalry* (New Haven, London, 1984), 20 – 1.

[12] Charny's *Le Livre de Chevalerie* was printed by K. de Lettenhove in his *Oeuvres de Froissart*, I, parts 2 – 3 (Brussels, 1872), 463 – 533. 'ainsi comme l'on doit honorer bonnes gens d'armes et ainsi comme il appartient a eulx de si tres-noble oevre comme de fait d'armes de guerre qui passe tous autres, excepte Dieu servir' (p. 466). Charny goes on to distinguish jousts (individual encounters between *gens d'armes*), tournaments (encounters between teams of *gens d'armes*), and war: 'Et pour ce doit – l'en priser plus et honorer gens d'armes pour la guerre que nulles autres gens d'armes qui soient'; and this is because 'ces deux mestiers d'armes [i.e., jousts and tournaments] sont tous compris ou fait d'armes de guerre'. (Charny, 466; cf. 473).

[13] Concentrating on the years before 1188 has the effect of emphasizing that period in William's life when he was the ideal young knight and minimizing that even longer period when he was the ideal mature knight. In general, historians of chivalry have been attracted to the type of behaviour appropriate to the young man — the knight errantry and the individualism — and in consequence have tended to neglect the more prudential behaviour of the knight with responsibilities. What the *History* makes clear is that although good knights were expected to behave differently at different stages of their career (*HGM* 11,247 – 56), nonetheless they all belonged to a single military society governed by a single code of honour. Within that society it was the experienced knights who wielded power and who, not surprisingly, were the ones to be listened to. Charny, 475: 'Car par raison ils en doivent miex parler, aprendre et conseiller que li autre, car ils ont veu et sceu, fait, este et essaie en toutes manieres d'armes'.

[14] Gransden, 345.

[15] On the basis of these passages Duby, 111 – 37, provides a fine analysis of tournaments. Cf. G. Duby, *Le Dimanche de Bouvines* (Paris, 1973), 111 – 28. It is as a tournament champion that the Marshal leaves his mark in R. Barber, *The Knight and Chivalry* (London, 1970).

counted, and the fact is that the *History* gives well over twice as much space to war as it does to tournaments. Thus Duby is quite right to say that the stage on which William and his fellows move is the theatre of war.[16] Yet, though he then offers us a long and excellent analysis of tournaments, he says very little about war, and that little, as I shall make clear, is mostly rubbish.[17]

But if the historian of chivalry takes Geoffrey de Charny's order of priorities seriously, then should he not look carefully at the paragon of chivalry at war? As Maurice Keen writes, 'if ever a knight lived up to Geoffrey's principle of chivalrous prowess, it was surely William Marshal'.[18] Yet, so far as I know, no historian of chivalry has tried to do so. Perhaps, it might be thought, because they have left that side of William's life to the specialists, to the historians of war. But if we look at Contamine, at Verbruggen, at Lot, at Oman, we find that they have not done so either.[19] So we reach the curious conclusion that neither the historians of war, nor the historians of chivalry, nor indeed the modern biographers of William the Marshal have made any real attempt to investigate the Marshal's military career. It is all the more curious in view of the traditional opinion that medieval warfare was, in essence, knightly warfare.[20] All the more curious, too, in view of the considerable interest in the relationship between war and chivalry.[21] For where could we hope to find out what a thirteenth-century writer thought knightly warfare was, or chivalry was, if not in the pages of the *History of William the Marshal*? This, then, is my intention in this paper: to see how war was perceived by an extraordinarily well-informed vernacular author, writing in the 1220s, and writing, I imagine, for an audience who themselves knew a great deal about war. Thus I am not so much concerned with what really happened as with what this author said had happened. Naturally, I too shall see in the *History of William the Marshal* exactly what I want to see.

I begin where Maurice Keen left off. The year is 1188. William has returned from the Holy Land and has entered the service of King Henry II: 'De sa maisne le

---

[16] 'Ce fut entouré de guerriers que Guillaume vécut et agit. Ils occupent tout son souvenir': Duby, *Guillaume*, 68 – 9.

[17] All we get are passing references to Montmirail, Arras and Milli (out of the 1400 lines which the poet devoted to the war of 1192 – 9), and a page on the battle of Lincoln, mostly taken up by William's pre-battle speeches (out of more than 2500 lines on the war of 1215 – 17).

[18] Keen, 21. Charny's oft-repeated principle was 'Qui plus fait, miex vault.'

[19] The only reference to William in P. Contamine, *War in the Middle Ages* (trans. M. Jones, London, 1984), 216, is to the tournaments of his day. According to J. F. Verbruggen, *The Art of Warfare in Western Europe during the Middle Ages* (trans. S. Willard and S. C. M. Southern, Amsterdam, 1977), 14, the *History* is 'very useful', but he attempts no analysis of it and uses it chiefly to illustrate tournament practice. He also claims (p. 16), on grounds which are not clear to me, that the author of the *History* failed to understand what happened at Fréteval (1194), when William was in command of a force which Richard I held in reserve. So far as I can see there is only one brief footnote reference (on Bouvines) in the whole of F. Lot, *L'Art Militaire et les Armées au Moyen Age* (Paris, 1946), i. 229, n. 8. As might be expected, C. W. Oman, *The Art of War in the Middle Ages* (London, 1898), 407 – 13, merely used the *History* in his reconstruction of the battle of Lincoln. So did T. F. Tout, 'The Fair of Lincoln and the "Histoire de Guillaume le Maréchal" ', *EHR* xviii (1903), 240 – 65.

[20] E.g., the title of M. Howard, *War in European History* (Oxford, 1976), ch. 1, is 'The Wars of the Knights'.

[21] See M. Vale, *War and Chivalry* (London, 1981). However, as its subtitle — 'Warfare and Aristocratic Culture in England, France and Burgundy at the End of the Middle Ages' — indicates, this is principally concerned with a different period.

retint / de ses hals consels le fist mestre'.[22] Presumably it was his new position in the royal household which allowed William, in his turn, to recruit new servants, among whom was John of Early, the man whose memories or *mémoires*, or both, served as the basis around which a professional *trouvère* composed our history.[23] So, for several reasons, the year 1188 is an important one in the life of the Marshal. It is also the year in which he gave his first recorded advice on how to make war.

King Philip II of France has launched an attack on the castle and town of Gisors. It failed; indeed, in the course of it a charge of the supposedly invincible French knights, lances lowered, was twice beaten off by the spears of Henry's 'boen servant' — not the kind of thing that is supposed to happen in medieval warfare before the battle of Courtrai in 1302 — and the disgruntled Capetian army, after demonstrating its prowess by chopping down the famous elm of Gisors, withdrew into Capetian territory and dispersed.[24] As soon as he heard this news, William goes to speak to his lord:

> Listen to me sire. Philip has divided and disbanded his troops. I advise you to disperse your men too, but to give them secret orders to re-assemble at a given time and place. From there they are to launch a *chevauchée* into the territory of the king of France. If this is done in force, prudently and promptly, then he will find he has to suffer far greater damage than the loss of one elm. This will be a better and a finer deed.

'By God's eyes', said the king, 'Marshal, you are most courteous ('molt corteis') and have given me good advice. I shall do exactly as you suggest.' And he did. He ordered his army to disband and then quietly to muster again at Pacy. It crossed the frontier and burned and ravaged all the land between there and Mantes. William des Barres and some other knights of the French king's household, then based at Mantes, did their best to prevent it, but they had been deceived by the initial manoeuvre and were hopelessly outnumbered. At the end of the day Henry's men marched into Ivry, loaded down with plunder and well-satisfied with themselves. The poet then reports a conversation between Henry and his warlike son Richard, in which they agree to give all the credit for this day's work to the Marshal's good advice.[25]

In the very next episode, later that same year, Henry decided to surprise his enemies by launching a mid-winter attack from Chinon. His orders to his men were that they should ride day and night until they reached the vicinity of Montmirail; then they were to burn and destroy everything in sight, sparing nobody, seize the town, sack it and burn it. And, led by the Marshal, that is exactly what they did. On

---

[22] *HGM* 7308 – 9.

[23] *HGM* iii. vii – xiv; Gransden, 346; M. D. Legge, *Anglo-Norman Literature and its Background* (Oxford, 1963), 306 – 8.

[24] *HGM* 7436 – 781, esp. 7738 – 69. The dispersal of the French troops is confirmed by William the Breton in *Oeuvres de Rigord et de Guillaume le Breton*, ed. H-F. Delaborde (Paris, 1882 – 5), i. 189.

[25] *HGM* 7782 – 852.

their return the Old King declared himself well-pleased with the results of their *chevauchée*.[26]

And so it goes on. Sometimes it is William who is on the receiving end, as in 1218 when the Welsh prince, Morgan of Caerleon, ravages the Marshal's lands, burning (we are told) twenty-two churches in the process.[27] Whether, as on these occasions, we are given details, or whether we get no more than a casual, passing reference to the 'doing of damage', it is clear that the poet, like the authors of *chansons de geste*, regards these ravaging expeditions as the normal business of war.[28] It is clear, too, that the poet understood the dual function of the raid: to gain plunder and to put pressure on the enemy. In his own words, 'for when the poor can no longer reap a harvest from their fields, then they can no longer pay their rents and this, in turn, impoverishes their lords'.[29] It is clear, too, from the way he tells the stories of the Gisors and Montmirail episodes, that the well-organized *chevauchée* was one which took the enemy by surprise. The intention was not to seek out the enemy's knights and meet them in a head-on clash of arms. On the contrary, the aim was to send his armed forces in the wrong direction, and then, in their absence, to destroy his economic resources, the fields and flocks of his people. This was how the Marshal made war, and this is how the Marshal said war should be made. And note the poet's language. When the Marshal offered this good advice, he was 'molt corteis'.[30] This, in other words, is chivalrous warfare.

How does the Marshal's advice fit in with Duby's view that William 'was blessed with a brain too small to impede the natural vigour of a big, powerful and tireless physique'?[31] It does not, of course, and Duby nowhere mentions this example of William's military advice. On the other hand, he does cite another case in which William had advice to offer. In 1197 Count Baldwin of Flanders was laying siege to a town (probably Arras) when King Philip approached with a relieving army. The Flemish barons recommended using the communal carts together with their militias as a kind of barrier fortress, a retreat before which the knights could safely offer battle to the French. William, however, opposed this. In his view the carts should be left behind while the knights moved out in battle array, ready to confront the enemy in open field.[32] This, claims Duby, was the characteristic attitude of the true knight: temerity has dethroned prudence.[33] But this is a hopelessly one-sided

---

[26] *HGM* 7872 – 8048. Note the use of the word 'chevalchie' (line 8047, as earlier in line 7792) and the verbal form 'chevacha' (line 7835) and 'chivalchiez' (line 7886).

[27] *HGM* 17,748 – 864.

[28] I doubt if a line recurs more frequently than variants of 'maint ennui li fist et maint mal' (*HGM* 148, 282, 367, etc.). That the authors of *chansons de geste* also regarded ravaging as commonplace was pointed out by M. Bennett, 'The Status of the Squire: the Northern Evidence', in *The Ideals and Practice of Medieval Knighthood*, ed. C. Harper-Bill and R. Harvey (Woodbridge, 1986), 4. For further comment on the function of ravaging, see J. Gillingham, 'Richard I and the Science of War in the Middle Ages', in *War and Government in the Middle Ages. Essays in Honour of J. O. Prestwich*, ed. J. Gillingham and J. C. Holt (Woodbridge, 1984), 78 – 91.

[29] *HGM* 659 – 69.

[30] *HGM* 7800.

[31] Duby, *Guillaume*, 186. This judgment is at the heart of Duby's summing-up of the Marshal's career and reputation.

[32] *HGM* 10,783 – 840.

[33] Duby, *Guillaume*, 107. He made the same point, on the evidence of the same episode, in Duby, *Dimanche*, 136.

interpretation of this incident. For one thing, leaving the carts behind is presented not as a bold gesture of defiance but as a tactical device; the role of the carts and their troops is to prevent the townspeople making a sortie and taking the besiegers in the rear. For another, when Philip's scouts reported the reception which Count Baldwin, in conformity with William's advice, had prepared for him, he decided to withdraw and leave Arras to its fate.[34] So is this an episode which illustrates chivalrous temerity? Or is it one which emphasizes knightly caution? The poet, incidentally, approved Philip's decision. For him, too, there was no wisdom in risking battle where one had no clear-cut advantage.[35] There is further evidence of the poet's own attitude to battle in his account of Bouvines. Once again we find the French under Philip retreating in order to avoid an engagement, and if this time they win the day it is only because the over-confident allies forced a battle before the bulk of Otto IV's forces had had time to come up. In doing this they had gone against the count of Boulogne's advice. 'Let them go', he had said, 'for the land will then be ours for the taking', and it is clear that the poet agreed. 'If they [i.e. the allies] had only waited until the morrow', he writes, 'then they would have won great honour.'[36] Contrast this with Duby's dictum on the knight: 'Honour compelled him to appear intrepid, even to the point of folly.'[37] One of the odd things about Duby's view of the knight at war is that it is at odds with his own analysis of the knight in training for war. For he points out that in tournaments victory was the reward not of ardour but of discipline.[38] Not that he seems to be aware of this contradiction; sadly, these days, Duby seems to be blessed with a brain too small to impede the natural facility of his tireless pen.[39]

An episode which is peculiarly revealing of the pre-occupations of modern historians is the *History*'s account of Richard I's campaign in the Beauvaisis in 1197. What all modern writers seize upon is the moment when the Marshal threw himself into the assault on the castle of Milli and went up the scaling-ladder like a young man.[40] Duby uses this remarkable display of courage and prowess by a man in his fifties and, in Duby's words, 'already creaking at the joints', in order to characterise the Marshal's good service in Richard's wars.[41] But what he does not

---

[34] *HGM* 10,827 – 32, 10,867 – 81.

[35] *HGM* 10,882 – 90.

[36] *HGM* 14,746 – 800.

[37] Duby, *Guillaume*, 107. When medievalists say this kind of thing it is hardly surprising that a modern historian should write of the 'old chivalry of the feudal host in which every man charged for himself, concerned as much with personal honour as with victory': Howard, 16.

[38] Duby, *Guillaume*, 123. It is, of course, now conventional to emphasize the close similarity between tournaments and real engagements, and, therefore, the value of the sport as training for war — a point made by Roger of Howden in the twelfth century, Geoffrey de Charny in the fourteenth and, most recently, by Juliet Barker in the twentieth. See J. R. V. Barker, *The Tournament in England 1100 – 1400* (Woodbridge, 1986), esp. 17ff. One additional point could perhaps be made: that tournaments trained men to fight together in small groups of friends. For the importance of this in war, see J. Keegan, *The Face of Battle* (London, 1976), 51 – 2, 71 – 2, citing the findings of the study of human behaviour in combat made by the US Army Historical Service.

[39] Harsh words perhaps, but no harsher than his own judgment on William Marshal, who is in no position to answer back. And given the astonishing achievement of Duby's early writings, the relatively poor quality of his recent works is doubly distressing.

[40] *HGM* 11,169 – 231.

[41] Duby, *Guillaume*, 171.

point out is that William's actions were criticized as being foolhardy and inappropriate — and criticized by none other than Richard I, the king whom the poet calls 'le meillor prince del monde'.[42] At least both Painter and Crosland, in their much fuller accounts of this incident, do find space for Richard's criticism, yet neither they, nor (so far as I can see) anyone else has thought it worthwhile to set the incident in the context of the campaign.[43] And yet, again, the context is one of secret orders, an undercover muster and then a sudden attack, in this case by two columns operating in tandem. One column, under Richard's personal command, having taken Milli by surprise, was able to capture it by assault; the other column, consisting of the *routiers* under Mercadier's command, succeeded in capturing one of Richard's great enemies, the bishop of Beauvais, and took so many other prisoners that, according to the poet, there was no room anywhere to put one's feet.[44] Now the *History* reports all of this, but not modern historians. This suggests that the thirteenth-century view of knightly warfare was both more complex and more comprehensive than that of modern writers. Clearly, like modern scholars, our thirteenth-century author was drawn to the compelling image of the middle-aged knight on the scaling ladder, but unlike them, he did not allow that image to fill his mind to the exclusion of everything else.

As in these episodes, so also in many others. Time and again we hear of one commander trying to surprise his opponent. Indeed, the first military action in the *History* occurs when King Stephen raced to the relief of Winchester in 1141 and took the empress Matilda so much by surprise that she was forced to 'hitch up her skirts' and ride like a man.[45] According to the poet, Stephen's next coup was to surprise the garrison of Newbury. Here, indeed, the word 'surprise' occurs three times in the space of twelve lines.[46] Time and again the author emphasizes the rapidity of troop movements. A commander in a hurry might persuade his troops to press on after dinner, as when King Richard rode to the relief of Verneuil in 1194.[47] We hear, too, of night marches, as in the attack on Montmirail, and as used by William's father, John Marshal, to ambush Patrick of Salisbury's men outside Winchester in 1141.[48] Or by Henry II when, in 1173, he strove to capture his rebellious eldest son. Although Henry's swoop failed to capture the Young King, it created such a state of panic in the rebels' camp that they had to resort to the emergency measure of having him hastily knighted by the best man immediately to

[Handwritten left margin:] it is a pity that we have no treatise similar to the numerous Renaissance and early modern

[Handwritten across middle:] Arts of War to establish exactly what is permissable and what isn't. But the sources we have do hint at defensive ma[...] [...]ring (fencing, armour), offensive [...]

---

[42] *HGM* 11,247 – 56, 11,766. Curiously, Duby refers to Richard's reproach at Milli elsewhere in his book (p. 124) in his discussion of tournaments. But, as already noted, Duby allows discipline and self-discipline a far greater place in tournaments than in war. Similarly, although Duby mentions another occasion when William's rash actions (on the bridge at Montmirail) were criticized by the best knights present, Baldwin de Béthune and Hugh de Hardincourt (*HGM* 7996 – 8003), he goes on to draw conclusions which do not require him to modify his view of what constitutes 'proper knightly behaviour': Duby, *Guillaume*, 109.

[43] Painter, 111; Crosland, 78.

[44] *HGM* 11,106 – 280.

[45] *HGM* 183 – 225.

[46] *HGM* 200 – 11.

[47] *HGM* 10,453 – 63.

[48] *HGM* 299 – 354. In consequence Earl Patrick's men were not wearing armour when attacked and were routed, losing a great deal of baggage. But twenty-seven years later this lesson seems to have been forgotten, this time with fatal consequences for the earl. See below, 11.

[Handwritten notes among footnotes:] (in the Strategicon, a Byzantine treatise, there are many instances. Though [...] far from western Chivalry it is not beyond chivalric warriors of W. and central Europe to use sim[...] gen[...]

[Handwritten bottom:] — > i.e. rolling carcasses (thrown into a city to spread disease), sieges to "starve the population into surrender", etc. — ambushes, etc.

hand, that is our hero.[49] All this was in accord with the maxim of Vegetius: 'courage is worth more than numbers, and speed is worth more than courage'.[50]

Inevitably, then, we constantly find commanders haunted by the fear of being taken by surprise.[51] Naturally, in these circumstances, the competent commander was acutely aware of the importance of good reconnaissance. The *History* contains several object lessons on how to carry out effective reconnaissance. In 1189, for example, Henry II, at bay at Le Mans, sent William out on patrol in the early morning mist; the Marshal made sure they got close enough to the Capetian forces to obtain accurate information about their numbers and disposition, and he resisted the temptation to pick up easy plunder so as not to jeopardise what was essentially a news-gathering mission.[52] In another example we hear how in 1202 William Marshal and the earls of Salisbury and Warenne, having ridden out themselves to check information which their scouts had brought them — that Philip Augustus had given up the siege of Arques — at once decided that discretion was the better part and beat a hasty retreat when they realised that the Capetian, taking advantage of a concealed valley, had sent against them a well-armed intercepting force under the command of William des Barres.[53] One of the other lessons of that episode — that a good commander should check the accuracy of information coming in — is further developed in the account of how Richard the Lionheart, by good reconnaissance, using both local knights and his own eyes, was able to take Philip by surprise at Gisors in 1198 and come within a hair's breadth of capturing him.[54]

It is against a background of assumptions like this that the poet tells the story of the climax of William's career, the war of 1216 – 17. When, on the very day of the child Henry III's coronation, William is informed of a threat to his own castle at Goodrich, he at once sends a force of knights, sergeants and crossbowmen on a night march to its relief.[55] During their march to Winchester in the spring of 1217, the earl of Salisbury and the young Marshal — for whom, of course, the *History*

---

[49] *HGM* 2024, 2038 – 9, 2161 – 2.

[50] Cited by Contamine, 252. On the use of Vegetius see Contamine, 210 – 11, and Gillingham, 'Richard I', 82 – 7, and the works cited there. Thus Ross was wide of the mark when he suggested that, even at the time of writing, 'Vegetius was hopelessly out of date': D. J. A. Ross, 'The Prince Answers Back: "Les Enseignements de Theodore Paliologue" ', in *Ideals and Practice*, ed. Harper-Bill and Harvey, 165. Eternal common-sense principles — R. C. Smail's description of Vegetius's strategic maxims — do not date.

[51] *HGM* 524, 12,235 – 40, 14,746. These lines refer to Stephen at Newbury in 1152, to Philip Augustus when withdrawing from Arques in 1202, and to Philip again on the eve of Bouvines. See also below, 10.

[52] *HGM* 8381 – 478.

[53] *HGM* 12,251 – 314.

[54] *HGM* 10,924 – 11,012. Note also that William of Poitiers, himself an old soldier, in his life of William the Conqueror compares William favourably both with the great generals of antiquity and with modern commanders in that William was prepared to go out on reconnaissance patrol himself, instead of leaving it all to subordinates. Obviously there were risks, but accurate information was all-important. 'Fuit illorum et est ducum consuetudinis, dirigere non ire exploratores: magis ad vitam sibi, quam ut exercitui providentiam suam conservarent. Guillelmus vero cum viginti quinque, non amplius militum comitatu promptus ipse loca et incolas exploravit': Guillaume de Poitiers, *Histoire de Guillaume le Conquérant*, ed. R. Foreville (Paris, 1952), 168. Even in a tournament 'scouts' were useful, as when at the great tournament of Lagny (1180) the seneschal of Flanders kept a squadron of thirty knights clear of the *melée* until a knight sent him word of the precarious plight of the Young King: *HGM* 4935 – 51.

[55] *HGM* 15,352.

was written — take good care to avoid being ambushed.[56] Later that year, Prince Louis of France, because he feared a sudden attack on London, hastily abandoned his siege of Dover.[57] And as for the two critical battles of 1217, one of them, Lincoln, may have reminded the old man of his tournament years, but even a work in praise of the Marshal makes it clear that it was the brilliant reconnaissance work of Peter des Roches which created the decisive advantage. By finding a hidden entrance the bishop of Winchester enabled the royalists to take the French so much by surprise that their master of artillery was killed by men he believed to be on his own side.[58] The old man's last charge captures the imagination, but it was only the icing on the cake.[59] Incidentally, so far as I can see, it was also the first time since Drincourt in 1167 — exactly fifty years earlier — that William had charged into battle, so rare an event was the battle charge of the heavily-armoured knight. No wonder the old fellow was so out of practice that he forgot to put on his helmet.[60] Similarly, at least the way the *History* tells it, it was not audacity but deviousness which won the battle of Sandwich in 1217. By ensuring that his cog was lightly laden and therefore rode high in the water, William enabled his sergeants to throw potfuls of blinding chalk-dust into the eyes of the unfortunate French.[61]

The use of this method, clearly with the poet's approval, raises the question of what was, or was not, considered unchivalrous. Just as the kinds of tournament tricks which Philip of Flanders employed seem to have been regarded as perfectly respectable behaviour,[62] so also in war there was clearly nothing dishonourable about deceiving the enemy, particularly if it permitted one to ravage his lands without interruption.[63] Was anything unchivalrous? In a tournament it would appear that it was unchivalrous to make off with the prize which another knight had taken, especially when that other knight was William — though even this seems to have been a debatable point of honour.[64] And what about in war? In passing, the poet makes it clear, as one would expect, that it was dishonourable to surrender a castle all too readily, as the defenders of Carrickfergus did in 1210, and honourable to resist stoutly, as William de Silli did at Le Mans in 1189, and William Mortimer at Verneuil in 1194 and at Arques in 1202.[65] Equally to be expected is his disapproval of the anxiety of some of the French knights at Gisors in 1198 to save their own necks — behaviour all the more reprehensible because it jeopardised the safety of

[handwritten margin note: ⇒ can it seems that some historians like Co read "chivalry" in the context of later perceptions of honour]

---

[56] *HGM* 15,920 – 4.

[57] *HGM* 17,069 – 84.

[58] *HGM* 16,629 – 42.

[59] In his account of Lincoln, Duby, *Guillaume*, 182 – 3, goes straight from the Marshal's speech to the Marshal's charge. In this version there is no room for Peter des Roches, 'qui fu mestre cel jor de conseillier nos genz': *HGM* 16,998 – 9.

[60] *HGM* 16,597 – 604. More generally, on the rarity of the charge in a pitched battle, see Gillingham, 'Richard I', 80 – 1, 91.

[61] *HGM* 17,381 – 404. *[handwritten: ⟶ stratagem]*

[62] *HGM* 2723 – 9, 4821 – 916.

[63] For an explicit justification of both deception and ravaging by a fourteenth-century canonist, see Honoré Bonet, *The Tree of Battles*, ed. G. W. Coopland (Liverpool, 1949), 154 – 5. And as he puts it (p. 154), 'if sometimes the humble and innocent suffer harm and lose their goods, it cannot be otherwise'.

[64] *HGM* 3965 – 4284. For similar quarrels after real fights see M. Keen, *The Laws of War in the Late Middle Ages* (London, 1965), 164 – 6.

[65] *HGM* 14,276 – 8, 8878 – 86, 10,468 – 80, 12,044 – 55.

their king.[66] But there are only two occasions when the poet goes out of his way to call a course of action shameful. One was the killing of Earl Patrick in 1168, struck down from behind when he himself was unarmed.[67] The other takes us back once again to 1167 and to Drincourt — to William's first experience of war. As the count of Flanders moved up to attack the town, so the constable of Normandy prepared to move out. Seeing him go, the chamberlain, William's lord, called out, 'Sire, it would be great shame on him who lets this town burn.' Later on, the poet describes the constable's departure as 'villainous', and says why — because it put the town in great danger of being plundered and burned to the ground.[68] Undoubtedly it is true that the ensuing fight at Drincourt is described in language very like that used to describe a tournament — as Meyer, Crosland and Duby have all emphasized[69] — but it clearly was very much more than two teams of knights having fun by playing at war. A town and its inhabitants were to be saved from destruction, and it was this purpose which made the fight a notably honourable one. Equally, of course, there was nothing dishonourable about the intentions of the attackers. In a similar situation William would do exactly the same.[70] What was shameful was for the knight whose role it was to defend the people to fail to do so when the moment came.[71] Fortunately no one behaved shamefully at Lincoln, but the message, made explicit in William's two speeches to his men, was still essentially the same one. They were fighting not only for their honour but also for their wives,[72] their children and their land, even for the very existence of their country.[73] Thus, in William's last war, as in his first, we find the same message: war is not fought for the sake of individual gain, whether glory, reputation or material reward, but for

tournament —> ceremonial.

---

[66] *HGM* 11,025 – 30. Their headlong flight when Richard attacked 'like a ravenous lion' (*HGM* 10,993) was not what Charny called 'du beau retraire seurement et honorablement', in his section on 'comment l'en met sus une chevauchee pour guerrier et courre sus a ses ennemis': Charny, 473.

[67] *HGM* 1636 – 52. Contrast this with William's own behaviour when confronted by an unarmed Lionheart in 1189. 'By the legs of God, Marshal, do not kill me. That would be wrong for I am not in armour.' 'No, I will not kill you. I leave that to the Devil', replied the Marshal, running the future king's horse through with his lance and killing it on the spot. 'That was a fine blow', concludes the poet: *HGM* 8839 – 50.

[68] *HGM* 854 – 5, 1124 – 8.

[69] *HGM* iii. 18, n. 4; Crosland, 24 – 5; Duby, *Guillaume*, 88.

[70] What mattered was that the war should be a legitimate one. 'If on both sides war is decided upon and begun by the Councils of the two kings, the soldiery may take spoil from the kingdom at will': Bonet, 154.

[71] E.g. Charny, 465, 512. For Ramon Lull's view that chivalry was instituted to discipline and defend the people, see Keen, 8 – 11; Vale, 22f.

[72] One of the ways in which Duby minimizes the (admittedly small) role of women in the *History* is by consigning William's wife to the margins: Duby, *Guillaume*, 49, 167. But this is to ignore totally her role in William's council, particularly important when matters involving her own inheritance, notably in Ireland, were being considered: *HGM* 13,386 – 9, 14,095 – 100 (an interesting reversal of traditional male-female roles). And even in a vital affair of state — when William is deciding who should succeed him as Henry III's guardian — he calls the countess to counsel him: *HGM* 18,032. On the subject of the wife's role as adviser in *chansons de geste*, see P. S. Gold, *The Lady and the Virgin* (Chicago, London, 1985), 8 – 18.

[73] *HGM* 16,137 – 96, 16,277 – 310. And it was in the middle of the battle of Lincoln, as Duby, *Guillaume*, 68 – 9, rightly points out, that the poet places his profession of faith in the worth of chivalry. 'Que est donques chevalerie? / Si forte chose et si herdie / e si tres costos a aprendre / Que nuls malveis ne l'ose enprendre': *HGM* 16,859 – 62.

the common good — a thoroughly conventional message, and one which the *History* shares with the didactic treatises on chivalry.

If the proper purposes of knightly war were thoroughly conventional, so too, I believe, were the methods of knightly war. The kind of war William fought — and by definition this was the kind of war the best knights fought — was a war full of ravaging, punctuated quite often by attacks on strong-points but only rarely by pitched battles.[74] The *History* describes seventeen sieges but only three or four battles. Moreover, William in a remarkably long lifetime of warfare was present at only two battles.[75] If you had to fight then you fought hard, but always before you fought you tried to catch your enemy offguard, and often you preferred not to fight at all. This, of course, is not at all the impression which, as we have seen, continues to be fostered by the kind of nonsense that Duby writes on the subject. In reality, knights like William Marshal saw themselves as engaged in a deliberately destructive type of warfare, a warfare characterized by watchfulness, deviousness and sudden swoops. These are not the methods that we are inclined to associate with the word 'chivalrous'. We are inclined to assume that there is a contradiction, an inherent tension, between the ideals of chivalry and the nasty reality of war, and to sympathise, I suppose, with the words of the Limousin troubadour Girart de Bornelh, a contemporary of the Marshal:

> I used to see the barons in beautiful armour, following tournaments, and I heard those who had given the best blow spoken of for many a day. But now honour lies in stealing cattle, sheep and oxen, or pillaging churches and travellers. Oh, shame upon the knight who drives off sheep, robs churches and travellers, and then appears before a lady.[76]

But, with the exception of robbing churches, these are precisely the methods of making war which the *History* advocates. Read, for example, William the Breton's account (in other words, the victim's account) of precisely that raid which William Marshal advised Henry II to undertake in 1188.[77] If, as Malcolm Vale has pointed out, there is no sign of any tension between ideal of chivalry and reality of war in the mid fifteenth-century writings of Oliver de la Marche, equally there is no sign

[74] Cf. C. Gaier, *Art et organisation militaires dans la principauté de Liège et dans le comté de Looz au Moyen Age* (Brussels, 1968), 216.

[75] The sieges are Winchester (1141), Newbury (1152), Limoges (1184), Le Mans (1189), Windsor, Nottingham and Verneuil (1194), Arras (?1197), Milli (1197), Arques and Mirebeau (1202), Kilkenny (1207 – 8), Rochester (1215), Winchelsea, Winchester, Mountsorrel and Lincoln (1217). The battles are Bouvines (1214), Lincoln and Sandwich (1217), and possibly, on the grounds that it might well have involved the greater part of the forces active in a particular theatre of war (i.e. eastern Normandy in 1167), Drincourt. I do not count Fréteval (1194) or Gisors (1198), since on both occasions Philip ran for cover and made no effort to fight. Nor do I count Gisors (1188), since neither Henry II nor Philip allowed the greater part of their forces to get involved in the fighting. See above, 5. Thus whether William was present at one or two battles depends on whether or not one counts Drincourt as a battle — and most historians seem to regard it as only a skirmish.

[76] *Sämtliche Lieder des Trobadors Giraut de Bornelh*, ed. A. Kolsen (Halle, 1910) n. 65, pp. 414 – 15; cited by Keen, *Chivalry*, 233 – 4.

[77] Guillaume le Breton, *Philippidos*, Book 3, lines 286 – 309.

of it in the *History* either. There is really no question, as is sometimes suggested, of the chivalric ethic being gradually eroded in the later Middle Ages by the increasing savagery of war.[78] Of course, this is what contemporaries believed. In the words of the fourteenth-century canonist Honoré Bonet,

> In these days all wars are directed against the poor labouring people and against their goods and chattels. I do not call that war, but it seems to me to be pillage and robbery. Further that way of warfare does not follow the ordinances of worthy chivalry or of the ancient custom of noble warriors who upheld justice, the widow, the orphan and the poor. And nowadays it is the opposite that they do everywhere, and the man who does not know how to set places on fire, to rob churches and usurp their rights and to imprison priests, is not fit to carry on war. And for these reasons the knights of today have not the glory and the praise of the old champions of former times.[79]

But the *History of William the Marshal* makes it crystal clear that, when on the offensive, at least one much-praised champion of former times went to some trouble to ensure that his wars were 'directed against the poor and labouring people and against their goods and chattels'.

All this, it seems to me, is to reinforce Maurice Keen's point that the tendency of chivalry was not to limit the horrors of war, but 'rather to help make those horrors endemic'.[80] This is partly because, as he says, chivalry presented knightly conduct in an idealizing light, and this therefore had the effect of prompting men to seek wars. In this interpretation the horrors of war are looked upon as an inevitable and regrettable side effect of going to war. But is it entirely right to treat them merely as side effects? Surely, what the *History* shows is not just that the chivalric ethic of the thirteenth century already took the horrors of war for granted. What it also shows is that 'pillage and robbery' were central to chivalrous war-making. The good knight regretted them only when it was his dependants who were the victims. When he was on the attack then pillage and robbery were not simply taken for granted, rather they were actually approved of as the right, the proper, the courteous way to make war by 'the best knight in the world', the man whose life was held up as a model for all good men to follow. Since these were the methods advocated by the 'patron saint' of chivalry, it is perhaps not after all surprising that, as Matthew Paris reports, when William's tomb in the New Temple was opened in 1240, his body was found to be 'putrid and, so far as could be seen, detestable'.[81]

---

[78] Vale, 157 – 61. Similarly, *c.* 1200, troubadour poetry cultivated at the court of Montferrat expressed a knightly ethos in which courtly and martial values were felt to be in harmony — and the latter dominant. See A. Barbero, 'La Corte di Montferrato allo specchio della poesia trobadoura', *Bolletino Storico Bibliografico Subalpino* (Turin, 1983), 641 – 703, esp. 664 – 89. I owe this reference to the kindness of Maurice Keen.

[79] Bonet, 189.

[80] M. Keen, 'Chivalry, Nobility and the Man-At-arms', in *War, Literature and Politics in the Late Middle Ages*, ed. C. T. Allmand (Liverpool, 1976), 45.

[81] Paris, *CM* iv. 495.

The Legates Guala and Pandulf

Fred A. Cazel, Jr.

The minority of Henry III has long been recognized as a period with special characteristics and achievements. The legations of Guala and Pandulf comprise one of its special characteristics, all would agree, but the role of the legates in its achievements is not subject to the same agreement. In 1904 G. J. Turner wrote of Guala as 'That great man', who 'laboured incessantly in the cause of the young king', and he spoke of 'the supremacy of Pandulf'.[1] Kate Norgate, in 1912, also wrote of Pandulf's 'supremacy', and gave Guala full marks for supporting William the Marshal in his regency.[2] In turn, in 1226, Helene Tillmann defended the 'supremacy of Guala', though she did not deal with Pandulf's legation.[3] Sir Maurice Powicke, on the other hand, in *King Henry III and the Lord Edward* devoted two paragraphs to Guala and Pandulf who, he says, 'acted as the responsible agents of the pope', but his history of the minority essentially ignores their activity.[4] Most recently, Jane Sayers in her *Papal Government and England during the Pontificate of Honorius III 1216 – 1227* has it that 'Much, if not all, depended on the actions of the pope's representative, the legate Guala', and that 'On the death of the Marshal on 14 May 1219 it was Pandulf who secured the necessary governmental transition, "captured" the administration and secured the great seal'.[5] Clearly, not all these historians can be right, and the legates' roles require further study.

Part of the divergence of views derives from the writers' subjects. Sayers's concern with papal government naturally leads her to emphasize the role of the legates who were the representatives of the papal suzerain of Henry III. Similarly, Tillmann's concentration on the papal legates before 1218 inclined her to stress the role of Guala. Powicke, by contrast, wrote in the tradition of national history; he wished to show what Englishmen had accomplished in the thirteenth century towards the shaping of their political traditions. For his purposes the legates were really extraneous. Only Turner and Norgate have focused on the minority as their main subject. Of these two, Turner's study is rather episodic and somewhat

---

[1] G. J. Turner, 'The Minority of Henry III. Part I', *TRHS* new ser. xviii (1904), 255, 290. All manuscript references in this paper are to documents in the PRO.
[2] Kate Norgate, *The Minority of Henry III* (London, 1912), 72, 103, 112.
[3] Helene Tillmann, *Die Päpstlichen Legaten in England bis zur Beendigung der Legation Gualas (1218)* (Bonn, 1926), 110 – 11.
[4] Powicke, *Henry III*, i. 45 – 7.
[5] J. E. Sayers, *Papal Government and England during the Pontificate of Honorius III 1216 – 1227* (Cambridge, 1984), 167, 174.

15

revisionist. Norgate's book is still the most balanced and thorough account of the period, so far as the printed sources of her day would allow her to go.

The sources are, of course, crucial. The traditional account of the reigns of John and Henry III was chiefly based on the St. Alban's chroniclers, Roger of Wendover and Matthew Paris. While they have long had their critics, since the First World War they have come under increasingly heavy attack for their local patriotism and xenophobia. Turner further pointed out that almost all the important monastic chroniclers of the minority, including those of St. Alban's, came from the east Midlands and East Anglia,[6] their geographic location affecting their coverage of events. The *Histoire de Guillaume le Maréschal* and the *Histoire des ducs de Normandie et des rois d'Angleterre* fortunately provide a different perspective on events, lay and Continental. And the royal records have added greatly to our knowledge, some of them having been published since Turner and Norgate wrote. Perhaps the records of greatest value are to be found in the class of Ancient Correspondence. In the seventeenth century Prynne published some of these incoming letters to the chancery from bundles he found in the White Tower.[7] The Public Record Office in the nineteenth century vastly enlarged the collection and named it Royal Letters; from this collection Dr. Shirley published his two volumes under that title in the Rolls Series. Still more have been added in this century, and the class renamed; from these additions new evidence can now be brought to bear on the legates' roles.

To start with, it must be clear that the legates' roles were plural. The two men were very different in their personalities, in their careers, and in their conceptions of their tasks. Nor was there any lack of changes to thrust new tasks in their way. Guala was a cardinal, sent in 1215 by Innocent III to support King John against the baronial rebels. His previous experience as a legate was not in England but in Italy and in France; even so, he failed to prevent the invasion of England by Prince Louis of France. His first half-year was spent chiefly in whipping the English Church back into obedience to Rome and to support of the king. Then John died and Guala had to cope with the minority of the heir to the throne, a very different and more difficult situation than any that could have been foreseen. Fortunately, he saw the need for an English regent, and the old Earl Marshal took on this Herculean role. By contrast, Pandulf had extensive previous experience in England, having been papal nuncio there in 1211, 1213 and 1215. For his diplomatic success he had been rewarded with the bishopric of Norwich, but he delayed his consecration until the end of his legation. When the papal chamberlain, Cencio Savelli, was elected Pope Honorius III, Pandulf was made one of two papal chamberlains in succession. He was thus a man of considerable importance in the papal curia, though not a cardinal, and his appointment to succeed Guala in 1218 was natural. After six months in England his role, too, was drastically altered when the Marshal fell mortally ill and surrendered his regency into the hands of the legate. In consequence, the rest of Pandulf's legation was taken up with the details of governance as Guala's never was. The differences between the two legates and the changes over time require that their legations be studied separately.

---

[6] G. J. Turner, 'The Minority of Henry III. Part II', *TRHS* 3rd ser. i (1907), 205 – 6.

[7] William Prynne, *An Exact Chronological Vindication of Our Kings' Supreme Ecclesiastical Jurisdiction over All Religious Affairs* (London, 1665 – 8), iii. 44 – 70.

If Guala kept a register, it has not survived, and his itinerary is very poorly known.[8] Of about 950 days spent in England, on only sixty-eight days can he be located. His own letters account for only nine of those days, royal records for sixteen, and various narrative accounts for the remainder. For his first six months, while John was still alive, his location on only five days is certain. His known concerns were all ecclesiastical: the excommunication of the rebels and invaders and their supporters, and the collection of procurations to support himself. No one has suggested that during this period Guala exercized any papal powers in the government of England; he was there to help John, not to try to supersede him. Their relations appear to have been good, and John listed Guala first among the executors of his will. But the succession of John's heir as a minor created a new situation: Guala was the representative of a pope who took very seriously his powers and responsibilities as the suzerain of the boy-king. At the coronation of the young king, the legate presided over the bishops at the altar, as befitted an ecclesiastical ceremony. The king made his homage to the pope. But the legate does not appear to have desired to govern England or, at any rate, he accepted the need for a lay regent and offered the Marshal the crusader's indulgence if he would take up the task. It was the Marshal who entrusted the person of the king to the bishop of Winchester, Peter des Roches, and the royal records make it clear that the administration of government and the prosecution of the war were within the regent's authority. On his part, the Marshal accepted papal suzerainty, of which the legate was the representative, but he took to himself the title of 'ruler of the king and of the kingdom'.

As before John's death so after it, Guala's concerns remained heavily ecclesiastical: all of his surviving ten letters deal with the absolution and deprivation of rebellious clergy,[9] and the narrative sources relate such matters as his proclamation of a kind of crusade against the rebels and his refusal to include the clergy in the Treaty of Kingston (1217). He participated in all the great councils of the period: the first meeting at Bristol where Henry's first Charter of Liberties was issued, the negotiations with Louis, the council which agreed, after much discussion, on the terms of the second Charter of Liberties. He held conferences with Llywelyn of Wales and Alexander of Scotland. On all of these occasions he played the part of the king's principal counsellor; on the documents that issued, his attestation led all the rest, and his seal was occasionally used to fortify that of the Marshal. The great bulk of royal documents, however, were sealed with the Marshal's seal until November 1218, when a royal seal was struck. The first letters patent under the new seal limited its use so that no grant in perpetuity would be made before the king came of age. That document was witnessed by the legate, the two archbishops, the Marshal and the justiciar in the presence of (*coram*) twelve bishops, nine abbots, eight earls and fifteen barons, named as meeting in 'common council.'[10] One can easily visualize that meeting: the boy king at the centre, with the legate, the archbishops, bishops and abbots on his right, while to his left sat the Marshal, the justiciar, the earls and the barons.

---

[8] H. G. Richardson, 'Letters of the Legate Guala,' *EHR* xlviii (1933), 250; Tillmann, 118 – 20; I have been able to add five additional dates to his itinerary.

[9] Richardson, 'Letters', collected six of Guala's official letters; I have been able to add four more.

[10] *PR 1216 – 25*, 177.

Guala was as supreme in the English Church as papal powers could make him, but whatever powers he may have claimed in secular affairs, he did not act as if he were supreme. He took little part in the war; indeed, he seems to have spent the autumn and winter of 1216 – 17 in the Severn valley. In April he was at Chichester, and there he arranged a truce with the Earl Warenne.[11] Sometime before 9 May he took 50 marks scutage from the canons of Osney and gave the money to serjeants he sent to strengthen the garrison at Dover.[12] In May he joined the regent's army in its march towards Lincoln, but he turned back at Newark and awaited the outcome of the battle at the strong fortress of Nottingham. His principal contributions to the war effort were his granting of the crusader's indulgence to the men who fought for the young king and his condemnation of their enemies. In June 1217 he joined the regent in ordering Robert de Gaugy to restore Newark castle to the bishop of Lincoln. Guala probably saw this as a matter of ecclesiastical property,[13] but, in any event, Robert ignored the orders of both regent and legate, and it was not until July 1218 that the Marshal ousted him by military action. The castle was turned over to the bishop of Winchester until the legate should notify him of the disposition he wanted to be made of it.

This is the only castle Guala seems to have really concerned himself with, although Turner and Powicke thought otherwise.[14] They relied upon two pieces of evidence: (i) Falkes de Breauté's *Complaint* of 1225 to the pope, in which he said that Peter de Maulay received Corfe castle in custody from both King John and the Legate Guala;[15] and (ii) a letter of Pandulf to the vice-chancellor in May 1219, asking him for the 'form of peace' (unqualified) and the 'form under which Lord Guala gave castles into custody, if you have it, or you should inquire diligently from those who know and write back to us what you find out'.[16] This letter shows that Pandulf did not know if such a form existed, or even if Guala had given castles into custody, and it will not bear the weight previously given it. Falkes's *Complaint* is too biased, furthermore, to be accepted at face value, and since no one else who lost castle custodies claimed commissions by the legate, it seems very doubtful if Peter de Maulay had such a commission. Possibly, Falkes may have been referring to the general agreement at the council of Bristol in November 1216 that all of John's officers, including castellans, should continue to hold their offices.

When Henry fitzCount surrendered the county of Cornwall and the castle of Launceston to the king in 1220, the letter patent recording this deed says he had them 'of the bail of Lord Guala, once legate of England, and of William Marshal and others of the council of the lord king'.[17] In other words, the giving of castles and other royal offices was done by the regency council, not by the legate or the regent alone, though they were the leading members. When Guala wanted Peter de Maulay to deliver prisoners from Corfe castle, he associated with himself, in one case, the archbishops of Dublin and York, the bishops of Winchester, Bath, and Worcester, and the Marcher lords, Walter de Lacy, John of Monmouth and Hugh

[11] *PR 1216 – 25*, 110.
[12] *PR 1216 – 25*, 63.
[13] *PR 1216 – 25*, 71.
[14] Turner, 'Minority. Part I', 284; Powicke, *Henry III*, i. 55.
[15] *Memoriale Fratris Walteri de Coventria*, ed. W. Stubbs (RS, 1872 – 3), 260.
[16] *Royal Letters*, i. 117.
[17] *PR 1216 – 25*, 266 – 7.

de Mortimer, and, in the other case, the bishop of Winchester and William Marshal.[18] Guala may be regarded as the first counsellor, but he ruled with the other members of the council, and most especially with the regent and with the king's guardian, the bishop of Winchester. This is hardly supremacy. And yet Guala deserves better than the faint praise he received from Powicke. As he himself says in a letter written soon after he resigned his legation, he had laboured as much as he was able to secure the peace and the unity of the king and the kingdom.[19] His severity towards the English clergy should not be allowed to cancel out his real contribution to the reconstruction of the English polity in the minority of Henry III.

To turn now to Pandulf, who proclaimed his legation on 2 December 1218.[20] His legation would last till July 1221, a few months longer than Guala's stay in England. Overall, his itinerary is better known than Guala's because some fifty of his own letters have survived, chiefly in the Ancient Correpondence. But datable references to his activities in the record and narrative sources are only about half as numerous as to those of Guala. Since his letters are found to be almost entirely from the period between April 1219 and October 1220, both the first four months and the last nine of his legation are very poorly documented. Furthermore, Pandulf only dated his letters by the day and month and not by the year, and this practice has led to some differences of opinion about their date. On the whole, however, external criteria make it possible to assign annual dates with a considerable degree of confidence to all but a very few. His activity, of course, can be known without precise dates. During his first few months, for example, the chronicles tell us that he was undoing some of Guala's severity towards the clergy: he delivered thirteen clerks from the prison to which they had been confined by Guala, and he is said to have restored their benefices to other clerks whom Guala had suspended or deprived.[21] But on 3 April and 12 April 1219 he may be found at Reading,[22] at the time when the old Marshal had moved to his manor of Caversham across the river. There, as he prepared to die, William delivered the regency of the king and kingdom into Pandulf's hands. Within two weeks the collection of the legate's letters at the chancery began to grow, enabling us to see how the government of the minority functioned under his leadership.

Perhaps the most important of his letters for assessing his role are the first ones. Shirley printed seven letters sent by the legate to the vice-chancellor and the treasurer in April and May, but he dated them to 1220 and failed to appreciate their significance.[23] This was to be the contribution of Powicke in his article of 1908 on 'The Chancery in the Minority of Henry III', where he proved that these letters were written in 1219 and that they showed Pandulf seeking to 'capture' the administration.[24] By controlling the use of the great seal, and by restricting the payment of monies out of the treasury, he hoped to establish his supremacy in the government. A related letter from the justiciar, Hubert de Burgh, to the treasurer and the vice-chancellor makes it clear that Hubert was resisting the legate's attempt

---

[18] *Foedera*, I. i. 146; *RLC* i. 335b.

[19] SC1/1/28.

[20] Ralph of Coggeshall, *Chronicon Anglicanum*, ed. J. Stevenson (RS, 1875), 186.

[21] 'Annales prioratus de Dunstaplia', in *Ann. Mon.* iii. 52, 53; *PR 1216–25*, 185.

[22] *Registres de Grégoire IX*, ed. L. Auvray (Paris, 1896–1910), ii. 741; *RLC* i. 390.

[23] *Royal Letters*, i. 112–13, 117–21.

[24] F. M. Powicke, 'The Chancery in the Minority of Henry III', *EHR* xxiii (1908), 220–35.

and that he believed he had the other officers' support.[25] Hubert wrote that the legate had sent two of his clerks to see the justiciar and to assure him that Pandulf would act throughout with Hubert's counsel; the justiciar says he replied that if the legate would accept the counsel of the treasurer and vice-chancellor, he in turn would accept the legate's. Pandulf wanted Hubert to come to meet him at Cirencester, but the justiciar told the messengers that he was returning to London, and they said the legate would come to Windsor to meet him. That meeting may or may not have been held; ten days later the legate was still sending his orders to the vice-chancellor not to leave the exchequer. This was a direct challenge to the justiciar, who had been attesting most royal writs since the Marshal's resignation.[26] On the basis of these letters Powicke thought that Pandulf had wrested control of the government from Hubert, but Powicke did not know that there is another letter, not published by Shirley, that concludes the series with a clear surrender of the legate's claims. On 11 June the legate wrote to the vice-chancellor in these words:

> By authority of these present we command you that you should do what the lord bishop of Winchester enjoins you *viva voce* and you should go with the justiciar as the same bishop will enjoin you on our part.[27]

The references to the bishop of Winchester indicate that this surrender was negotiated by him, with the result that he was provided with a share of the highest authority as the honest broker between the legate and the justiciar. A kind of triumvirate was formed.

Succeeding letters show how this triumvirate functioned. Pandulf hated London and seems to have preferred to spend his time in the west. There he received visits from, and took counsel of, others of the magnates. If he wanted letters issued under the royal seal, however, he had to write to the justiciar, or to the bishop of Winchester, or to the two of them, and give his reasons. Shirley wrote: 'we find him writing to the justiciar and to Des Roches, as the haughtiest of the Plantagenets might have written to his humblest minister'.[28] It is true that he writes briefly and frequently uses forms of *mando*, but haughtiness is in the eye of the beholder. Certainly, he did not always get his way and was sometimes annoyed when he did not. But Peter des Roches and Hubert de Burgh were quite strong enough to stand up to him. They spent more time at Westminster, especially at the sessions of the exchequer, and through their visitors, both official and unofficial, learned things that the legate did not know. Some of the letters and petitions from royal suitors to be found in the Ancient Correspondence are addressed to each of them or to both of them, and occasionally to them and the legate. It is clear that such people expected the three of them to work together, and in one letter Pandulf wrote that he awaited the justiciar's advice because he did not want to be accused of making decisions by

[25] *Royal Letters*, i. 116.
[26] *PR 1216–25*, 119 ff.; *RLC* i. 390b, ff.
[27] SC1/6/37.
[28] *Royal Letters*, i. xx.

himself.[29] When the legate, in his ecclesiastical role, provided a new bishop of Ely and sent him to the king for the royal assent, the king wrote to the justiciar: 'we would have given him our assent, but he suggested we send him to you for your counsel'.[30] The bishop-elect saw the advantage of seeking the justiciar's counsel, even though he had been chosen by the legate. Again, when the seneschal of Poitou and Gascony resigned and a replacement had to be found, the choice was put in Hubert's hands, perhaps because he himself had been seneschal of Poitou in John's reign. Pandulf was disturbed that it took Hubert so long to make a choice and accused him of 'wandering over the seas and the mountains, seeking those things that cannot be had'.[31] Nor did he like Hubert's choice, but he went along with it. To some degree, each of the three played his own hand. But they were all counsellors of the king, whose interests they put first.

No more than Guala was Pandulf supreme in the government of the minority. He did not 'capture' the administration nor secure the great seal. Though there was no English regent as such, Hubert de Burgh and Peter des Roches had taken the Marshal's place as the leader of the English magnates. Pandulf was accepted as first among the counsellors of the king, and as such he rather took the place of the archbishop of Canterbury. Stephen Langton seems to have felt the loss of place in both Church and State very keenly, for he won from the pope a promise that he would not send another legate to England as long as Langton lived.[32] Even later, in 1230, when Henry III decided to ask the pope for a legate, it was the churchmen who were most exercized by this threat to their independence.[33] The laity resented papal provisions as abrogations of their rights of patronage, and clergy and laity alike were moved by xenophobia. But in the troubled early years of the minority Guala and Pandulf had worked hard for the peace and unity of the realm, and they deserve praise for their realism in recognizing their limitations in dealing with the English polity. The popes might have grandiose notions of papal lordship, ideas which led the papal legates in Sicily during the minority of Frederick II to fail miserably in their efforts to govern that kingdom, and which gave the legate Pelagius the leadership of the Fifth Crusade that he led to disaster. But in England Guala and Pandulf accepted the English magnates as their colleagues and learned to work with them. Even after their legations were over they continued to promote English interests at the papal curia and elsewhere. One might more justly say that Guala and Pandulf were co-opted into the English ruling class than that they dominated it.

---

[29] Prynne, 49; also *Foedera*, I. i. 158.
[30] SC1/1/106.
[31] *Royal Letters*, i. 76, 79; Prynne, 48, and *Foedera*, I. i. 162; SC1/2/15; SC1/1/182.
[32] 'Ann. Dunstaplia', *Ann. Mon.* iii. 74.
[33] *Royal Letters*, i. 379 – 80.

Castles and Politics in England, 1215 – 1224*

Richard Eales

The subject of royal castle policy, and the political importance of castles in general, tends to flit uneasily in and out of the narrative history of twelfth- and thirteenth-century England. At times of crisis like episodes of revolt and civil war the issue demands attention, and estimates must be made of the number and distribution of castles, who held them in fee or in custody, their strategic value, state of preservation and preparedness for defence. Such snapshots of the territorial *status quo ante bellum* can be used as the starting point for subsequent military events. Campaigns and sieges also provide the most crucial evidence for many archaeologists, who study castles primarily as architectural forms evolving in response to the demands of military technology. Yet these pictures can only be interpreted properly against the background of longer term changes and policies pursued through intervening years of peace. The aim here is to set the events of 1215 – 24 in a wider perspective of twelfth- and thirteenth-century development.

I

The period 1154 – 1216 has been the subject of detailed study by R. Allen Brown, which remains the most sustained attempt to relate castle policies to more general politics so far attempted for medieval England.[1] His conclusions provide a useful checklist for the subsequent period. Cumulative totals in the pipe rolls of 1155 – 1215 show a minimum expenditure of £46,000 on royal castles (including those temporarily in the king's hands), an average of £780 a year. The expenditure was maintained fairly consistently from decade to decade after about 1165, following a rise from lower figures in the early part of Henry II's reign, when the exchequer was auditing much smaller sums. The annual average over all of Henry's reign was £650, rising to over £1,000 under John, though much of this increase must have been accounted for by inflation in building costs. Such sums were

---

* I should like to thank David Carpenter and Charles Coulson for reading and commenting on a draft of this paper.

[1] R. A. Brown, 'Royal Castle-Building in England, 1154 – 1216', *EHR* lxx (1955), 354 – 98; idem, 'A List of Castles, 1154 – 1216', *EHR* lxxiv (1959), 249 – 80; *The History of the King's Works, Vols. I – II The Middle Ages*, ed. R. A. Brown, H. M. Colvin, A. J. Taylor (London, 1963), especially i, 51 – 81. The figures which follow are taken from the tables in Brown, 'Royal Castle-Building', 377 – 98. The pipe rolls do not of course provide a complete account of all royal expenditure.

adequate to rebuild royal castles in stone on a large scale as well as to carry out immediate repairs: 30 castles had over £100 spent on them under Henry II and 26 under John. But many others were still substantially defended by timber and earthworks in 1215, and this must have been a matter of choice, because the concentration of resources on a few key sites was an equally clear feature of the Angevin period. Over two-thirds of the £21,000 spent by Henry II went on 7 fortresses (Dover, Newcastle, Nottingham, Orford, Scarborough, Winchester and Windsor); well over half of John's £17,000 on 9 (Corfe, Dover, Hanley, Harestan, Kenilworth, Knaresborough, Lancaster, Odiham and Scarborough). Few of these were entirely new sites, but all were transformed. Dover alone cost £6,600 between 1180 and 1191, while £2,880 for the Tower of London appears in one year's account (1189 – 90). There is little sign of nationwide strategic planning and castles of the interior were as liable to be strengthened as those that had a role in border defence. The Welsh March, in particular, took only a low proportion of expenditure. On the whole, it is better to explain the selection of key sites in local or regional terms. For example, it has been plausibly argued that the new castle of Orford was constructed after 1165 to oppose the power of the Bigod family in East Anglia, and in particular to out-build their nearby fortress of Framlingham.[2] Work at Rochester, Dover, Canterbury and the largely new castle of Chilham in the early 1170s might be ascribed to unsettled conditions in Kent after the *dénouement* of the Becket affair, and so on.[3]

Angevin policy towards the custody of royal castles shows a steady drift towards the installation of accountable officials in place of baronial and hereditary castellans, but the overall picture was patchy and many of the latter survived, even being reinstated on occasion after periods of disturbance.[4] The key periods for changes in the control of castles, 'ownership' as well as custody, were the early years of Henry II's reign, the mid-1170s after the suppression of the great revolt of 1173 – 4, and the latter part of John's reign. Brown has shown clearly how large numbers of royal castles were re-possessed, and baronial castles seized and sometimes demolished in these episodes. But he has also emphasized (and this is perhaps his central conclusion) that the process of royal aggrandisement was continuous and statistically imposing: '255 baronial and 49 royal castles in 1154, a ratio of nearly 5 to 1; 179 baronial and 93 royal castles in December 1214, a ratio of just under 2 to 1. . . . The alteration in the balance of power in terms of castles which took place in these years was almost entirely the result of direct action by the Crown at the direct expense of the baronage.'[5] To assess the real significance of these changes, though, it is necessary to look to what happened after December 1214.

Many historians have also assumed that this practical success of the Angevin kings went hand in hand with the establishment of firm customary rights over castles and castle-building. Thus J. C. Holt has argued that 'Title to castles was

[2] R. A. Brown, 'Framlingham Castle and Bigod', *Procs. of the Suffolk Institute of Archaeology*, xxv (1952), 127 – 48.
[3] R. Eales, 'Local Loyalties in Norman England: Kent in Stephen's Reign', *Anglo-Norman Studies* viii (1985), 107 – 08.
[4] J. Beeler, *Warfare in England 1066 – 1189* (New York, 1966), 161 – 92, 283 – 92, 439 – 46, on Henry II's reign.
[5] Brown, 'List', 249 – 58, quotation at 256 – 7.

markedly less secure than title to land' and that among the reasons for this were 'the need to license private castle-building' and 'a prerogative right of seizure' by the Crown, both traceable back to the Norman 'Consuetudines et Justicie' of 1091.[6] According to this model, Henry II in the 1150s was destroying 'the adulterine, or unlicensed, castles of the Anarchy',[7] and reviving a royal power to control castle-building which had been acknowledged in the reigns of his predecessors. The feudal right to demand the temporary cession of a vassal's castles in time of need or as a test of loyalty, Holt's 'prerogative right of seizure', often called 'rendability' in the context of French customary laws,[8] has not been identified with such confidence in England, though there is one episode in 1176 which is otherwise hard to explain. In that year, according to both Howden and Diceto, Henry II at the Council of Windsor 'took into his own hands' all the castles of England and Normandy, ecclesiastical as well as baronial.[9] Any such assertion of right must have remained largely theoretical, and probably served as a cover from which the king could strike at individual targets in the aftermath of the 1173 – 4 revolt, but the mere fact that it was made is striking enough. It can be concluded that these customs of feudal jurisdiction over castles were known in Norman and Angevin England. They could indeed have been independently introduced from France at later dates — 1176 may represent one such attempt — as well as indigenously evolved since the days of William I. What must remain unlikely is that the resultant range of traditions was ever assimilated or enforced as a common body of customary law in twelfth-century England. Whatever the cumulative practical consequences of the Angevin kings' treatment of castles between 1154 and 1214, that treatment was too arbitrary and opportunistic to be regarded as a consistent policy or to establish generally accepted legal powers as a platform on which later rulers could build.

II

The course of the civil war of 1215 – 17 bears out a number of conclusions about the military role of castles in conditions of serious warfare, when substantial forces were in the field. It is well understood that castles could not physically block communications routes, or oppose the passage of armies larger than their own garrisons. But even a mobile army faced a cumulative danger from leaving unsubdued castles on its route of march, while a commander like Louis of France, who aspired to rule England, had to make territorial gains permanent and that meant capturing all the castles sooner or later. He was in rather the same position as his father Philip in Normandy in 1203 – 4. The main issue at stake was the order in which he could proceed. One possibility was to aim for a knockout blow: a pitched

---

[6] J. C. Holt, 'Politics and Property in Early Medieval England', *Past and Present* lvii (1972), 25 – 7, quotation at 25.

[7] Brown, 'List', 250. For the concept of 'adulterine' castles, see 39 – 40 below.

[8] C. L. H. Coulson, 'Rendability and castellation in medieval France', *Château Gaillard: Etudes de Castellologie médiévale*, vi (1973), 59 – 67, is an introduction to this subject.

[9] See discussion and references in Brown, 'List', 253 – 4; D. J. C. King, *Castellarium Anglicanum* (New York, 1983), i. xxiv.

battle if that were possible, otherwise a series of attacks on the greatest centres of enemy power, in castles and towns. The alternative was to make easier gains in less well-defended territory, so as to build up a momentum of conquest and isolate the difficult targets before risking assault. In this way Philip Augustus delayed his attack on Rouen in 1204 until he had received the submission of western Normandy, and John never seems to have contemplated an open advance on London at the end of 1215 or early in 1216. Overt military operations had to be conducted in concert with propaganda and opinion, particularly in a civil war in which many men were uncommitted and awaiting the outcome. William Marshal is said to have advised John not to hazard his kingdom on a single battle by opposing Louis's landing in Kent in May 1216.[10] Prolonged warfare was a progressive testing of loyalties as well as an attempt to gain military success by piecemeal stages.

In this process, castles had an immediate function as rallying points and as centres for the stockpiling of money and equipment, but when they came under attack the most important benefit they conferred was time, and the tying down of enemy units.[11] Prince Louis kept much of his army before Dover between July and October 1216, and again in May 1217 while the other half of his forces was being decisively defeated at Lincoln. Lincoln castle itself, under its royalist castellan Nicholaa de la Haye, had been besieged with varying seriousness by Gilbert de Gant since July or August 1216. Windsor castle also held off a baronial siege for two months in the summer of 1216 with a garrison commanded by Engelard de Cigogné, until it was lifted in September by John himself. Louis made the classic mistake of committing his forces and then not pushing his attacks to a conclusion. Whatever his reasons for abandoning the siege of Dover in October 1216 and granting the defenders an extended truce until the following Easter while he looked for easier gains elsewhere, it was a blow to the confidence of his allies and possibly a crucial error. The most famous of successful sieges was John's capture of Rochester at the outset of the civil war, in October and November 1215. But even that success, after which according to the Barnwell Annalist 'there were few who would put their trust in castles', was bought at significant cost.[12] It took almost seven weeks, and a large sum from the king's resources, if not the imaginative 60,000 marks estimated by Ralph of Coggeshall.[13] John occupied the next six months with highly successful raiding campaigns in the North and in East Anglia, during which many rebel castles were surrendered to him, but in the end he failed to suppress the baronial opposition before Louis landed with major French reinforcements in May 1216. The time factor had proved to be vital.

Financial resources were also crucial in a war in which both sides employed mercenary troops on a large scale. Insofar as they were garrisoned and had control

---

[10] Dunstable annals, in *Ann. Mon.* iii. 46. Compare the tactical judgements of W. L. Warren, *Henry II* (London, 1973), 117–37, on 1173–4; idem, *King John* (London, 1961), 113–15, on 1203–04, 269–70, on 1215–16.

[11] No attempt has been made to provide full references for all narrative examples below. Clear accounts of the civil war can be found in S. Painter, *The Reign of King John* (Baltimore, 1949); idem, *William Marshal* (Baltimore, 1933); Warren, *King John*; K. Norgate, *The Minority of Henry III* (London, 1912). I have also made use of an unpublished dissertation by N. A. Hooper, 'The War of 1215–1217 between King John and the Rebel Barons', for which I would like to thank the author.

[12] Barnwell annals, in *The Historical Collections of Walter of Coventry*, ed. W. Stubbs (RS, 1873), ii. 227.

[13] *Radulphi de Coggeshall Chronicon Anglicanum*, ed. J. Stevenson (RS, 1875), 176.

of their immediate areas, castles were bases for collecting vital revenues, regular or irregular. The latter, under the general name of *tenseries*, often amounted to free plunder, though it could be dressed up as exceptional taxation, fines for misconduct, or the confiscation of rents and produce from enemy-held estates. The struggle for resources could also be waged negatively; assets which could not be carried off could at least be destroyed and so rendered unavailable to the enemy, as John wasted the Scots borders in January 1216. Castle garrisons had sometimes to collect their revenues in competition with their opponents. While John was in the North during the winter of 1215 – 16, his commanders around London detached forces to raid in East Anglia and replenish their supplies, with great success according to the chroniclers. Two lesser captains paid 450 marks of profit into the royal treasury, after one such expedition.[14] Even uncaptured castles could be weakened and deprived of some of their usefulness by these means. Towns, which always needed open markets and free access to their hinterlands, could similarly be coerced by the garrisons of surrounding castles or by raiding forces, if they were in a position to disrupt supplies. Clearly this was John's long-term plan to soften up London.

The events of 1215 – 17 also suggest that the military importance of minor castles was sometimes very low. During John's victorious tour of the North in December 1215 to February 1216 some fortresses of moderate strength like Castle Donnington surrendered to detached troops on request, once it was known that a royal army was operating within reach. Louis enjoyed similar success in June 1216, taking Reigate, Guildford, Farnham, Winchester, Odiham and Porchester in succession within four weeks, and once again the lesser castles surrendered in the wake of the greater ones.[15] It is also notable that at least a quarter of the 270 or so English castles known from documentary evidence at this time were not set in defence or used in the war, or at least do not appear in the sources. Many others played no significant part.[16] Even larger fortresses could not be expected to sustain serious attack for long unless they had been adequately manned and prepared. In time of war the long-term investment of castle building had to be augmented by short-term mobilization of resources of all kinds. Rochester in 1215 was held by a force variously estimated at between 95 and 140 knights with other troops in support, though it seems clear that there was no time to lay in adequate provisions. Hubert de Burgh's garrison at Dover in 1216 was also said to contain 140 knights.[17] Such forces bear no relation to the size of any permanent 'castle-guard' arrangements, even those which, as at Dover and Rochester, could draw on substantial feudal resources. In most cases, despite clause 29 of the Magna Carta, which provided that tenants should be allowed to do their castle services in person if they wished, obligations survived as cash payments in the early thirteenth century, and there is no evidence that the events of 1215 – 17 breathed life into an obsolete system.

---

[14] *Coggeshall*, 177 – 8; Paris, *CM* 639 – 41, 645 – 6; *RLP* 169.
[15] Paris, *CM* ii. 639; *RLC* i. 251, on Castle Donnington. *Histoire des Ducs de Normandie et des Rois d'Angleterre*, ed. F. Michel (Paris, 1840), 172 – 4, is the best account of the 1216 campaign.
[16] Comparing figures given in Brown, 'List', 261 – 80, and Painter, *Reign of John*, 352 – 3 with narrative events.
[17] *Histoire des Ducs*, 157; *Coggeshall*, 176; *Walter of Coventry*, ii. 226; Paris, *CM* ii. 621; for Rochester. *Histoire des Ducs*, 170; for Dover.

But no castle, whatever the state of its walls and provisions, could be held unless it had a loyal castellan and the morale of the defenders was sustained. Defiance like that of Hubert de Burgh at Dover or William de Albini at Rochester was recognized as heroic but it was not dishonourable, having delayed the attacking forces for a while and appealed in vain for outside relief, to surrender upon terms. Even the immediate surrender of a weak castle might be seen as no more than a recognition of the inevitable. But many castles changed hands for other reasons. Belvoir capitulated to John in December 1215 because its lord William de Albini was a prisoner in his hands and was threatened with death. John de Lacy surrendered Pontefract to the king in January 1216 when he changed sides and pledged his loyalty, his relative Earl Ranulf of Chester interceding for him.[18] Giving up castles in such circumstances was like giving hostages (John actually provided his brother Roger on this occasion), an earnest of good intentions. Rather different were the desertions John experienced in the summer of 1216 when the tide was flowing the other way after Louis's landing in England. The earls of Warenne, Arundel and Salisbury and the count of Aumâle all went over in a concerted move at the end of June, taking their castles with them. Hugh de Neville, who was in command of the royal castle at Marlborough, shortly afterwards betrayed it to Louis, and others followed.[19]

The Angevin castle policy of the 60 years up to 1215 can be re-assessed in the light of these events. It is clear that the mere token possession of large numbers of fortresses, of varying quality and preparedness, was not a decisive asset. It was of no value to have 90, rather than 50, castles, unless one had 90 loyal commanders and the resources to hold them. The dividing line between royal and baronial castles was always blurred by disputed claims, such as that over Bristol maintained by the earl of Gloucester since it was taken by the Crown in 1175. There were also attempts, some of them successful, to establish hereditary tenure by custodians. During the open season for complaints against the Crown which followed John's acceptance of Magna Carta in 1215, such claims were brought in respect of several major royal castles: Hertford, Colchester, York, Hereford, Trowbridge and the Tower of London. The first two at least were conceded.[20] In the civil war between two rival claimants to the throne distinctions were further eroded. Rochester became a *casus belli* at the outset when the constable maintained by Archbishop Stephen Langton, Reginald de Cornhill, would not surrender the castle to the king, but gave it up to baronial forces advancing from London. Yet Rochester was a royal castle, though in theory, and to a large extent in practice, in the permanent custody of the archbishop since 1127.[21] It might seem an obvious device to shift royal castles into the hands of officials, trusted *curiales* and military professionals and away from aristocratic custodians in time of crisis, but this was not a certain remedy. Among those who deserted John in the last months of his life were some of

---

[18] Paris, *CM* ii. 639; for Belvoir. *Histoire des Ducs*, 163, for John of Lacy.

[19] *Histoire des Ducs*, 174 – 6.

[20] *Earldom of Gloucester Charters*, ed. R. B. Patterson (Oxford, 1973), 3 – 8; *Accounts of the Constables of Bristol Castle*, ed. M. Sharp (Bristol Rec. Soc., xxxiv, 1982), xx – xxiii, 70 – 5; M. Altschul, *A Baronial Family in Medieval England: The Clares 1217 – 1314* (Baltimore, 1965), 27 – 8, 77, 127; Holt, 'Politics', 26 – 7.

[21] *Regesta Regum Anglo-Normannorum, ii (1100 – 1135)*, ed. C. Johnson and H. A. Cronne (Oxford, 1956), no. 1475. *King's Works*, ii. 807 summarises subsequent changes.

his intimates and officials like Warin fitz Gerold, chamberlain of the exchequer, John fitz Hugh and Hugh de Neville, taking their castles with them, though the royalist cause was preserved for John's son by the loyalty of many others.[22]

Angevin kings were of course aware of the potential dangers, and that is why their castle policies from the 1150s onwards were marked as much by the concentration of resources on selected key sites as by the sheer accumulation of fortresses. Some of those in royal possession had only negative value: by keeping them in his own hands the king was preventing anyone else modernizing them or making greater use of them. For the same reason at least 30 baronial castles confiscated by the Crown between 1154 and 1214 were demolished rather than retained as they stood. In time of war the same logic of finite resources applied: in January 1216 John issued instructions for Tamworth castle to be dismantled.[23] It might be suggested that John's record total of 'royal' castles in December 1214 represented a dangerous overstretching of his resources, or at least a dubious gain to set against the accumulating resentments of those from whom castles had been taken, ecclesiastics as well as laymen. Clause 52 of Magna Carta stated these grievances very clearly. Sidney Painter took as indicative of the strength of John's position at the outset in September 1215, the fact that of 209 castles 'that seem certainly to have been used during the civil war . . . John and his men held 149 castles against 60 held by his foes'. Painter then proceeds to narrate John's gains over the following six months, yet strangely fails to draw conclusions from the fact that none of this won the war for him, or saved him from the dramatic reversals that overtook him in 1216.[24] The obvious conclusion is that it was necessary for the king to have a loyal body of servants to whom royal castles could be entrusted, but also one which could be employed without alienating the greater noblemen on whose support the king also relied.

Despite everything, including the general unpopularity of the Poitevins shown all too clearly in Magna Carta, John's cause and that of his son was preserved by his and William Marshal's ability to get military commanders like Fawkes de Breauté, Engelard de Cigogné and Peter de Maulay to work reasonably well with his chief baronial supporters. Conversely, Louis's collapse from what was still a very strong position in the spring of 1217, though brought about by the fortunes of battle at Lincoln, was prepared by the recurrent tensions between his English allies and the men he brought over from France. In March 1217, when Louis temporarily returned to France to seek reinforcements, his cause was deserted by William, earl of Salisbury and William Marshal the younger, who were followed by over 100 lesser men. According to Roger of Wendover, Marshal was disaffected because he had been refused custody of the royal castle of Marlborough, while Louis's French followers were busy advising him that the English were traitors and could not be trusted.[25] In this climate the sustained attempts of the regent to win back support, by a combination of individual persuasion and general pronouncements like the reissue of Magna Carta, began to make real headway.

[22] *Histoire des Ducs*, 175 – 6; *RLC* i. 277; *RLP* 190.
[23] Brown, 'List', 261 – 80. *RLC* i. 244; for Tamworth, which is one example of many. See C. Coulson, 'Fortress-policy in Capetian tradition and Angevin practice. Aspects of the conquest of Normandy by Philip II', *Anglo-Norman Studies*, vi (1983), 33 and n. 31.
[24] Painter, *Reign of John*, 352 – 3, 362 – 73.
[25] Paris, *CM* iii. 11 – 13.

Clearly major castles served many functions and formed crucial points around which the civil war of 1215 – 17 was fought. But equally clearly the fluctuations of loyalty and confidence which were crucial in determining the outcome were far too dynamic to be predicted from the initial balance of territorial power as expressed in control of castles. And even after the build up of royal finances, war preparations and access to mercenary troops which had taken place between 1208 and 1214, the ultimate dependence of royal government on the loyalty of the aristocracy had again been displayed in 1215 and its aftermath. Any royal castle policy in the subsequent period had to take these broader considerations into account.

III

The sudden, and in some ways unexpected end to the civil war in 1217, with the Treaty of Kingston and Louis's departure from England in September following rapidly on the sea battle off Sandwich in August, inevitably had the effect of freezing in place the territorial dispositions of the winning side.[26] William Marshal as regent and the papal legate Guala could only rule with and through the agency of great noblemen like Ranulf, earl of Chester and William, earl of Salisbury, and John's leading officials and military commanders headed by Hubert de Burgh and Fawkes de Breauté. From 1217 the earl of Chester held the shrievalties of Shropshire, Staffordshire and Lancashire, grouped strategically around his independently-administered earldom of Chester. De Burgh held office as sheriff in Kent, Norfolk and Suffolk, and was custodian of the royal castles of Dover, Canterbury, Rochester, Orford and Norwich. De Breauté held the shrievalties of six midland counties: Bedfordshire, Buckinghamshire, Cambridgeshire, Huntingdonshire, Northamptonshire and Oxfordshire, along with their attendant royal castles. A little lower down among the hierarchy of royalist commanders, Philip Marc at Nottingham, Engelard de Cigogné at Windsor, Peter de Maulay at Corfe, and many others, also wielded tremendous power within more limited areas, based on the same combination of office and custody of royal castles.[27]

Inevitably, the holding of important castles had assumed an enhanced importance during the years of civil war. John was already making increasing use of regional castle treasuries, at Corfe, Bristol, Nottingham and elsewhere, to handle war finances in the second half of his reign.[28] As conflict broke out in 1215 and the central administration ceased to operate, trusted local commanders were given more and more freedom to operate independently. Castles were set in defence and garrisons built up by custodians who were able to draw on any local revenues within reach, augmented where necessary by *tenseries* and the licensed or

---

[26] On the treaty, see J. Beverley Smith, 'The Treaty of Lambeth, 1217', *EHR* xciv (1979), 562 – 79. Accounts of events 1217 – 1219 in Norgate; Painter, *William Marshal*.

[27] *PRO Lists and Indexes, IX List of Sheriffs in England and Wales* (reprinted with corrections, New York, 1963), 117, 72, 67, 86, 1, 12, 92, 107.

[28] J. E. A. Jolliffe, 'The Chamber and the Castle Treasuries under King John', in *Studies in Medieval History Presented to Frederick Maurice Powicke*, ed. R. W. Hunt, W. A. Pantin, R. W. Southern (Oxford, 1948), 117 – 42.

unlicensed seizure of rebel lands and their revenues. The civil war of 1215 – 17 did not see the same recrudescence of small-scale castle building as in Stephen's reign, but the sub-contracting of royal power to local military commanders, in units centred on major fortresses, served a similar purpose to the creation of new earldoms by Stephen and Matilda in the conditions of the mid-twelfth century. Writing about the counties of the far north, J. C. Holt drew a close parallel with the events of the 1170s: 'In a crisis Border government tended to dissolve and reform along different lines, especially around the great castleries of Carlisle, Bamburgh and Newcastle, and around escheats and custodies temporarily in the hands of the Crown.'[29] As in 1173 – 4, so in 1215 – 17, 'the supra-shrieval authority of royal castellans and custodians' was tolerated by the king and was sustained by whatever means were available.

The difference in 1217 was that there was no king of full age to restore control (or to put it more realistically, to arbitrate between competing claims and allow the balance of central and local authority to re-stabilize) as Henry II had done in the 1150s and 1170s. Many sheriffs and officials were reappointed to their positions by the regency government in the later part of 1217, as the civil war came to an end. Others, especially castellans, seem to have regarded their appointments by John as valid until the new king came of age, or even argued that they had taken oaths to that effect on assuming office. In the first months of the new reign, and while war still raged, the Marshal entertained some such notion; for instance, in October 1216 William de Ferrers, earl of Derby was granted the royal castle of Peak to hold until the king reached the age of fifteen.[30] Such grants almost ceased in the course of 1217, mostly because the leaders of the minority government were no longer committed to a fixed date for Henry's majority, but ideas of this kind, once current, were not easily dispelled. The minority has thus been seen as a period when there was a real danger that royal government and its territorial power would be fragmented. The narrative has been written by some historians as a series of small castle wars through which the minority governors averted the threat, culminating in the crisis of 1223 – 4 when the custody of over 30 royal castles was re-allocated by Hubert de Burgh on the king's behalf. Sir Maurice Powicke argued that during the Marshal's regency the danger was all too apparent, 'so long as half a dozen barons and military experts ruled from their strongholds nearly a score of shires in the midlands and west of England . . . What was needed was a general resumption of castles by the crown, and a redistribution which would emphasize their dependence on the crown. The change was effected between 1221 and 1223.'[31]

The general question raised by such views is whether the threat to royal government was potentially as great as has been supposed. A full examination would have to take into account the social and economic tensions of the period, the progressive definition and implementation of Magna Carta and the readjustments consequent on the loss of further territories in France. The specific question most relevant here is whether the control of castles was such a crucial indicator of

[29] J. C. Holt, *The Northerners: A Study in the Reign of King John* (Oxford, 1961), 200 – 01, and 241 – 50 on the resultant consequences after the civil war.

[30] G. J. Turner, 'The Minority of Henry III, Part I', *TRHS* new ser., xviii (1904), 280 – 4; Norgate, 280 – 6. *PR 1216 – 25*, 1; on Peak castle: the king's fifteenth birthday is the most plausible interpretation of 'usque in quartumdecimum annum etatis nostre completum.'

[31] F. M. Powicke, *King Henry III and the Lord Edward* (Oxford, 1947), i. 55 – 6.

territorial power, or such a vital factor in the political outcome, as Powicke and others have assumed.

In the early years of the minority the regency government of William Marshal accepted the need to work within the balance of territorial power bequeathed to it on the conclusion of peace in 1217. The aim was certainly to rebuild royal income and set the administrative system to work again, by such measures as the general eyre of 1218 – 19, and to restore lands as they had been held before the civil war, in accordance with the terms of the Treaty of Kingston of September 1217. Lesser men accordingly found themselves pursued for their debts and impleaded for land to which they had a dubious or recent claim. But the powerful were handled with great caution.[32] Aware of his limited room for manoeuvre, he tried to achieve as much as possible by agreement, though in the last resort open defiance had to be suppressed in case it proved infectious. Brian de l'Isle, who had been instructed to surrender Peak castle to William de Ferrers, and had perhaps resisted the Marshal's instructions, was given Knaresborough castle instead in May 1217, and was allowed to appoint a deputy when he went on crusade the following year. Later in 1217 a dispute arose over the custody of Lincoln castle, which was claimed by William, earl of Salisbury after his appointment as sheriff of the county in May 1217. For a time he may have succeeded, but not surprisingly he was resisted by Nicholaa de la Haye who had held the castle as hereditary castellan and defended it in the civil war. In October 1217 she seems to have recovered both the castle and the county, but by the end of the year a compromise had been reached: William was confirmed in office as sheriff while Nicholaa retained the castle. At times the Marshal could achieve his ends by persuasion and his personal prestige. In June 1217 Fawkes de Breauté wrote to Hubert de Burgh to complain about the seizure of some lands in his custody by the regent's servants, emphasizing that he was tolerating such intrusion and prepared to negotiate about it only because the Marshal was involved. At other times he was prepared to accept a temporary reverse. In February 1218 William de Forz, count of Aumâle, already a potential trouble-maker, was ordered to surrender the royal castles of Rockingham and Sauvey, but no action was taken after he failed to obey.[33]

After the Marshal's death on 14 May 1219, the pressure for stronger measures in such cases increased. Already on 10 May 10 the legate Pandulf, to whom the Marshal wished to leave some kind of supervisory authority over the government, wrote to Ralph Neville, the vice-chancellor asking on what terms the legate Guala, his predecessor, had granted the custody of castles.[34] In the autumn of 1219 the dispute over Lincoln broke out again, and Fawkes de Breauté was ordered to

[32] For recent analyses of the general political problems involved, see J. C. Holt, *Magna Carta* (Cambridge, 1965), 269 – 92; R. C. Stacey, *Politics, Policy and Finance under Henry III, 1216 – 1245* (Oxford, 1987), 1 – 44.

[33] *PR 1216 – 25*, 1, 4, 7, 15, 64, 190; for Peak and Knaresborough. *PR 1216 – 25*, 65, 117, 130; *King's Works*, ii. 705; for Lincoln. *Royal Letters*, i. 4 – 5; for Fawkes de Breauté. *PR 1216 – 25*, 136; for Rockingham and Sauvey. Stacey, 10 – 22, is a useful short summary of events to the end of 1220. David Carpenter has suggested that de Breauté's letter should be re-dated to June 1219, in which case it would refer to William Marshal the younger.

[34] *Royal Letters*, i. 117; if the date is emended from 1220 to 1219 as proposed by F. M. Powicke, 'The Chancery during the Minority of Henry III', *EHR* xxiii. (1908), 229 – 31. Stacey, 15, appears to prefer Shirley's dating.

garrison the castle to dissuade William of Salisbury from violent action. Measures against William de Forz were stepped up: in November 1219 royal letters were sent to the men of Yorkshire, Lincolnshire and four other counties warning them that he was detaining Sauvey and Rockingham against the king's will. The younger William Marshal's custody of Marlborough and Fotheringay castles was also coming under pressure. Fotheringay was part of the lands of David, earl of Huntingdon, but on the earl's death in June 1219, his estates had been taken into the king's hands, while Marlborough was actually a royal castle.[35] A more concerted campaign against castle custodians was shaped in 1220, by agreement between the leading ecclesiastics and secular figures of the administration. In May 1220 Pope Honorius III wrote several letters to the legate Pandulf, urging that bishops and others who held royal castles should surrender them, and more specifically that no one should hold more than two royal castles.[36] On 17 May, the young Henry had been re-crowned at Westminster. According to the Dunstable annalist the barons present took an oath on the day after the ceremony that they would surrender their castles on the king's command and render account for them; also they would make war on anyone who refused to obey and had been excommunicated by the legate.[37] This symbolic act was followed by a royal progress through the Midlands, culminating in Henry's arrival at Rockingham towards the end of June. Though preparations for a siege had been begun in case of need, the personal presence of the king had the desired effect and William de Forz's garrisons submitted, both there and at Sauvey.[38] Henry then went straight on to Canterbury for a second symbolic ceremony, the translation of the relics of Thomas Becket on 7 July, after which Archbishop Stephen Langton, having reasserted the king's position as well as his own, departed for Rome.

From 1221 onwards Hubert de Burgh was able to increase the pressure for recovery of the royal castles as his own position strengthened. In November 1220 William Marshal finally relinquished Fotheringay castle, probably to an agent of the justiciar.[39] There followed the futile revolt of the count of Aumâle in December and January 1220 – 1 in Lincolnshire which was crushed by an army led by the justiciar. This confirmed de Forz's loss of royal castles the previous year, and compelled him also to give up Castle Bytham, which his own vassal (and ex-rebel) William de Coleville had been trying to recover judicially since 1217. Otherwise the count was forgiven because of his faithful service to King John in the civil war, an excuse which in his case was now wearing thin.[40] In 1221 Peter de Maulay was

[35] *PR 1216 – 25*, 201; for Lincoln. *PR 1216 – 25*, 257 – 8; *Royal Letters*, i. 56 – 8; for Sauvey and Rockingham. *RLC* i. 397; for Fotheringay.

[36] *Royal Letters*, i. 121, 535 – 6.

[37] Dunstable annals, in *Ann. Mon.* iii. 57.

[38] Barnwell annals, in *Coventry*, ii. 244 – 5. *PR 1216 – 25*, 238, 240; for negotiations with William de Forz, and royal proclamation of the surrender on 29 June. Fawkes de Breauté was allowed £100 for his expenses at the 'siege' of Rockingham: *RLC* i. 439.

[39] After receiving four royal requests to do so between June and Nov.: *PR 1216 – 25*, 236, 257, 272; *RLC* i. 429, 442. See Stacey, 21 – 2, on other interests in Fotheringay, which was seized by William de Forz in his subsequent rebellion.

[40] Above, notes 33, 35, 38. R. V. Turner, 'William de Forz, Count of Aumale: An Early Thirteenth-Century English Baron', *Procs. of the American Philosophical Soc.* cxv (1971), 232 – 43, is a full account of his career through the minority. See also B. English, *The Lords of Holderness, 1086 – 1260* (Hull, 1979), 40 – 7; and the reappraisal in Stacey, 22 – 4. Bytham was demolished by the royal army.

compelled to surrender his custody of Corfe castle after being accused in the royal court at Whitsun of plotting treason. Fawkes de Breauté later, probably rightly, accused Hubert de Burgh and his allies of trumping up this charge for their own purposes.[41] Further piecemeal recoveries continued during 1222, but towards the end of 1223, following a successful campaign against Llywelyn on the Welsh March which had strengthened an alliance between Hubert de Burgh and William Marshal, the justiciar was ready for more drastic action.[42] Since the summer of 1223 he had been in possession of papal letters declaring Henry to be of age and ordering those who had lands or custodies from the king to be prepared to surrender them. When in November he had these letters proclaimed and ordered the resumption of Gloucester and Hereford castles, the party opposed to the justiciar took this as a warning shot and began to raise arms. In the event they only accelerated change. The 'opposition' Christmas court at Leicester was outnumbered by those who rallied to the king and de Burgh; the potential rebels headed by the earl of Chester backed down and a major redistribution of castles and shrievalties followed in January and February 1224.[43] In the wave of complaints and judicial cases against the dispossessed which followed now that they were vulnerable to attack, Fawkes de Breauté seems to have been singled out for particular attention, which drove him into his disastrous revolt in June 1224.[44] Bedford castle, in which his brother William had imprisoned a royal judge, was besieged for eight weeks in July and August. The defenders, surrendering *in extremis* were hanged at the king's personal wish. Once again, as with William de Forz in 1220 and 1221, the man who risked rebellion found no allies to join him; once again the personal presence of the king, even a king who was a minor or a figurehead, counted for a great deal. De Breauté threw himself on the king's mercy and was exiled, taking his grievances to the papal court, to which is owed the preservation in writing of his side of the story.

Like so many other things in Henry III's minority, the recovery of the royal castles can be regarded either as an evident need of royal government, or as the product of factional manoeuverings. Both of these approaches have some validity and the balance between them is hard to draw. On both political sides there were mixed motives. It was perhaps desirable that those who acted in the king's name should succeed in recovering the royal castles, but having recovered them they could only hand them on to other custodians more loyal to the justiciar and his colleagues. Even the Marshal had put his own friends and allies in positions of power, and had been expected to do so. This was a matter of degree: such use of patronage was only dangerous when it passed beyond acceptable limits. Against

---

[41] Stacey, 24–5. Peter des Roches, bishop of Winchester (who held the custody of Winchester, Southampton and Porchester castles until Jan. 1224) was also accused. This episode begins de Breauté's *querimonia* addressed to the papal court in 1225, and preserved with the Barnwell annals in *Coventry*, ii. 259–72.

[42] R. F. Walker, 'Hubert de Burgh and Wales 1218–32', *EHR* lxxvii (1972), 473–6, on the 1223 campaign. For narrative accounts of the 1223–4 crisis, see Norgate, 200–17; Powicke, *Henry III*, i. 55–60; Stacey, 27–30.

[43] *PRO, List of Sheriffs. Royal Letters*, i. 508–16 (Appendix II), brings together the main changes between Nov. 1223 and Mar. 1224.

[44] Narrative of the revolt and siege in Norgate, 223–4, 230–49, 296–9; Powicke, *Henry III*, i. 60–6; Stacey, 30–2. The castle was demolished despite the protests of its would-be hereditary castellan William de Beauchamp: *Royal Letters*, i. 236; *King's Works*, ii. 559.

this background, the castellans in office in 1217 had a reasonable claim, based on past loyalty, to be regarded as the natural upholders of the new king's authority, at least until he came of age. After the Marshal's death in 1219 they also had good reason to fear that if they left office voluntarily they would be unrewarded for their past services and brought to account by men prejudiced against them. Their possession of royal castles provided a kind of security, symbolic as well as military, for their other possessions and general political position.

This emphasizes the crucial point that the recovery of royal castles in the minority cannot be seen as a discrete issue. It spilled over into other areas of politics. Castles and shrievalties were often held together, and, in 1223 – 4, redistributed together. But, in peace as in war, all castles were only of limited value unless they carried with them sufficient services and income to be self-supporting, and preferably profitable. Lesser men and professional administrators, who could not afford to run castles from their own resources as part of broader political ambitions, were all the more aware of this. In February 1220 Hugh de Vivonne, constable of Bristol castle refused to surrender the barton, the bundle of property and jurisdiction which went with the castle, to the earl of Gloucester until he received the alternative revenues he had been promised.[45] The cost of running a castle included in the first instance building and maintenance of the fabric, but the recurrent cost of stocking and wages were just as important, and rapidly escalated to enormous burdens if a castle were to be kept in any sort of war readiness.

Destruction in the civil war did create an important need for repair and rebuilding at several major fortresses.[46] At Dover the outer gate which had been undermined in 1216 was now closed up and a completely new gatetower constructed. At least £4,865 was spent between Michaelmas 1217 and Easter 1221, though as much as two-thirds of the total may have been used to sustain the garrison. Another £1,290 went on building costs between 1221 and 1225. Repairs at Lincoln also began early, in 1217 and 1218, with at least £500 spent by 1220. By 1219 work was underway at Rochester, though the major repair of the keep, which was eventually to cost over £500, was only authorized in 1226. At Windsor, Northampton, Hertford, Marlborough and other sites too, the backlog of remedial work from the civil war continued through the 1220s, though gradually giving way to more general improvements, like new mural towers at the Tower of London and a new barbican at Bristol. The Welsh March was an area of special strategic need, for Llywelyn the Great's enhanced power was also a consequence of the civil war in England. The royal campaign in 1223 headed by Hubert de Burgh resulted in the construction of a major new royal castle at Montgomery. At least £3,300 was spent between 1223 and 1228, though again this was divided between building costs and the pay of the garrison. Subsequent royal campaigns in Wales in 1228 and 1231 were also associated with new castle works.[47]

It might seem as though, within the tight financial constraints of the minority regime, resources were being concentrated upon the most important castles in

---

[45] *Royal Letters*, i. 90 – 1; *Accounts of the Constables of Bristol Castle*, liv – lv. There was no question of surrendering the castle itself, as stated by Stacey, 14.

[46] Figures which follow are from *King's Works*, ii. 633 – 4, 705, 807 – 08.

[47] Walker, 'Hubert de Burgh', 465 – 94; *King's Works*, i. 111; ii. 739 – 40, 775 – 6.

accordance with strategic need. This, though, is only a partial view. The treatment of specific castles owed as much to individual influence as to overall planning. Hubert de Burgh's personal prestige was obviously identified with Dover, which he had defended against Louis's attacks, and he was well placed to lavish funds on it. Between 1217 and Easter 1221 he accounted for the works in person. Among the revenues committed were the entire renders of Kent, Norfolk and Suffolk, the counties of which de Burgh was sheriff. At Northampton, held by Fawkes de Breauté, over £300 was spent on the castle between 1217 and 1219; at Nottingham Philip Marc obtained a writ in 1219 to cover £213 which he had spent on building and repairs.[48] Such operations were arguably necessary by any definition of the needs of national defence and royal government. It was, after all, the most important castles which were most likely to have been seriously attacked and seriously defended in the civil war, and to have been entrusted to powerful custodians by John in the first place. But custodians who retained their influence and local authority after the conclusion of peace in September 1217 were the best placed to carry them through and inevitably, in the process, their own personal priorities and ambitions entered the picture. Both claimants to the disputed castles of Lincoln are found receiving allowances for work on it: William, earl of Salisbury £374 in 1217, and Nicholaa de la Haye £130 between 1218 and 1220. How the money was spent on the ground, and by whom, is not clear.[49] Such costs had always been met from local revenues whenever possible, and in the conditions of the early minority custodians were often able to retain for local use part of the revenues for which otherwise they would have had to account at the exchequer. William de Forz appears to have paid nothing in respect of the farms of Rockingham and Sauvey between receiving them in December 1216 and surrendering them in June 1220.[50] Even on the Welsh borders, where royal castle building appears most clearly geared to national strategic needs, it was also deeply interwoven with Hubert de Burgh's own personal ambitions, all the more so as his grip on the royal administration strengthened in the 1220s. Montgomery castle, built during the royal campaign of 1223 and lavishly funded, was put in the justiciar's custody and granted to him for life in 1228. The success of that operation was largely the work of William Marshal's campaign in the west. He recovered Cardigan and Carmarthen from Llywelyn, who had held them since 1215 and had been granted their custody when he did homage to Henry III in 1218. The Marshal was then given charge of the two castles and seems to have spent heavily on restoring them, but he lost the custody in 1226, and in 1229 both were granted in perpetuity to Hubert de Burgh, to hold for the service of five knights.[51] The three linked border castles of Grosmont, Skenfrith and White Castle, first granted to de Burgh by John in 1201 and recovered by him in full fee by a decision of the royal court in 1219, were also massively rebuilt subsequently, though there is no documentary evidence to furnish precise dates.[52] Ambitious moves of this kind prepared the way for the justiciar's downfall in 1232, and already in 1228 the derisory nickname of 'Hubert's Folly' (*stultitia Huberti*)

[48] *King's Works*, ii. 633, for Dover; ii. 751, for Northampton; ii. 757, for Nottingham.
[49] *King's Works*, ii. 705.
[50] *PR 1216–25*, 240.
[51] Walker, 'Hubert de Burgh', 465–94; *King's Works*, ii. 590, 600, 739–40; *CChR 1226–57*, 74, 100; *PR 1225–32*, 186, 276.
[52] *King's Works*, ii. 657–8, 837, 854; *RLC* i. 386, 398.

given to the abortive castle begun by the royal army invading Wales in that year was an indication of growing hostility.[53]

Work on castle fabric was accomplished by equally variable costs for stocking and wages. It is hard to generalize about 'garrisons' because the term is so ambiguous and covers such a variety of arrangements. When castles were prepared for war, costs would rise rapidly, but this could mean in effect that a lord or the king was temporarily basing part of his forces (and their supplies) in a castle, rather than furnishing a garrison for the sole purpose of defending it. When the war moved elsewhere, so would the men. When peace returned such forces were run down rapidly, even in major royal castles in the thirteenth century, to a token military presence with an attendant staff of watchmen and janitors. But castles did not serve purely military purposes, and this too is reflected in their running costs. Bristol castle in 1224 – 5 contained 4 knights, 3 sergeants and 13 squires, with 25 horses and a large number of servants, but Bristol was a major administrative and accounting centre with an enduring strategic importance in relation to Wales and Ireland. It was also a prison, in which at this time Henry III's cousin Eleanor of Brittany was kept in secure but honourable captivity.[54] The extreme case of military expense in the minority years is Dover, whose large paid garrison is known to have cost about £1,000 a year between 1221 and 1228, and is unlikely to have been on a smaller scale in previous years. Such exceptional provision could be regarded as meeting a national need at a crucial strategic point, but it also once again reflected and bolstered the power of the justiciar, who also held the royal castles of Rochester and Canterbury, to which he received life grants in 1228 after he became earl of Kent.[55] When Peter de Maulay was removed as constable of Corfe in 1221, the exchequer allowed 7,000 marks to cover his expenses there since Louis's landing in England in 1216, an indication of the running costs of another major royal castle.[56] It is no wonder that those who controlled such sums, and attendant patronage, as long as they had revenues to draw on, were reluctant to relinquish office.

Because of the cost of putting a castle in readiness for defence was so great, it was both a warning sign to others and a declaration of political intent. The royal letters of November 1219 announcing that William de Forz was holding Rockingham and Sauvey castles against the king's will accused him also of fortifying them and stocking them with grain from the surrounding countryside. In April 1220 the legate Pandulf wrote to Hubert de Burgh urging that similar measures should be taken against William Marshal in respect of the royal castle of Marlborough which he was fortifying, that is preparing for war. The legate urged that he be ordered to stop, and others banned from aiding him 'sine domini regis speciali licentia et mandato'. Evidently, rumours of this kind were in constant circulation.[57]

---

[53] Walker, 'Hubert de Burgh', 476 – 91; D. Carpenter, 'The Fall of Hubert de Burgh', *Journ. British Studies*, xix (1980), 1 – 17; Paris, *CM* iii. 159.

[54] *Accounts of the Constables of Bristol Castle*, xvii – xxxvi, 6.

[55] *King's Works*, ii. 633; *CChR 1226 – 57*, 74, 27 April 1228. This grant of Dover, Rochester and Canterbury castles for life promised 1,000 marks a year from the exchequer for maintenance (and another 200 for Montgomery): 'in case of war or rebellion the king shall give him further help in money that he may be able to keep the said castles'.

[56] *King's Works*, ii. 620. In 1217 – 18 there were still 12 knights and 112 serjeants at Devizes: *RLC* i. 467.

[57] *Royal Letters*, i. 56 – 8, 100 – 01.

The recovery of royal castles in Henry III's minority was also associated with the broader political issue of royal policy towards baronial fortification. Some of the royal castellans ejected by Hubert de Burgh in the 1220s can be classified as foreign adventurers or military professionals with nowhere else to go. Even Fawkes de Breauté can be regarded in this light, though with his marriage in 1215 into the Redvers lands of the earldom of Devon he appeared to have successfully made the transition into the English aristocracy until the disaster of 1224. But others were building on an existing power base. It was the pattern of lands and loyalties he already possessed which made William de Forz's detention of royal castles so threatening. The extreme case of this is the massive territorial power of the earl of Chester, which could have made the brief wars of 1221 and 1224 infinitely more dangerous if he had moved into open rebellion instead of eventually surrendering his royal custodies. The castle of Beeston which Earl Ranulf built around 1225 blatantly defended Cheshire from England rather than from Wales and was perhaps a symbolic act of defiance, but the earl had too many interests in the rest of England to fall back on a policy of local separatism, though his relations with the royal government were very distant for most of the 1220s.[58]

In such conditions, leading political figures were concerned at any reports of castles being fortified or constructed. Fawkes de Breauté received a letter from William Souder and Nicholas de Thebotot, perhaps in 1219, to tell him that Gilbert de Gant was rapidly strengthening his castle at Folkingham in Lincolnshire, and that it was said he had 'licentiam de domino rege et de comite de Salesbire' for his activities. De Breauté's concern arose from its nearness to his own castle of Oakham, which was specified in the letter, but he was also involved with the earl of Salisbury in the dispute over the custody of Lincoln castle. Folkingham was much nearer to Castle Bytham, 10 miles or so to the south-west, which William de Forz was withholding from William de Coleville between 1217 and 1221.[59] Under 10 miles north of Folkingham was Sleaford castle, which with Newark 20 miles or so further to the north-west, belonged to the bishop of Lincoln. The bishop had turned the castles over to John at the outset of the civil war, but orders were given in June 1217, following the battle of Lincoln, that they be returned to him. William de Albini at Sleaford seems to have complied, but Robert de Gaugi at Newark ignored both this and three further letters from William Marshal in the next two months, though he was promised that all his reasonable claims would be met and he would be well provided for, perhaps by a post elsewhere. By March 1218 the Marshal was issuing orders for a force to be raised to recover the castle, but action was again postponed until finally the task was accomplished by a brief siege in July 1218. Even then the Marshal's moderation was evident: according to Wendover, de Gaugi was allowed to reach a kind of settlement with the bishop and was compensated, or repaid, for the food and stocks he had assembled within the castle.

---

[58] *Annales Cestrienses*, ed. R. C. Christie (Rec. Soc. of Lancashire and Cheshire, xiv, 1887), 52 – 5; R. Eales, 'Henry III and the End of the Norman Earldom of Chester', in *Thirteenth Century England I*, ed. P. R. Coss and S. D. Lloyd (Woodbridge, 1986), 101 – 08. It seems clear that Ranulf was also rebuilding Bolingbroke castle in Lincolnshire during the 1220s.

[59] *Royal Letters*, i. xliii, 64. The editor, Shirley, misidentifies the site as Fillingham, north of Lincoln, but 'distat ab Ocham tredecim leucas ad dextram viae versus Lincolniam'. For potential interests of Salisbury, de Forz and others, see above pp. 32 – 3, nn. 33, 35, 40.

Personal considerations were not absent from this incident either. Early in 1218 the bishop of Lincoln gave William Marshal 100 marks for his own use to revive his interest in the recovery of the castle.[60] The minority government's general aim of restoring property seized during the civil war and resolving outstanding claims thus had to be pursued with close attention to the complexity of local interests in a disputed area like Lincolnshire. The recovery of castles presented certain specific problems, but their re-allocation was an important symbol of the return to normality after the civil war.

The other specific obligation taken on by the royal government in relation to castles was stated in the new final clause of the 1217 reissue of Magna Carta: 'all adulterine castles [*castra adulterina*], that is those built or rebuilt since the beginning of the war between the lord John our father and his barons of England, shall be destroyed immediately.'[61] This specific and limited definition does not support the view that 'adulterine' should be equated with 'unlicensed', in the sense of contrary to a universal system of royal authorization applicable to all castles. Executive action in the following years usually corresponded closely with the Charter provision: for example, Anstey castle in Hertfordshire was ordered to be returned to the condition it was in before war broke out. It survived as a castle, and is referred to again in 1225.[62] The most detailed illustration of the issues involved comes from a letter written by Richard de Umfraville to Hubert de Burgh in 1220, replying to a royal letter querying the status of his castle at Harbottle in Northumberland. Contrary to information which had reached the king, his castle was not adulterine but had been built in the time of Henry II with the help of the whole *comitatus* of Northumberland and the bishopric of Durham. It was valuable in the defence of the Scottish border and more than nine leagues distant from the royal castle of Bamburgh: 'non sit adulterinum, cum constructum fuerit per assensum et praeceptum domini regis Henrici, ad utilitatem tam regis quam pacis regni.'[63] This is a comprehensive range of justifications for possession of a castle, possibly intended to screen the real issue, that de Umfraville had carried out adulterine (that is, wartime) improvements to it. The reference to Henry II might be read as an appeal to a specific licence or royal grant but, if so, nothing specific about it was preserved. Probably it should be seen rather as a claim of long tenure since Henry II's day. Further south, on the Tyne, de Umfraville found that his castle of Prudhoe was challenged by Philip of Oldcotes's construction of another nearby at Nafferton. He complained to the king that Nafferton was a new castle, and orders were issued for it to be demolished, though this was only done in 1221 – 2, after its owner's death. Philip de Oldcotes, joint-sheriff of Northumberland and keeper of the bishopric of Durham, was another of the recalcitrants of the post civil war period, who ignored numerous orders to surrender Mitford castle to

---

[60] *PR 1216 – 25*, 68, 71, 81, 85, 121, 164. *RLC* i. 602, for the 100 marks. Paris, *CM* iii. 33 – 4. G. J. Turner, 'The Minority of Henry III, Part II', *TRHS* 3rd ser., i (1907), 224 – 34, is still the best general account of the episode.

[61] Text in Holt, *Magna Carta*, 357.

[62] *RLC* i. 350; *PR 1216 – 25*, 543.

[63] *Royal Letters*, i. 140 – 1. See also Holt, *Magna Carta*, 279.

Roger Bertram between September 1217 and his eventual compliance under threat of excommunication in 1220.[64]

In nearly all of these cases, though Richard de Umfraville was put to the defence of his castle at Harbottle, the onus of proof was on anyone who claimed that an existing castle was illegal or objectionable, the 'adulterine' clause forbidding wartime building from becoming permanent being the usual grounds. Evidence for a positive system of licensing, by which all castles would be required to have specific royal approval, remains very thin, though so-called 'licences to crenellate' do survive on the chancery rolls from their beginnings in John's reign. Ten such grants survive from before 1216: seven from 1200 and 1201, all on the charter rolls, and one each from 1202, 1203 and 1204 enrolled as letters close.[65] Nor did Henry III's minority see any proliferation of 'licences', either to establish new rights or confirm old ones. Six were issued for England and Wales between 1216 and 1231 but only one pre-dated 1227. It appears as a royal letter to Ranulf, earl of Chester in 1221, ordering him not to hinder Fulk fitzWarin from fortifying Whittington castle in Shropshire, as Fulk had 'undertaken by his charter that he would never commit any misconduct by means of the castle so as rightfully to be reputed as transgressor of his fealty'.[66] The others were grants to the burgesses of Montgomery (1227), Henry de Audley for Red Castle in Shropshire (1227), Maurice de Gant for Beverstone in Gloucestershire (1229), Hubert de Burgh for Hadleigh in Essex (1230) and Robert de Tattershall for Tattershall in Lincolnshire (1231).[67] All of these were apparently new works except Beverstone, which was allowed to 'stay and remain', perhaps a case of an adulterine castle which had gradually been rendered acceptable by the passage of time, but for which the unusual assurance of a specific grant was thought worth procuring. This exiguous evidence only goes to support the conclusion that though in practice royal intervention in baronial castles could be justified on a variety of grounds, as it had been in the twelfth century, it still did not rest on any defined legal basis and should not be regarded as a system of control.

IV

The balance of political forces in early thirteenth-century England was such that the possession and relative distribution of castles was not in itself decisive. Even in war, as the events of 1215 – 17 showed, castles were valuable assets only insofar as they were inherently strong, well supplied and prepared for defence, and entrusted to a loyal commander and garrison. The first of these required prior investment,

---

[64] *RLC* i. 379; *PR 1216 – 25*, 287 – 8, 291; B. Harbottle and P. Salway, 'Nafferton Castle, Northumberland', *Archaeologia Aeliana*, 4th ser., xxxviii (1960), 130 – 5. Holt, *Northerners*, 244 – 6, on Philip of Oldcotes's activities in these years.

[65] *Rotuli Chartarum in Turri Londoniensi asservati*, ed. T. D. Hardy (London, 1837), 60, 70, 89, 103; *Rotuli de Liberate ac de Misis et Praestitis, regnante Johanne*, ed. T. D. Hardy (London, 1844), 32, 34 – 5, 104.

[66] *RLC* i. 460. It is of course stretching a point to call this mandate a 'licence'.

[67] *CChR 1226 – 57*, 10; *PR 1225 – 32*, 138, 260, 417 and 422, 435.

usually over a prolonged period, as stone castles grew more and more elaborate. The others required a prompt response to emergency conditions and sensitivity to the political attitudes and loyalties of one's own men, as well as potential allies and enemies. Merely to acquire or build castles did not ensure security unless accomplished without creating too much local opposition while leaving adequate resources for other costs. Kings, magnates and lesser men alike had to balance the future advantages of investment in fortification against all the other long-term and short-term calls on their finances. When war broke out, castles could be sustained in a brief conflict by pillaging but over any length of time this was liable to prove counter-productive by alienating local populations and powerful neighbours. And whatever the current conclusions of military historians about the balance between technologies of attack and defence in this period, no castle was ever invulnerable. Castles were held because their defenders were motivated to hold them when they came under attack in the hope of eventual gains. The prolonged sieges of Dover and Lincoln in 1216 – 17 only assumed the importance they did against the background of dynamic changes in political fortunes elsewhere. A king or lord who failed to provide acceptable leadership risked losing such loyalty, and many of his castles might become peacetime assets only, liable to fail him in a crisis when they were most needed.

If the value of castles appears so relative and provisional even in time of war, this is all the more true for the subsequent period of pacification. The real threat which faced the minority government in the years after 1217 was the gradual insidious alienation of royal offices, rights and incomes while they were in the hands of men who had partially escaped from central control.[68] The custody of royal castles was only part of the problem and the recovery of them was only part of the solution. It was evidently linked with the staged process through which the king came of age, in 1220, 1221 and 1223. It was linked also with the mounting pressures on royalists to disgorge most of their land seizures and other gains made during the war. In some respects the royal government actively restored order, a process reflected in the records of the *curia regis* and eyre circuits from 1218 onwards. In other respects it presided over the return of more stable conditions, ratifying local agreements shaped by ransom payments, family alliances and individual bargains of every kind. Nor was the minority government itself always united or able to follow consistent policies. At every stage the interests of individuals, officials or powerful supporters in council and country had to be taken into account.

Seen in this context the recovery of the royal castles symbolized the success of Hubert de Burgh and his allies in re-asserting royal rights on a much broader front. But the question remains: could the castles have been used to defy the justiciar after all? Such a conclusion is implicit in Powicke's view that if de Burgh and Stephen Langton had not prevailed in 1223 – 4, 'this development would have changed the course of history in incalculable ways. It would have made the castle the embodiment, not the instrument, of power, and given a new strength to what in fact became, in the greater part of thirteenth-century England, an old-fashioned place of business or the object of architectural experiment.'[69] The restraint and ultimate loyalty of the baronial group, especially Ranulf, earl of Chester, led them to give

---

[68] As recent research has generally confirmed. See the survey in Stacey, 6 – 12.
[69] Powicke, *Henry III*, i. 51.

way when they could have made a stand. But these arguments are not really convincing. Rather, it was the case that Hubert de Burgh, with ecclesiastical support, the declaration of the king's majority, and a careful calculation of baronial allegiances, had outmanoeuvered his opponents. The testing of strength at the Christmas courts of 1223 made the point; Earl Ranulf and his allies accepted the inevitable, judging that by fortifying their castles they would only risk greater losses. Fawkes de Breauté's fatal rebellion in 1224 displayed the consequences of over-reliance on castles and inadequate calculation of the other factors involved. The siege of Bedford bore out the tactical value of the castle very well, as it held up a massive royal army for almost two months, but in the meantime de Breauté's political support, instead of strengthening, withered away completely.[70]

If the political role of castles in Henry III's minority has sometimes been overstated, it has usually been underestimated for his majority rule down to 1258. Except for sporadic warfare on the Welsh March, which briefly spilled over into domestic politics in 1233 – 4, this was a generation of internal peace, but the investment in 'architectural experiment' was still considerable. H. M. Colvin estimated royal expenditure on castles during the whole period 1216 – 72 at £85,000, an average of £1,500 a year. Though much of this went on residential building in the great palace castles of Windsor (about £15,000), Winchester and the Tower of London (almost £10,000 each), the remainder was sufficient to complete the process of rebuilding in stone which had been initiated before 1216, on almost every site still thought worth fortifying. Apart from Dover, there was a growing concentration on Wales, where Degannwy castle alone cost up to £10,000, and royal power was consolidated by the acquisition of the earldom of Chester and its castles in 1237.[71] Custodial arrangements show a nice balance between loyalty and authority on the one hand, and economy on the other.[72] Probably this had been true in earlier periods too, but the process can be demonstrated more clearly from the fuller records of the thirteenth century. Individual cases must be scrutinized to see which motive was predominant: sometimes castles might be removed from the sheriff and put in the care of a powerful nobleman or *curialis* for reasons of security, sometimes this was done because such a man could relieve the king of running costs, while the castle itself was left in the hands of an underpaid deputy. Concentration on fewer sites meant that some castles were effectively alienated to save money, as Sauvey was in 1235, or demolished, as Bedford was after the 1224 siege.[73] Henry III's family policy also emerges clearly, with grants to Richard of Cornwall and Simon de Montfort culminating in the creation of Edward's great apanage in 1254. As far as royal policy towards baronial castles is concerned, the striking fact is that between 1232 and 1251 no 'licences to crenellate' appear on the chancery rolls at all. Though it is always possible that some grants were made and not enrolled, this general picture strikingly confirms that the unsystematic

---

[70] Above, n. 44; R. A. Brown, *English Castles* (3rd edn., London, 1976), 191 – 4. G. H. Fowler, 'Munitions in 1224', *Bedfordshire Hist. Rec. Soc. Trans.*, v (1920), 117 – 32, gives some idea of the resources employed.

[71] *King's Works*, i. 110 – 15; ii. 624 – 6.

[72] D. Carpenter, 'The Decline of the Curial Sheriff in England 1194 – 1258', *EHR* xci (1976), 1 – 32, esp. at 27.

[73] *CPR 1232 – 47*, 100, grant of Sauvey to Hugh Paynel 'provided that the said Hugh will maintain the castle and buildings at his own cost'. Above, n. 44.

inheritance of royal rights over castles had yet to be systematized, even in a more legalistic age.[74] In 1258, Henry's baronial opponents were anxious to gain control of key royal castles and to safeguard themselves from the danger of foreign invasion, but they advanced no complaints about royal interference with castles in general.[75]

Many of the elements which composed royal castle policy in the thirteenth century closely parallel those of the pre-1216 period. Seen in a longer perspective, the events of the crisis years 1215 – 24 serve to highlight the enduring forces which both shaped and set limits to the importance of castles in twelfth- and thirteenth-century England.

[74] I am grateful to Dr. Charles Coulson for giving me access to his unpublished handlists of royal licences to crenellate.
[75] *DBM* 80 – 1, 102 – 03, 112 – 13.

Knighthood and the Early Thirteenth-Century County Court

P. R. Coss

In an important recent study Dr. Palmer has taught us to understand just how professional were the county courts, especially by the end of the reign of Edward I.[1] They were dominated by the lawyers, the pleaders and attorneys, who were often, in addition, the stewards and bailiffs of the lords and responsible for the judgements of the court. Characterized by their aristocratic allegiances and a high level of ability, these lawyers 'made the county court a professional and legally respectable institution, rather than the amateur court presented by historians'.[2] Even in the early thirteenth century, he argues, these courts were dominated by the aristocracy through 'their chosen and changeable delegates', their stewards.[3]

Any re-assessment of the functioning of the county court during this period must turn, to some degree at least, on the question of suit, and Palmer has reinforced Maitland's view on the relative paucity of suitors in the thirteenth century. Many of the tenurial obligations to attend would seem to have applied to the biannual great courts only, and with withdrawal of suit a constant factor there is every reason to believe that the number of suitors was declining throughout the century. The reign of Edward I appears to have been critical: 'Suitors played little or no role in normal county procedure by around 1300'.[4] Even in earlier reigns, however, it seems that, for the most part, ' "the great counties" or "general counties" were not very large assemblies', leaving aside 'the thinly attended meetings that are holden month by month'.[5] This relative paucity of suitors must undoubtedly have further strengthened the stewards, present as it were in their professional capacity, reaffirming the position which their greater knowledge of law, custom and procedure must naturally have given them. The way was thus prepared for the domination of the court by the professionals at the close of the century, when suit had become a negligible factor.

What I want to re-examine here, however, is not the county court of the reign of Edward I, which Palmer has done so much to illuminate, but the county court as it existed at the beginning of the thirteenth century. His *exposé* of some of the weaknesses in the traditional interpretation of the county court offers a valuable

---

[1] R. C. Palmer, *The County Courts of Medieval England, 1150 – 1350* (Princeton, 1982), chs. 3 – 5. In preparing this essay I have drawn upon the expertise of Dr. P. A. Brand. I am most grateful to him for sharing his knowledge with me.

[2] Ibid. 112.

[3] Ibid. 136.

[4] Ibid. 86.

[5] F. Pollock and F. W. Maitland, *The History of English Law Before the Time of Edward I* (2nd edn., Cambridge, 1968), i. 542 – 3, 548.

corrective, and it is one we should take on board. Unfortunately, however, in doing this, Palmer has produced an anachronistic picture. In essence he has projected back into the past not only the Edwardian county court but also the social structure of fourteenth-century England. If we follow him here our chances of correctly understanding the evolution of local society will be minimal. I wish to draw attention to the distortions which are present in Palmer's analysis, and then to offer, albeit briefly, some observations on the role and status of the early thirteenth-century knight through the medium of his relationship to the county court.

The heart of the problem seems to lie in Palmer's concern to demonstrate that the origins of the legal profession lie not at Westminster but in the counties during the course of the twelfth century.[6] This leads him to over-professionalize practitioners in the law at too early a date, and consequently to create rigid distinctions which are inapplicable to the society of early thirteenth-century England. Often the problem arises from a matter of emphasis which culminates in distortion. Two famous cases are re-examined, the first to illustrate the role of the steward, the second to debunk G. T. Lapsley's famous treatment of the *buzones* of the county court, 'on whose nod', says the author of 'Bracton', 'the votes of the others depended'.[7] The two cases are, of course, the Lincolnshire case which resulted in Theobald Hautein and Hugh de Humby making a stand on Magna Carta in the royal court in 1226, and the Gloucestershire case of false judgement of 1212. In Palmer's analysis, stewards and lawyers quickly become synonymous and are then used in contradistinction to knights. When defining lawyers he writes:

> I consider a person involved in legal activities a professional lawyer when, for a period of years, that person appears to be spending the major part of his time in legal functions and deriving the greater part of his income from these activities or, at least, from the investments made from that income, and when that person possesses a specialized knowledge differentiating him from laymen.[8]

Most assuredly, under this definition, the pleaders of the county court at the close of the thirteenth century were lawyers, and many of the contemporary stewards appear to have been drawn from the same ranks. Without doubt, very few stewards were knights by this time. In the early thirteenth century, however, it is a different matter. It is doubtful, too, whether one can draw a clear distinction at this date between those possessing and those lacking specialized knowledge. Even if we can, it is certainly the case that we will not find knights exclusively on the one side rather than the other.

Concerning the *buzones*, these are no longer to be regarded, we are told, as 'a standing group of country gentlemen active and influential in the affairs of the

---

[6] R. C. Palmer, 'The Origins of the Legal Profession in England', *The Irish Jurist*, xi (1976), 126–46. For an alternative viewpoint, see P. A. Brand, 'The Origins of the English Legal Profession', *Law and History Review*, v. no. 1 (Spring 1987), 31–50.

[7] Henry of Bracton, *De Legibus et Consuetudinibus Angliae*, ed. G. E. Woodbine, trans. S. Thorne (Cambridge, Mass., London, 1968–77), ii. 327.

[8] Palmer, *County Courts*, 89.

county and its court', and as 'men qualified by their lands and their knighthood to discharge these functions, and chosen it would seem rather than others equally qualified by reason of their taste and aptitude for such business'.[9] Of course not! 'They were the kind of people included in the vague category of lawyers: seneschals, bailiffs, pleaders, attorneys'.[10] Now, it is doubtful whether this is a legitimate category at all, vague or otherwise. But Palmer goes on: 'They were, it is true, called knights of the shire in certain procedural contexts along with many other Gloucestershire residents. That should not, however, be taken to mean that they were knights "girt with the sword" '.[11]

Here, quite clearly, an anachronistic concept is being employed. It is borrowed from a later age, when knights were relatively few and when members of parliament could be drawn equally well from social groups immediately beneath them. In the context of the early thirteeenth century, however, the concept has no validity whatsoever. Admittedly, we are not normally informed that knights were 'girt with the sword', though on one occasion, at least, this does occur: a defendant in the royal court in 1225 claimed that two carucates in Shepperton (Middlesex) had been adjudged to him during the reign of King John by a jury of twelve belted knights ('legales milites gladios cinctos').[12] The importance of knighthood in these 'procedural contexts' is most clearly demonstrated, however, in a case from Warwickshire which reached the royal court in 1225.[13]

Roger Levelaunce and his wife had sued Richard de Gloucester for five hides at Wolverton. Richard had essoined twice of sickness on the way to court, and then of bed-sickness. The sheriff was therefore instructed to send the required four knights to view him. The plaintiffs claimed that these four knights were unable to see the defendant who had, in fact, risen through others who were not knights. If this were the case, then the defendant would have been deemed to have risen without licence and would have lost his case. The truth of the matter, however, seems to have been this. The sheriff had elected (or perhaps chosen, 'elegit') only three knights in full county and ordered the hundred sergeant, John de Tysoe, to summon a fourth who was not present in court. When the three knights arrived at Wolverton, Richard de Gloucester would not let them in on the grounds that there were only three, the requisite fourth knight being missing. They therefore failed to make the view. Subsequently, however, the fourth knight and three other men (who were not knights) were ordered to make the view by the hundred bailiff. The latter confessed that he had done this through his own foolishness and that the sheriff was not at fault. A number of irregularities had occurred here. Both parties had shown themselves to be aware of correct procedure, however, and were equally willing to pounce on any lapse that would give them an advantage. What they were agreed upon was that the viewers *de malo lecti* must be actual knights, not nominal knights chosen to satisfy the necessary procedure. The author of 'Bracton' agrees, and in

---

[9] G. T. Lapsley, 'Buzones', *EHR* xlvii (1932), 187, 193.

[10] Palmer, *County Courts*, 134.

[11] Ibid.

[12] *CRR* xii. no. 356. There seems to be no particular reason why the profession of arms should have been made explicit here. Flower was inclined to see it as 'an Homeric epithet', employed by 'an eager suitor': C. T. Flower, *Introduction to the Curia Regis Rolls, 1199–1230* (Selden Soc., lxii, 1943), 440.

[13] *CRR* xii. 43–4.

fact includes this case in his own discussion of correct and incorrect procedure.[14] They must be *milites*, he insists, not *liberi homines*, nor even a combination of the two. The judges took the same view. In 1207 the electors of a grand assize jury in Dorset were amerced for choosing jurors who were not knights.[15] Of course, one might argue that these instances indicate that such anomalies did occur. Even so, they can hardly have been widespread. 'Knight of the shire', then, was not valid as a concept in the way Palmer uses it, and without that legitimacy it is very doubtful whether the employment of non-knights can have been at all common.

With these observations in mind, let us follow Palmer's trail. That the stewards did indeed play a major part in the deliberations of the early thirteenth-century county court is indicated by the famous Lincolnshire case which reached Westminster in 1226.[16] The dispute began when the sheriff, unable to complete the cases before the court on a single day, told the stewards, knights and others ('dixit senescallis, militibus et aliis de comitatu') to return early the following morning to hear the pleas and make the judgements. The following day he duly ordered the stewards and knights who were outside the shire house to enter and complete the business. On their refusal — on the grounds that the county court should be held only for one day — the sheriff postponed the cases to the wapentake court. When the courts of the ten wapentakes of Kesteven duly convened at Ancaster, the sheriff heard the postponed cases and told the knights to make the judgements. Led, or stirred up, by Theobald Hautein and Hugh de Humby, the knights and others responsible for making the judgements refused to do so other than in the county court. One of them, however, sided with the sheriff. He was Thomas fitzSimon, steward of John Marshal.

Beyond a doubt, then, the stewards played a leading role among the judges of the county courts. At Lincoln the sheriff referred twice to stewards and knights, in that order. There are, moreover, several indications in this case that behind the stewards lay baronial power. At Ancaster Theobald Hautein informed the assembly that he had come from the royal court where he had spoken with the archbishop, the earl of Chester and other magnates, and that before three weeks were out a writ would arrive forbidding such injuries in the future. He and Hugh de Humby later informed Thomas fitzSimon that they would shortly be seeing his lord and that they would tell him how his steward conducted himself in the county court. Where precisely the initiative lay for the *débâcle* at Lincoln — as so often in such cases — is unclear, but it has been pointed out that it was during the settlement of the baronial rising in the following year that the king summoned knights from thirty-five shires to present their grievances against the sheriffs on matters arising out of Magna Carta.[17]

---

[14] Bracton, iv. 120.

[15] *CRR* v. 109; see also J. Quick, 'The Number and Distribution of Knights in Thirteenth Century England: The Evidence of the Grand Assize Lists', in *Thirteenth Century England I: Procs. of the Newcastle upon Tyne Conference, 1985*, ed. P. R. Coss and S. D. Lloyd (Woodbridge, 1986), 114 – 15.

[16] The case itself may be found in *CRR* xii. nos. 2142, 2312, and in *Bracton's Notebook*, ed. F. W. Maitland (London, 1887), iii. no. 1730. Discussion of this case from various viewpoints may be found in Pollock and Maitland, i. 549 – 50; J. C. Holt, *Magna Carta* (Cambridge, 1965), 279 – 81; J. R. Maddicott, 'Magna Carta and the Local Community, 1215 – 1259', *Past and Present*, cii (Feb. 1984), 33 – 4, 49.

[17] Maddicott, 'Magna Carta', 49.

Be that as it may, and allowing for both the primary role of stewards and the possibility of baronial influence on the courts through them, the Lincolnshire case also makes it clear that knights as well as stewards took part in the judgements. This is also shown in other cases cited by Palmer himself from later in the century. In Warwickshire and in Derby 'knights and stewards', in Devon 'stewards and knights' are said to have rendered the judgements.[18] There are cases on the curia regis rolls, moreover, which make plain the importance of knights in the county court in the early thirteenth century. In 1211 we hear of a judgement being put in respite in the Herefordshire county court because of the paucity of knights present and because of strife between those who were there: 'et quoniam pauci milites fuerunt ad comitatum tunc et contencio fuit inter illos qui interfuerunt, posuerunt judicium in respectum usque ad alium comitatum'. In 1222 Isabella Goer claimed that a false judgement in the county court of Oxford had deprived her of a knight's fee at Sibford. Only one of the four knights who were to bring the record of the case to Westminster had appeared. The sheriff was duly instructed to have the record brought by six knights of the county (court) other than those four, as it had been testified that virtually all of the knights of the county had refused to participate in the judgement that had been made: 'eo quod testatum fuit quod fere omnes milites de comitatu et surexerunt et noluerunt interesse judicio illi'. When the six knights and two of the original four appeared on the appointed day, the court listened to their rival testimonies. It seems that a minority had wished to give judgement in favour of Isabella's opponent, Simon de Barcheston, even though he was the son of the original plaintiff, who had, in fact, died during the delays to which the case had been subject. The majority of the knights present in the county court had then left, refusing to participate further, leaving the false judgement to be rendered by the sheriff, the two named knights and certain others ('quosdam alios'). The royal court gave seisin to Isabella as the knights of the county had disavowed the judgement ('quia milites de comitatu deadvocant judicium'). In 1236, during yet another case arising out of disaffection with a sheriff, this time of Devon, the defendants claimed that they had deferred judgement on certain matters in the county court because there were few knights there, and the bishop and other barons and magnates were absent ('eo quod pauci milites tunc ibi fuerunt et episcopus loci et alii barones et magnates tunc absentes fuerunt').[19]

Much of what Palmer says on the predominant role of the steward in these early years rests on the *Leges Henrici Primi*. In his reading of this, however, he may well have made an unwarranted assumption. The relevant chapters say that: 'If any baron of the king or of other lords is present in accordance with the law, at the county court, he may acquit all the land which he holds in his lordship in that county', and that 'the same is true if his steward is lawfully present'.[20] The assumption here is that the steward acquitted all the lord's tenants of attendance including those holding by military service. Maitland's view, shared by Sidney

---

[18] Palmer, *County Courts*, 128 – 9.

[19] *CRR* vi. no. 173; *CRR* x. 267, 344 – 6; *CRR* xv. no. 1983. I am grateful to Paul Brand for alerting me to these cases.

[20] *Leges Henrici Primi*, ed. L. J. Downer (Oxford, 1972), cls. 7.7, 7.7a. As Paul Brand has pointed out, the editor's translation of 'dominium' as lordship, rather than as demesne, at this point, is misleading.

Painter, that it was only the tenants of the lands held in demesne who were so acquitted, is surely the more tenable.[21] It might be added that the word *baro* as used here — and as illustrated by the qualification 'or of other lords' — covers a much wider group than those designated by the term in the thirteenth century. Many knights, then, may well have sent their bailiffs or stewards, but others will surely have attended in person. In short, even if the initiative often lay with stewards, and even allowing for a steady increase in their role as the century progressed, nonetheless during the early thirteenth century *knights who were not stewards* could also play a significant part.

I have italicized the phrase on purpose, for we next need to examine the social status of the steward. Of Theobald Hautein, Palmer says he was no 'ordinary suitor' to the court but 'a professional lawyer', on the basis of sporadic appearances as an attorney in the king's court.[22] In fact, he may well have been a steward himself, for he certainly was a decade earlier.[23] But whatever else he and Hugh de Humby may have been, they were certainly knights: both are found during the decade as knights of the grand assize for Lincolnshire.[24] And this was still commonly the case with stewards at this time.

Let us look a little more closely at the type of men who might become baronial stewards. As an example let us take four men who can be identified as stewards of the earls of Warwick in the early thirteenth century: William de Arden, William de Wilmcote, John Durvassal and Robert de Grendon. Of these, the best endowed in terms of land was undoubtedly the last. Robert de Grendon functioned for Earl Thomas de Newburgh (1229 – 42).[25] He was very solidly based in the north of the county, and of ancient lineage. His ancestor, Roger de Grendon, had held two fees of old enfeoffment, one at Grendon and Whittington of the Camvills, and another of the Marmions at Dordon and Warton. Robert was thus a figure of some local significance. Like the other stewards he was a knight of the grand assize during the 1221 – 2 eyre. He married well, bringing the manor of Shenston (Staffordshire) into the family and launching his son, another Robert — and in some respects a

---

[21] Pollock and Maitland, i. 546 – 7; S. Painter, *Studies in the History of the English Feudal Barony* (Baltimore, 1943), 86. For evidence, dating from the time of the *Leges Henrici Primi*, of the attendance of a steward acquitting specifically the demesne manors of his lord, see *Visitations and Memorials of Southwell Minster*, ed. A. F. Leach (Camden Soc., new ser., xlviii, 1891), 196. The composition between William de Lancaster and the hereditary sheriff of Westmorland in 1227, which Palmer, *County Courts*, 114 – 15 cites, should surely be seen in terms of a tendency to withdraw service in favour of franchise courts in the thirteenth century rather than the normal *modus operandi* indicated by the *Leges Henrici Primi*. The steward, here, is indeed to acquit the suit of William's knights and other men from William's lands, except where they are drawn into pleas or where they are necessary for afforcing the court. Interestingly, in the latter case the steward is to 'bring with him knights and other discreet and wise men from the land of Kendal in order to make the judgement.'

[22] Palmer, *County Courts*, 135.

[23] Theobald Hautein, who had joined the rebellion against King John, was the steward of Robert Grelley: see J. C. Holt, *The Northerners* (Oxford, 1961), 56, 59n., 60.

[24] Theobald occurs e.g. in 1222: *CRR* x. 276; Hugh in 1230: *CRR* xiv. 115. For further details of Theobald Hautein's life and career, see *The Registrum Antiquissimum of the Cathedral Church of Lincoln, VII*, ed. C. W. Foster (Lincoln Rec. Soc., 1953), 131 – 2. He held a knight's fee at Scredington of Gilbert de Gant. His successor, Robert Hautein, calls himself *miles* in a charter relating to the manor: ibid. no. 2104.

[25] *The Langley Cartulary*, ed. P. R. Coss (Dugdale Soc., xxxii, 1980), no. 311.

rather unsavoury character — into a local career further north, where he ultimately became sheriff of Shropshire and Staffordshire.[26]

In terms of lineage, however, the most illustrious was probably William of Arden, a steward of Earl Waleran (1184 – 1205).[27] Though precise identification is often difficult in the case of the Ardens, he was most probably William de Arden of Radbourne, a member of the famous Arden family — descendants of the Conquest quisling Turchil of Warwick — who became, by mediatization, important honorial barons of the earls of Warwick. The family's antiquity and its tradition of service and association with the earls are both suggested by the figure of the vavassour Heralt of Arden, the mythical steward of the mythical 'Guy of Warwick' in the thirteenth-century ancestral romance. William of Arden, however, was not the head of this family but a collateral holding principally one-tenth of a knight's fee at Radbourne.[28] A fortunate survival indicates that the steward could not have been the contemporary William de Arden who held of the Mowbray fee at Hampton-in-Arden and elsewhere and who was busily building up further estates around Temple Grafton in the early years of the thirteenth century.[29] This family was of more recent origin and owed its wealth to Robert de Arden, clerk, the incumbent of Hampton and archdeacon of Lisieux.[30] The name William de Arden occurs, in fact, eight times as a knight of the grand assize in the 1221 – 2 eyre as well as once as a knight bearing the county's record in 1214. Probably both William of Hampton-in-Arden and William of Radbourne (or his son, another William) are represented here. Incidentally, Thomas de Arden, head of the main Arden line, was also a knight at this same eyre.

William de Wilmcote and John Durvassal (*alias* Burnassal) were both stewards to Henry de Newburgh II, earl of Warwick (1213 – 29).[31] William, though extremely active in the grand assize, is a rather shadowy figure. He clearly took his name from Great Wilmcote in Aston Cantlow, where he was claiming the adowson in 1228. He must have acquired rather than inherited the estate, however, for it was of 'the lands of the Normans' and was taken from Brito the Chamberlain in 1205. It was clearly a small estate; in 1205 it was valued at only 42*s*. in fixed rent. It was probably identical with the messuage and carucate which John, son of William de Wilmcote, settled on Juliana, widow of William de Wilmcote, for life in 1295. In 1316 Great Wilmcote was called a hamlet of Aston Cantlow.[32]

---

[26] Sir William Dugdale, *The Antiquities of Warwickshire*, ed. W. Thomas (London, 1730), 1100 – 02; *VCH Warwickshire*, iv. 76 – 7, 190.
[27] HMC, *Report on the MSS of Lord Middleton* (London, 1911), 24 – 5; BL, Cotton Charter, xi. 39.
[28] *VCH Warwickshire*, vi. 199; Dugdale, 329.
[29] *VCH Warwickshire*, iv. 82; Dugdale, 952; *Warwickshire Feet of Fines, I*, ed. E. Stokes *et al.* (Dugdale Soc., main ser., xi, 1932), nos. 170, 178, 181. One of the charters of Earl Waleran which William de Arden the steward witnesses is a grant to William de Arden, son of Roger of Hampton-in-Arden.
[30] See esp. *Charters of the Honour of Mowbray, 1107 – 1191*, ed. D. E. Greenway. British Academy Records of Social and Economic Hist., new ser. i (London, 1972), nos. 330 – 8. There is no certain evidence for Dugdale's assertion that the Ardens of Hampton-in-Arden were another collateral of Turchil's line. I intend to deal with the history of the Ardens more fully elsewhere.
[31] *The Beauchamp Cartulary Charters, 1100 – 1262*, ed. E. Mason (Pipe Roll Soc., new ser., xliii, 1980), nos. 290, 299.
[32] *VCH Warwickshire*, iii. 37; Dugdale, 838; *Warwickshire Feet of Fines, II*, ed. E. Stokes *et al.* (Dugdale Soc., main ser., xv, 1939), no. 1109; *Feudal Aids. Inquisitions and Assessments Relating to Feudal Aids Preserved in the PRO, 1284 – 1431* (London, 1899 – 1920), v. 178.

Somewhat more secure was John Durvassal, who seems to have inherited Spernall from his father, William Durvassal. This estate seems to have comprised a demesne of two carucates and 40*s*. rent in 1246, assuming the land which he gave to his second son Roger — by-passing his heavily indebted heir William — to have been its entirety. John also held land at Buckley, near Henley in Arden, which he conveyed to the priory of Wootton Wawen, whilst his father had granted property at Great Alne to the abbey of Winchcombe. John was extremely active in the shire. In addition to being a prominent knight of the grand assize, he functioned as justice of the assize, justice of gaol delivery, as one of the commissioners for assessing and collecting the fortieth of 1232, as an assessor of tallage in 1235 and as commissioner under the Assize of Arms in 1242. He and John de Ladbrook held Warwick castle for the king in 1233 under a commission to assess any defects in castle defences in the county'.[33]

What can we say, then, of the stewards in general? First, it is true that they were prominent as knights of the grand assize and tended to function also in other capacities. They were, however, of varying backgrounds. They could still be, in the second quarter of the thirteenth century, the heads of fairly illustrious county families, or of others of less consequence but nonetheless established. They could be younger sons, or at least collaterals, of established families. Or indeed, they could well be more lowly figures who perhaps owed their status to service alone, which seems to be the case with William de Wilmcote. The balance between these types is likely to have varied, not only across time but from one lordship to another, though there is no reason to suppose the ministers of the earls of Warwick to have been strikingly atypical. Far from representing a segment of society outside of knighthood the stewards tend, in fact, to mirror its diversity.

With the stewards out of the way, we come to the *buzones* of the county court and Palmer's reassessment of the Gloucestershire false judgement case of 1212.[34] Without rehearsing this familiar case in detail, it should be recalled that the false judgement had been secured by tampering with the rolls. Thus the case concluded not only with the amercement of the county for false judgement and irregularities of procedure, but with the arrest of the knights of the county (court) who were accustomed to take part in false judgements and were *buzones* of the judgements ('Et milites de comitatu qui consueti sunt interesse falsis judiciis et sunt buzones judiciorum arestentur'). The plaintiff was also arrested. These *buzones* comprised William de Parco, Elias Cokerel and Hugh Mustel, the three knights who brought the false record to Westminster, and, for some reason that is not stated, two others, Walter de Aure and Philip de Beaumont ('alii buzones').[35] In his analysis Lapsley included both the plaintiff — on the grounds that he was clearly a figure of some influence in the court — and the fourth knight, one Geoffrey Martel, who ought to have carried the record to Westminster, with the others, but who claimed that he had not been present at the making of the judgement and was therefore ignorant of the case. There were thus seven men in all. The character of these *buzones*, as

---

[33] *VCH Warwickshire*, iii. 172; Dugdale, 756 – 7; *Warwicks. Feet of Fines, I*, no. 626.
[34] Palmer, *County Courts*, 130 – 5.
[35] The fullest discussion is in Lapsley, 'Buzones', 177 – 93. The case itself is to be found in *CRR* vi. 228 – 31. See also Flower, 'Introduction to the Curia Regis Rolls', 62 – 4.

Palmer rightly insists, is clearly an important matter. What he thinks of them in general we already know. Like Lapsley, whose view he is attacking, however, he seeks confirmation of his position from their biographical details. Palmer concentrates on two of them. Walter de Aure he finds to have been a fee-farmer at Aure and royal bailiff of the hundred of Newnham, although this is soon rendered 'bailiff and lawyer'. Philip de Beaumont functioned several times as a champion and was therefore 'more likely a lawyer than a self-respecting squire'. His traceable lands seem to have been largely acquired during his lifetime rather than inherited.[36] Oddly, these are the two whom the record does not specify as knights and whose role in this particular case seems tangential. With regard to the rest, Lapsley was able to show quite clearly that they were all active knights, involved in the grand assize and similar duties in the county. The most important of the five appears to have been William de Parco, who inherited from his father in 1194 and who held Bewper and an interest at Hardwick. He acquired further land from the Crown and rents in Gloucester from the earl of Hereford. Elias de Cokerel held principally at Cotes Cokerel where he possessed a half-fee. William de Eston, the plaintiff, was 'a man of substance and influence in the west country', whose chief interests appear to have been at North Aston (Oxfordshire) and at Cadbury and at Spaxton (Somerset), where he held in right of his wife. The other two seem to have been relatively obscure characters. Geoffrey Martel had been an active knight militarily in the service of the Crown. He had married one of three co-heiresses to property in Gloucestershire.[37] In the case of Hugh Mustel, however, Lapsley was unable to locate his interest. In short, the *buzones* of the court were a varied group, most of them knights, some perhaps not. They were variously endowed, and of varying background. They include, beyond doubt, men with some skill in the law. But if they are not all business-loving volunteers from among the country gentlemen, 'who manage the county business because they like the work',[38] equally they are not an exclusive category of lawyers.

I do not think, however, that we should leave the matter there, for the cases we have discussed give rise to important questions as to the nature of knighthood in the early thirteenth century. At this point I would like to refer, albeit briefly, to the results of my study of the situation in contemporary Warwickshire.[39] First, it is clear that knighthood was a widely shared social distinction. Secondly, the knights were of diverse interests and origins. Too much concern with knights' fees and with the military service owed to the Crown has caused us to concentrate on one major basis of knighthood, a problem compounded to some degree by the distraint of knighthood as it developed during the 1240s. The result is that we have applied an anachronistic model of knighthood to the later twelfth and early thirteenth centuries. Around 100 knights appear on panels or in the grand assize in Warwickshire between 1220 and 1232; of these, one-third or so can be categorized as either obscure or possessing only relatively minor interests in the county.

---

[36] Palmer, *County Courts*, 132 – 3. Palmer is surely right to criticize Lapsley's cavalier assumption that there was only one man bearing each of these names across the whole of England.

[37] A Geoffrey Martel was holding a half-fee at Stowell (Gloucs.) in 1235 – 6 and 1242 – 3, though this escaped Lapsley's notice: *Fees* i. 438, 819.

[38] Pollock and Maitland, i. 543.

[39] Detailed treatment will be found in my forthcoming book, *Lordship and Locality*.

Moreover, of the forty-one men who appear as knights of Warwickshire on the curia regis rolls between 1200 and 1210, the proportion of obscure and minor figures is as many as one-half. Notwithstanding problems of evidence and the imprecision of any sub-divisions one might devise, these proportions are very high. The *militulus* was clearly alive and well in early thirteenth-century England.

It is not just a question, however, of lesser endowment. Other features are apparent which help to account for this complex situation. One is the phenomenon of younger sons and collaterals. Another is the prevalence of interests, many of them minor, acquired by marriage. A third feature is service, of various kinds. In addition to the stewards of the earl of Warwick, we find, for example, William de Flamville, who had been steward to William de Hastings, and William Huse, who seems to have been in the service of Robert Marmion of Tamworth. Two others were, or had been, royal falconers. These features are not, of course, mutually exclusive, and two or three of them might be combined in the same individual. Their property, too, was of diverse origins. Some of it derived undoubtedly from the profits of service, and often the result of direct investment. Neither should one exclude from consideration the probability of household knights and ex-household knights holding rent income of various types. In truth, knighthood at this date was variously supported and had a variety of components, including a basis (whether exercized or not) in the profession of arms, an emphasis on service, and status conferred by wealth and/or relationship to the great. Naturally, there was an important ministerial element. Service was not something which arose in opposition to knighthood, or even alongside it, but was of its essence. Knighthood was permeated with it. Local society was becoming more literate and more professional, or perhaps we should say semi-professional, but it is often difficult as yet to delineate discrete categories among men, and virtually impossible to do so with the knights. The lesser knights, in fact, do not seem, on the whole, to predominate in the grand assize. Quite the contrary: it is more often the solidly based who are most active in the community — on the grand assize, on the various panels of knights, as justice of assize and gaol delivery, as coroner and so on. But again this was by no means exclusively so. The truth of the matter is that contemporary knights were neither strictly amateurs nor strictly professionals, but semi-professional because service was part of the knightly ethos, part of what conferred status, and because service was itself gradually becoming more professional.

There is another sense, too, in which Palmer's view is neither entirely accurate nor yet entirely false. Suit, if not completely decadent, was certainly declining in the early thirteenth century, and the number of knights present in the county court must often have been small. During the Gloucestershire false judgement case, for example, it was twice stated that the case had been postponed in the county because of poor attendance at court. Moreover, as we have seen, one of the four knights who was sent to Westminster with the record failed to attend. This was not unusual. As often as not when we hear of panels of knights on the curia regis rolls, we find that one or more (or even all) of them failed to make the view, to confirm the essoin, or even to elect the jurors. Again, the problems with the essoin *de malo lecti* in the Levelaunce case seem to have arisen because of difficulties, first, in electing a full panel of knights in the county court, and second, in getting the panel to expedite the matter effectively. As Dr. Maddicott says, men found the meetings of local courts 'vexatious, expensive and open to exploitation', and this surely applied to county courts as much as any others.[40] This is not to deny that the county could be an effective channel of communication between the Crown and the governed, nor that it could become a vociferous forum of opposition to the government. These things have been convincingly demonstrated.[41] But it is ironic, nonetheless, that one of the examples so often cited to show the county court in operation — the Lincolnshire case of 1226 — had as one of its major issues the desire to limit the session of the county court to a single day: to restrict, that is, the duration of the very body that is supposed to have expressed their solidarity! Many a sheriff, like the sheriff of Lincoln in 1226, must have found it difficult to conduct the business and must have been tempted to bend the rules in order to operate effectively at all. As we have seen at Warwick in the previous year, the sheriff ordered the appointment of a fourth knight who was not present to make up the requisite panel for the view *de malo lecti*. What I am saying is that, for the most part, local society operated at some remove from the county court. The majority of its meetings, then, were not large gatherings of knights and freeholders eager to take part in 'self-government at the king's command', to use that hackneyed phrase. It would probably be truer to say that most knights avoided the detailed business of the court except where their interests, personal or shared, were concerned, and except when called upon to act when their status was specifically required — and not invariably even then. We can hardly avoid the truth of Maitland's supposition that 'the ordinary business of the court was transacted by a small group of active men'.[42]

One final point should be made. Actions of false judgement, such as the Gloucestershire case of 1212 and the Oxfordshire case of 1222, strongly suggest that justice in the county court could be partial. Although in these particular instances matters were clearly put right — and we should not undervalue the capacity to circumvent corruption — it nevertheless remains the case that a variety of corrective and preventative processes had to be built into the developing legal system to make it workable. Even the 'royal benefit' of the grand assize, replacing trial by battle, was not necessarily equally beneficial for all. The prior of Coventry, for instance, complained in the royal court in 1201 that the Leicestershire county court had refused him a view of eight carucates of land at Packington, for which an action of right had been brought against him, and that he had been threatened there and forced to plead against his will. He elected to defend his land through his champion 'because he feared that they would judge his land away from him' ('et quia verebatur prior ne forisjudicarent eum de terra sua predicta, optulit defendere illam per Henricum hominem suum'). He then went immediately to the justiciar and complained that the county intended false judgement against him. As a result the record of the wager of the duel was summoned to Westminster, and the case, it was decided, should proceed there. Clearly, the prior of Coventry had no faith in the integrity of the county court of Leicestershire, which is presumably why he chose not to invoke the procedure of the grand assize.[43] In 1214 the prior of Warwick complained that although he had opted for battle in a case involving two virgates at

---

[40] Maddicott, 'Magna Carta', 36.
[41] Ibid. *passim*; J. C. Holt, 'The Prehistory of Parliament', in *The English Parliament in the Middle Ages*, ed. R. G. Davies and J. H. Denton (Manchester, 1981), 1–28.
[42] Pollock and Maitland, i. 553.
[43] For the full details, see *CRR* i. 445–6; and Flower, 'Introduction to the Curia Regis Rolls', 67–8.

Pillerton (Warwickshire), and the duel had been waged in proper fashion, it was being prevented locally from taking place.[44] One is reminded of the example of trial by battle later in the century, to which V. H. Galbraith drew attention, when the champion of the abbey of Bury St. Edmunds lost his life. A chronicle account tells us that the monks had opted for trial by battle rather than the grand assize because they suspected the countryside of being inclined towards, and related to, their enemies ('patriam habentes suspectam utpote adversariis nostris familiarem et affinem').[45]

Perhaps the religious were particularly vulnerable to collusive action, but it was not only they who needed to be wary of the inclinations of the countryside. Take the case between two north Warwickshire knights, Thomas de Arden and John de Bracebridge, which came to a conclusion in 1208.[46] Thomas sought a knight's fee at Kingsbury by right of inheritance from his distant ancestor, Turchil of Warwick, and his son, Siward de Arden, and offered to prove this by the body of his free man, that is to say by battle. John put himself on the grand assize. Thomas then argued that the grand assize ought not be held because they were both descended from the one stock ('de uno stipite'), viz. from Turchil. Glanvill tells us that because members of the same stock ought not to fight, the grand assize, which was deemed to be a substitute for trial by battle, was in such cases automatically invalidated. Had this been found to be the case, the issue would have been decided by inquiry of their relatives and, in case of deadlock, of the neighbourhood.[47] In fact, John de Bracebridge was able to show that although they were indeed both descended from Turchil, his right did not lie through him but through Turchil's second wife, Leveruna, whose own land this had been and from whom he was descended. Turchil's grandson, Osbert de Arden, had left three daughters who had succeeded in turn, the last of them being Amicia, wife of Peter de Bracebridge and John's mother.

So far, it is a textbook case, straight from the pages of Glanvill's treatise, as it were. It is now that we come across one of the procedure's in-built correctives, for John offered 10 marks to have a jury composed of knights from two counties, on the grounds that Kingsbury lay on the confines of Warwickshire and Staffordshire. Thomas offered the same for a jury from Warwickshire alone. John won the day, and two knights from each of the counties were to choose the twelve jurors. He also won the case.[48] Kingsbury is indeed in the far north of Warwickshire, although well within its border. The issue was, of course, the degree of objectivity, or rather partisanship, to be expected from the jurors. Bracebridge was probably no more influential in Staffordshire than Warwickshire; indeed, his family's roots were far away in Bracebridge (Lincolnshire). It was the authority and prestige of Thomas de Arden that was the real issue here. The senior representative of an ancient stock with estates not only in this locality but in several parts of Warwickshire, and in fact the overlord of many a knight, he was much better connected and much better

---

[44] *CRR* vii. 75.

[45] V. H. Galbraith, 'The Death of a Champion (1287)', in *Studies in Medieval History Presented to F. M. Powicke*, ed. R. W. Hunt, W. A. Pantin and R. W. Southern (Oxford, 1948), 283 – 95.

[46] *CRR* v. 241 – 2.

[47] For the procedure of the grand assize, see *Tractatus de Legibus et Consuetudinibus regni Anglie qui Glanvilla vocatur*, ed. and trans. G. D. G. Hall (Oxford, 1965), 26 – 8.

[48] *Warwicks. Feet of Fines, I*, no. 186.

positioned than the defendant in the case. He had, in fact, three chances of winning: through his champion, through inquiry of the Arden family or of the locality, and through a jury of north Warwickshire — each of which would seem to have given him a better chance than the means by which the issue was finally resolved.

We should be very wary, therefore, of assuming either that the county court in general necessarily administered equitable justice, or that the grand assize in particular was socially neutral. Further instances could be quoted, but the situation is perhaps expressed most graphically in 'Bracton', in the discussion of the writ *pone*, which transferred a case from the county to the royal court. This writ was rarely available to the defendant, except in certain circumstances: for example, where he has been long overseas, and presumably therefore not properly part of local society, or where the plaintiff is related to the sheriff or is his servant or close follower, or is very powerful and a *buzo* of the county.[49] Too much stress can be placed on the possibility of baronial interference in particular, and not enough of the tendency for judgements in general, to favour those with personal influence. Most important of all, we should resist any sense of the county court embodying the primeval spirit of free-born and liberty-loving Englishmen. When Richard Revel, in his famous case in the Somerset county court in 1204, stressed his and his family's local credentials as 'naturales homines et gentiles de patria', and the sheriff's lack of status there as an outsider ('adventicius'), he may well have been making a political statement about the over-zealous intrusion of royal officials into local affairs. A point that should not be overlooked, however, is that he hoped to win advantage thereby and to save the 60 marks that William Dacus was seeking by writ as damages for disseisin. In Richard's view the sheriff should recognize the status of himself, his father and his brothers, and deal justly with them ('ut eos inde juste deduceret').[50] When local men preferred to run local affairs, they did so not merely to keep a rapacious central government at bay but also to ensure that the local social order was reflected in, and social authority maintained by, the decision-making processes. It is necessary to say these things because the ghost of constitutional history still walks among us, as no doubt it long will.

---

[49] Bracton, iv. 59. Paul Brand has drawn my attention to the fact that neither of these clauses became standard.
[50] *CRR* iii. 129.

The Sheriff of Nottingham and Robin Hood:
The Genesis of the Legend?

David Crook

The discovery of a number of 'Robinhood' surnames earlier in date than the year 1300 has put an effective end to interpretations attempting to show that the legend of Robin Hood began only during the fourteenth century.[1] The rarity of such a combination of Christian name and surname to form a surname must mean that those involved in the creation of the names, and the recording of them, knew something of the outlaw figure, and they indicate that the legend was widely known in southern England in the later thirteenth century. In 1296 a Gilbert Robynhod paid tax at Fletching in eastern Sussex.[2] A year earlier in the common bench at Westminster a William Robynhod sued Roger son of Walter of Tilbrook to warrant him 2s. rent in Tilbrook (Huntingdonshire).[3] A year earlier still, in 1294 during an enquiry into the misdeeds of vagabonds before the king's justices, who were sitting at Winchester, a Robert Robehod who had been born at Sutton Scotney was among those indicted for stealing four sheep.[4] In the 1286 eyre in Suffolk the jurors of Blackbourne hundred reported that a steward had taken 10s. from a Gilbert Robehod to release him to pledges, when he was in fact repleviable by statute,[5] while in the 1272 Hampshire eyre the Fareham hundred jury said that John Rabunhod (or Robehod) was one of four men in the tithing of Roger le Page of Compton who killed John son of Simon after a quarrel in an inn at Charford.[6] The earliest reference of all — that in an exchequer memoranda roll of 1262 — indicates that a clerk working for a royal justice, in the chancery or at the exchequer itself, knew something of the legendary character, since he was aware of the real name of the man involved, William son of Robert Smith (le Fevre), and yet altered it to William Robehod, presumably as some sort of joke. William was a man from Enborne (Berkshire) accused of larcenies and harbouring who had fled the jurisdiction of the justices in eyre in that county in 1261. The prior of Sandleford was amerced the sum of 1 mark for seizing his chattels, which should have gone to

[1] See esp. J. R. Maddicott, 'The Birth and Setting of the Ballads of Robin Hood', *EHR* xciii (1978), 276 – 99; and J. G. Bellamy, *Robin Hood: An Historical Enquiry* (London, 1985); with the comments of J. C. Holt, *Robin Hood* (London, 1982), ch. 3; id., 'Robin Hood Revised', *Johns Hopkins Magazine*, xxxv (1984), xii – xvi; and id., review of Bellamy in *Albion*, xvii (1986), 79 – 80. Professor Holt has consistently championed a thirteenth-century date for the origin of the legend.
[2] Holt, *Robin Hood*, 65.
[3] CP 40/109, rot. 51. Unless otherwise stated, all manuscript references in this paper are to documents in the PRO.
[4] JUST 1/1301, rot. 12. For this and the following two references I am indebted to the kindness of Dr. H. R. T. Summerson.
[5] JUST 1/827, rot. 41d.
[6] JUST 1/780, rot. 18d.

the king, and it was during the process by which the debt was demanded against the prior, and then pardoned, that the form of the name was changed. It is to be supposed that the man who altered the name thought of Robin Hood as a criminal and fugitive.[7]

While, therefore, it seemed reasonable until recently to seek the origins of the legend about a generation before the first reference to 'rhymes of Robin Hood' in the B-text of Langland's *Piers Plowman*, written *c.* 1377 – 9, it is now apparent that a date some time before the year 1262 is required. Such a search leads in the first instance to the one known individual bearing the name who lived before that date, the Robert Hod who fled the jurisdiction of the king's justices for assizes and gaol delivery who sat at York under the leadership of Robert of Lexington in July 1225, and whose chattels were subsequently accounted for at the exchequer by the sheriff of Yorkshire.[8] We know nothing of that man save that he was a tenant of, or was subject to the jurisdiction of, the archbishop of York in Yorkshire, since the archbishop later claimed his chattels; Lexington's plea roll, which would have given the detail of the offence he was accused of having committed, has, like Lexington's other rolls, failed to survive.[9] He remains, as Professor Holt has pointed out, the only man called Robin Hood who is known to have been a suspected criminal,[10] and he lived long enough before 1262 to allow time for the development and dissemination of stories about him. He is the only realistic candidate already in the field, and he draws the enquirer towards Yorkshire at the end of the first quarter of the thirteenth century as a possible context for the origin of England's most durable legend.

The name appears in the Yorkshire account in nine successive pipe rolls from 1226 to 1234, six times as Robert Hod, once (in 1229) as Robert Hood and twice (in 1227 and 1228) as Hobbehod.[11] In 1227 'St. Peter' is inserted in the margin of the roll next to his name, and again in 1234, when the name is also preceded by a cross;[12] in the following year, it has been removed from the roll. It appears from this that the Church of St. Peter (in effect the archbishop of York) claimed and eventually was granted the chattels, which tells us that the fugitive was a tenant of the archbishop, or in some other way subject to his jurisdiction. That, and the fact that he committed or was thought to have committed some offence which caused him to flee, is all that we know about him.

Professor Holt, following a suggestion by Jeffrey Stafford, pointed out that Robert Hod's chattels were accounted for at the Michaelmas exchequer of 1226 by a sheriff of Yorkshire called Eustace of Lowdham, who held that office from 29 April 1225 to 26 May 1226, and who later, in 1232 – 3, was sheriff of Nottinghamshire and Derbyshire: 'He is the only known sheriff from whom there may have been a tenuous link to the only known outlaw bearing the name of Robin

---

[7] D. Crook, 'Some Further Evidence concerning the Dating of the Origins of the Legend of Robin Hood', *EHR* xcix (1984), 530 – 4.
[8] Holt, *Robin Hood*, 53 – 4.
[9] D. Crook, *Records of the General Eyre* (PRO Handbooks, no. 20, London, 1982), 16 – 17.
[10] Holt, *Robin Hood*, 54.
[11] E 372/70, rot. 1d; E 372/71, rot. 4d; E 372/72, rot. 14d; E 372/73, rot. 17; E 372/74, rot. 14; E 372/75, rot. 11; E 372/76, rot. 3; E 372/77, rot. 4; E 372/78, rot. 2.
[12] E 372/71, rot. 4d; E 372/78, rot. 2.

Hood, and he later became sheriff of Nottingham.'[13] Holt went on to say that, since he had concluded that the Nottinghamshire and Yorkshire tales of the sheriff and Robin Hood were probably distinct originally, identification of the prototype of the wicked sheriff of Nottingham, if indeed there was one, need not depend on his intervention in Yorkshire. That view has also found favour with Dobson and Taylor, and earlier with L. V. D. Owen. Nevertheless, his coincidence in time and place with Robert Hod is remarkable and it justifies a closer look at his life and career.

Eustace of Lowdham took his name from the village of that name in Nottinghamshire, only a few miles both from the river Trent and from the great minster church of the archbishops of York at Southwell. He was a clerk in the diocese of York who came to make a career in local government, first in the smaller of the two counties of the diocese, his native Nottinghamshire, and later in the larger, Yorkshire. All that is known of his parentage is that his father was called Herbert. In Michaelmas term 1220 he sued Philip son of Robert in a Hertfordshire plea of warranty of charter in the common bench at Westminster, appointing the Nottinghamshire men Godfrey Spigurnel, a chancery sergeant, and Henry of Gringley as his attorneys.[14] In an entry appointing a day for the case to be heard later in the same term he is referred to as 'Eustace son of Herbert'.[15] Perhaps the earliest record of him is in an undated grant by William Spicfat of Caythorpe to John, chaplain of Lowdham, probably made soon after 1200, of which, as 'Eustace of Lowdham, clerk', he was the first witness.[16] In 1207, as 'Eustace parson of Lowdham', he fell foul of King John, because in the pipe roll of that year he owed 15 marks, payable at 100s. per annum, for making a ditch at Lowdham 'in the manner of a deer leap' ('in modum saltorii').[17] It is quite likely that the fine was imposed by the king himself, since he visited Lowdham in August that year and since he took a close personal interest in forest matters;[18] it was probably on the same occasion that the lady of Lowdham, Emma de Beaufey, fined 100 marks to have seisin of her land in Lowdham of which she had been disseised 'on account of a certain ditch made against the forest without the king's licence'.[19] In November 1208 'Eustace clerk of Lowdham' was before the king's justices in eyre at Derby as defendant in a plea brought by Thomas son of Geoffrey concerning half a carucate of land at Lamcote in Radcliffe on Trent. They came to agreement by a final concord for which Eustace paid 3 marks, acknowledging the land to be Thomas's in return for an annual rent of 2s.[20] Probably somewhat later he was the first witness, his son Walter being the second, of a grant by Godfrey Angevin to Fulk of

---

[13] Holt, *Robin Hood*, 60 – 1.

[14] *CRR* ix. 208. For the connection of Eustace with Hertfordshire, see also *CR 1231 – 4*, 212. For Godfrey Spigurnel, who also had some sort of connection with Herts., see D. Crook, 'The Spigurnels of Skegby', *Nottingham Medieval Studies*, xxi (1977), 50 – 70.

[15] *CRR* ix. 217.

[16] HMC, *Middleton MSS* (London, 1911), 38 – 9.

[17] *Pipe Roll 9 John*, ed. A. M. Kirkus (Pipe Roll Soc., new ser., xxii), 24.

[18] J. C. Holt, *The Northerners* (Oxford, 1961), 159 – 60.

[19] *Rotuli de Oblatis et Finibus*, ed. T. D. Hardy (London, 1835), 379. At some point Emma made the manor of Lowdham over to King John by a charter which was in 1227 declared to be invalid: *CChR 1226 – 57*, 49. In 1236 she surrendered it to Henry III in reversion and he had gained possession by 1243: *CChR 1226 – 57*, 223 – 4, 310; *CR 1242 – 7*, 45, 49, 122.

[20] CP 25/1/182/2, no. 43; Crook, *Records*, 70.

Lowdham of land in Lowdham.[21] It is clear that, during the reign of John, Eustace was an established man of property and man of affairs in his native village and the surrounding district. It is therefore no great surprise to find him in the service of the local sheriff before the reign came to an end.

In the thirteenth century, and for long afterwards, the sheriff of Nottingham was responsible for two counties, Nottinghamshire and Derbyshire, which he administered from the castle built by the Conqueror on top of the great rock by the Trent at Nottingham. Derbyshire was in a position of subordination to its eastern neighbour. Until 1256, when a separate Derbyshire county court was established, the two counties shared a county court which met at Nottingham, while the county gaol for both counties was also at Nottingham and was normally delivered there.[22] From 1209 the sheriff of Nottinghamshire and Derbyshire was Philip Mark, who probably came from the Touraine just south of the Loire, and who served King John in England with several of his compatriots after the area was lost to Philip II of France in 1204.[23] By 1214 Eustace of Lowdham was Philip Mark's deputy and clerk, for after Michaelmas that year he accounted at the exchequer for the sixteenth year of the reign on Philip's behalf.[24] By then he may have been in the sheriff's service for some time, quite possibly since he first took office in 1209. He was almost certainly working for him by 1212, when 'Eustace the clerk' vouched for his master's expenditure of £107 in obtaining wine, grain and pork for the king, and in transporting them between York, Chester and Nottingham.[25] Before September 1213 he was renting a house from the king in St. Mary's parish below the gaol in Nottingham, presumably as a convenient *pied à terre* near his office in the castle. On 3 September that year the king granted the rent that he was accustomed to pay for the house to the Templars; the house was to become their free hospice in the town.[26]

The civil war which broke out between King John and the rebel barons in 1215, following the breakdown of the agreement reached at Runnymede in June that year, must have caused a conflict of loyalties for Eustace of Lowdham. In Magna Carta, John had agreed to remove his Poitevin followers from their offices in England and never to allow them to hold office there in future; Philip Mark and his relatives were among those specifically named.[27] Philip did not, however, relinquish the shrievalty, and he controlled the east Midlands for the king from Nottingham castle during the civil war. While he did so Eustace of Lowdham was not with him, since he took the side of his lord, John de Lacy, constable of Chester, a rebel, rather than that of his employer. Lacy had a mesne holding in Lowdham of the honor of Chester, and it was evidently through that holding that Eustace was connected with

[21] HMC, *Middleton MSS*, 54 – 5.

[22] D. Crook, 'The Establishment of the Derbyshire County Court, 1256', *Derbyshire Archaeological Journ.* ciii (1983), 98 – 106.

[23] J. C. Holt, 'Philip Mark and the Shrievalty of Nottinghamshire and Derbyshire in the Early Thirteenth Century', *Trans. Thoroton Soc.* lvi (1952), 8 – 24.

[24] *Pipe Roll 16 John*, ed. P. M. Barnes (Pipe Roll Soc., new ser., xxxv), 156.

[25] *Pipe Roll 14 John*, ed. P. M. Barnes (Pipe Roll Soc., new ser., xxx), 27.

[26] *RLC* i. 149. The rent paid by 'Eustace the clerk' seems to have been only 6*d.* per annum: *Pipe Roll 16 John*, 157; *Pipe Roll 17 John*, ed. R. A. Brown (Pipe Roll Soc., new ser., xxxvii), 31; *Pipe Roll 3 Henry III*, ed. J. Deas, P. M. Barnes, B. E. Harris, D. Crook (Pipe Roll Soc., new ser., xlii), 93.

[27] J. C. Holt, *Magna Carta* (Cambridge, 1965), 328 – 31.

him.[28] In May 1216 the king notified Philip Mark that at the petition of John de Lacy he had pardoned the arrears of the fine that Eustace had made for having his peace with the king because he had been against him with Lacy.[29] The latter had made his peace with the king in January 1216, so presumably Eustace had done so at about the same time.[30]

In the event, his momentary disloyalty to King John made little difference to his career under the young Henry III. To judge by the entries in the pipe rolls, it would appear that during the years of the king's minority Philip Mark accounted at the exchequer in person, since his is the only name that appears at the head of the account.[31] They do not, however, give an accurate indication of who accounted; the memoranda rolls of the two remembrancers, which begin to survive in a more or less regular sequence at that very point, do. What they show is that during the whole of the rest of the time that Philip held the shrievalty — that is until he was replaced by Ralph fitzNicholas, the household steward, on 28 December 1224 —[32] he only once appeared at the exchequer in person to render his account. From the time when the exchequer resumed its operations after the war in November 1217, Nottinghamshire and Derbyshire accounts were almost invariably rendered in Philip's name by 'Eustace of Lowdham, his clerk'.[33] Eustace was the accounting sheriff during the whole of that period while Philip was the titular holder of the office. Philip was in some ways, although to a far lesser extent, a regional military overlord in the same fashion as Fawkes de Breauté, who held six counties in the south Midlands and worked through acting sheriffs in all those counties until he fell, shortly before Philip, in the summer of 1224. Not only was Eustace of Lowdham the working sheriff of Nottinghamshire and Derbyshire from 1217 to 1224, he may often simply have been referred to as 'sheriff' — as many other deputy sheriffs were during that period —[34] although no indisputable evidence in his case has been found. A plea roll reference of Michaelmas term 1233 probably refers to his period as titular sheriff at about that time.[35] A grant to Thomas de Curzun of Kedleston (Derbyshire), which Eustace witnessed as sheriff of Nottingham, is undated but seems to be closely associated with another deed dated Easter 1232.[36] Another undated deed, of the prior of Lenton granting land in Sutton Passeys, which Eustace witnessed as sheriff, may not have been accurately dated by

---

[28] *Early Yorkshire Charters, III*, ed. W. Farrer (Yorks. Arch. Soc., Rec. ser., Extra ser., 1916), 190–1; W. E. Wightman, *The Lacy Family in England and Normandy, 1066–1194* (Oxford, 1966), 91.

[29] *Memoranda Roll 1 John*, ed. H. G. Richardson (Pipe Roll Soc., new ser., xxi, 1943), 144; Holt, *The Northerners*, 50.

[30] Holt, *The Northerners*, 1.

[31] *Pipe Roll 3 Henry III*, 91; *Pipe Roll 4 Henry III*, ed. B. E. Harris (Pipe Roll Soc., new ser., xlvii), 149; E 372/65, rot. 5; E 372/66, rot. 3; E 372/67, rot. 2d; E 372/68, rot. 16.

[32] *PR 1216–25*, 500.

[33] E 159/2, m.17d; E 368/1, mm.2, 6; E 368/3, m.2; E 368/4, mm.9, 13d; E 368/5, m.14; E 368/6, mm.17d, 23d; E 368/7, m.25d. The single exception was when Philip accounted in person for the sixth year of the reign on 1 May 1223: E 368/5, m.3. To judge by the famous letter of 1220 concerning the dispute involving Roger de Monbegon in the county court, Philip also ran the court through agents, although Eustace was not one of them: *Royal Letters*, i. no. 86.

[34] B. E. Harris, in introduction to *Pipe Roll 4 Henry III*, xi–xii.

[35] *CRR* xv. no. 508.

[36] *Descriptive Catalogue of Derbyshire Charters*, ed. I. H. Jeayes (London, Derby, 1906), nos. 1501, 1503.

its editor and could also belong to the early 1230s.[37] Four undated Rufford abbey charters in which he also witnessed as sheriff of Nottingham, two of them dated by their editor to 1212 – 13, cannot be placed with certainty before 1225, although some or all of them may have been made before that date.[38] For the present, it must suffice to suppose that by the mid-1220s he was closely enough associated with the office to be popularly known as 'the sheriff of Nottingham'.

The fall of Philip Mark at the end of 1224 presumably meant that Eustace was without a job, since the new sheriff, Ralph fitzNicholas, consistently employed Hugh le Bel as his clerk and undersheriff. Only four months later, on 29 April 1225, Eustace was appointed sheriff of Yorkshire.[39] On 27 November of that year he accounted for his shire at the exchequer for himself, as he had done so many times before on behalf of Philip Mark.[40] When the next Yorkshire account was rendered, however, he accounted for only three-quarters of the year, since he had by then been replaced by Robert of Cockfield, on 25 May 1226.[41] Robert was the steward of the justiciar, Hubert de Burgh, who at that time was consolidating his power over the government of the kingdom by placing his supporters in key positions; Hubert had already arranged for the custody of important castles in Yorkshire to be handed over to Cockfield.[42] During his year in office Eustace carried out the usual tasks performed by all sheriffs, such as keeping the king's buildings, paying his officials and making purchases for his use.[43] When he left office he was still in debt to the king to the extent of over £125; over £15 of that amount was pardoned in 1228 – 9, and he continued to pay off the rest at a fixed rate of £10 per annum.[44] Such arrangements were, however, perfectly normal, and his indebtedness did not prevent him from being a sheriff again, this time in his native Nottinghamshire. About 24 April 1233 he temporarily became sheriff in the place of Ralph fitzNicholas, and with the blessing of the latter.[45] The arrangement did not last long and had probably come to an end by mid-October 1233,[46] and Eustace never served as a sheriff again. He had been employed in a number of other capacities in Nottinghamshire and other counties north of the Trent. He had been a justice of gaol delivery for Nottingham gaol in 1227 and 1232,[47] a special assize justice in Nottinghamshire in 1229 and in Derbyshire in 1230,[48] an assessor of

---

[37] HMC, *Middleton MSS*, 55 – 6, where it is dated *c*. 1213 – 14, presumably because of the Pipe Roll evidence that he rendered the county account then: above, n. 24. The dating depends on the dates of prior R. of Lenton, to whom this may be the only reference, but he may be the Prior Roger who occurs in 1230 and 1231, just before Eustace's short period as titular sheriff: *Heads of Religious Houses in England and Wales, 940 – 1216*, ed. D. Knowles, C. N. L. Brooke and V. London (Cambridge, 1972), 119. When he served as clerk to the commissioners for the sale of cablish in Notts. and Derbys. in 1223 he was naturally not referred to as sheriff: *PR 1216 – 25*, 399.
[38] *Rufford Charters*, ed. C. J. Holdsworth (Thoroton Soc., Rec. ser., xxix, xxx, xxxii, xxxiv, 1972 – 81), nos. 174 – 5, 551, 631.
[39] *PR 1216 – 25*, 524.
[40] E 368/8, m.20; E 372/69, rot. 9.
[41] E 368/9, m.7; E 372/70, rot. 1; *PR 1225 – 32*, 38.
[42] *Ex inf.* Dr. D. Carpenter.
[43] E.g. *CLR 1226 – 40*, 33.
[44] E 372/72, rot. 14d; E 372/73, rot. 17d; E 372/74, rot. 14; *CR 1227 – 31*, 61, 156.
[45] *CR 1231 – 4*, 212.
[46] *CRR* xv. no. 508.
[47] *PR 1225 – 32*, 160, 516.
[48] *PR 1225 – 32*, 306, 443 – 4.

tallage in Derbyshire before 1231,[49] and a forest justice in Cumberland and Lancashire in that year.[50] After 1233 he was much less active and was probably mainly in retirement, although in 1234 he was again a special assize commissioner, in a Nottinghamshire and Yorkshire case,[51] and as late as April 1241 he was appointed to assess tallage in Nottinghamshire, Derbyshire, Lincolnshire and Yorkshire.[52] By then he was nearing his end, and in or about that year, for the safety of his soul, he made grants of 2s. rent in Horspool and two and a half bovates of land in Thurgarton to Thurgarton priory; he was dead by 1246 at the latest.[53]

In the later years of his life Eustace continued to acquire property in Lowdham. On 8 September 1235 he received six gifts of land and assarts there, four of them from Emma de Beaufey, and the lands of Robert son of Roger de Pascy in Gonalston, Thurgarton, Horspool, Hoveringham, Southwell and Newark.[54] According to the jurors of the Hundred Rolls inquiry in 1275, Eustace made a park at Lowdham in the reign of Henry III and blocked a highway at 'Bariltinhus' there with a bank or ditch; during Henry's reign he also made two assarts, of eight and a half acres and two and a half acres, in Emma de Beaufey's fee there.[55] Those properties were all in the south and east of Nottinghamshire, but he also had obtained a holding further north. On 13 November 1234 the king granted him and his heirs the rent of 30s. which Henry Corbin had in Carlton in Lindrick, for which he was to render 6d. yearly at the Easter exchequer.[56] Eustace is not known to have made any acquisitions in Yorkshire, and his appointment to the shrievalty of that county seems to be the calling-in of a professional administrator to fill a gap. Nevertheless, he did have a connection with Yorkshire through the lordship of John de Lacy. Our only evidence of his relationship with Lacy is that which indicates that he rebelled with him against King John in 1215 – 16.[57] Its obvious origin was the Lacy holding in Lowdham, and it is possible that it was John de Lacy's influence which secured Eustace the Yorkshire shrievalty in 1225. The centre of the large Lacy honor was at Pontefract; the Lowdham holding had been acquired from the earl of Chester towards the end of the reign of Stephen, and although it may not have been regarded as technically part of the honor of Pontefract, it had been closely attached to it ever since then.[58] It is possible that Eustace served John de Lacy as an official of his administration, but no evidence has been found which would confirm the suggestion. What is certain is that his son did so, and in a very senior capacity.

---

[49] *CR 1227–31*, 492.

[50] *CR 1227–31*, 574, 585.

[51] CP 25/1/283/10, no. 107; *Yorkshire Fines 1232–46*, ed. J. Parker (Yorks. Arch. Soc., Rec. ser., lxvii, 1925), 171.

[52] *CPR 1232–47*, 263; *CLR 1240–5*, 63; *CR 1237–42*, 303.

[53] Southwell Minster, MS 3,f.2r (I am indebted to Dr. T. Foulds for this reference); E 368/19, m.1; E 372/89, rot. 3.

[54] *CChR 1226–57*, 212. Eustace witnessed a grant by Emma of a meadow in Lowdham to Welbeck abbey: BL, MS Harley 3640, f. 92r.

[55] *RH* ii. 311; *The Sherwood Forest Book*, ed. H. E. Boulton (Thoroton Soc., Rec. ser., xxiii, 1965), 96.

[56] *CChR 1226–57*; E 372/79, rot. 3. It did pass to his heirs on his death: E 372/88, rot. 3; E 372/90, rot. 6; E 368/19, m.1.

[57] Above, and n. 29.

[58] Wightman, 91, 93; and map on p. 33; F. M. Stenton, *The First Century of English Feudalism* (2nd edn., Oxford, 1961), 271 – 2.

In 1232 John de Lacy was made earl of Lincoln, and the title was inherited on his death in 1240 by his son Edmund, a minor.[59] Edmund's steward was a man called Walter of Lowdham, to whom his father John had granted timber from his wood in Axholme shortly before his death, and who had earlier been a witness to some of John's charters.[60] In Hilary term 1248 in the exchequer, when described as Edmund's bailiff, Walter of Lowdham acknowledged receipt from the archbishop of York of all his lord Edmund's lands which the archbishop had held at farm.[61] A deed shows that Walter managed the estate on Edmund's behalf while he was under age. At an unknown date he came to an agreement as Edmund's steward to exchange with Adam de Neufmarché a small piece of land twenty perches of twenty feet long by ten feet wide below Adam's garden in Campsall and next to a windmill, subject to Edmund's agreement when he should come of age.[62] We have already seen that Eustace of Lowdham had a son called Walter,[63] and a Walter of Lowdham inherited Eustace's park at Lowdham and land in Carlton in Lindrick.[64] There can be little doubt that the steward of Edmund de Lacy was the son of Eustace of Lowdham.

Some of the demesne lands of the Lacy honor and the holdings of its sub-tenants lay in an area known as Barnsdale, which lay astride the Great North Road a few miles south-east of Pontefract on the way towards Doncaster.[65] Campsall, where Walter of Lowdham arranged Edmund de Lacy's affairs in such detail, was on the fringe of it. The primacy of Barnsdale in the early Robin Hood legend has been demonstrated by Holt, and by Dobson and Taylor, and Holt has suggested that the Lacy fee was important in the transmission of the legend both across into Lancashire and down into the south of England.[66] In Eustace of Lowdham we are dealing with a man who may have been a familiar figure in Barnsdale — as his son later certainly must have been, because of his attachment to the Lacy fee — a man, moreover, who, when he moved to York as sheriff in April 1225, later to account for the chattels of Robert Hod, fugitive, could well have been known in Barnsdale as 'the sheriff of Nottingham'. The property he later acquired in Carlton in Lindrick lay on the road which led from Nottingham through Sherwood Forest and Barnsdale to York. It was probably along that road that, as sheriff, he conducted from York to Nottingham £1000 given to the king's brother, Richard, by the king of Scots; the wages of the men who guarded it must have accounted for a large part of the £4 3s. 8d. that the operation cost.[67] Not only that, but one of his first tasks during his short period of office as sheriff of Yorkshire was to organize a manhunt for a wanted criminal. On 12 July 1225, at Winchester, the king and the justiciar

---

[59] *GEC* vii. 680. On the circumstances of the grant of the earldom, see R. Eales, 'Henry III and the End of the Norman Earldom of Chester', in *Thirteenth Century England I: Procs. of the Newcastle upon Tyne Conference, 1985*, ed. P. R. Coss and S. D. Lloyd (Woodbridge, 1986), 103 – 4.
[60] DL 25/2156; *CR 1237 – 42*, 281; DL 25/54, 55.
[61] E 368/20, m.6.
[62] DL 25/2156.
[63] Above and n. 21.
[64] *RH* ii. 311; C 132/2, no. 16; *CIPM* i. no. 36.
[65] For the Lacy estates in S. Yorks., see Wightman, 23, map; for Barnsdale and its extent, see Holt, *Robin Hood*, 83 – 6.
[66] Holt, *Robin Hood*, 53, and ch. 5; R. B. Dobson and J. Taylor, *Rymes of Robyn Hood: An Introduction to the English Outlaw* (London, 1976), 18 – 24.
[67] E 372/70, rot. 1.

authorized a writ to the barons of the exchequer to allow the sheriff of Yorkshire 40*s*. spent by him on the royal order to hire sergeants to 'seek and take and behead Robert of Wetherby, outlaw and evildoer of our land'.[68] When Eustace came to account at the exchequer in November 1225, the writ was set against the expenses of his farm; one of the other expenses he claimed was 2*s*. 'for a chain to hang Robert of Wetherby'.[69] From the following year's account we learn that a further 28*s*. was spent on the operation, and that the leader of the sergeants was a man called William the Vintner.[70]

Nothing further is known of Robert of Wetherby, of the nature of his crimes, or of the part of Yorkshire where Eustace of Lowdham's sergeants went to capture him. From the mention of the chain purchased to hang him, it must be assumed that he was in fact brought to justice; it probably also means that his body was put on display, hung up by the chain. From the nature of the measures taken to apprehend him, it is clear that he was no ordinary criminal. The hiring of a special group of sergeants paid by the king's principal agent in the county puts him well above the level of an ordinary murderer or robber, for whom the hue and cry of the neighbouring vills would have sufficed. He was probably a celebrity already in the district when the sheriff's men set out to fulfill their grim task. It is conceivable, but impossible to prove, that he and the fugitive Robert Hod were the same man. The possibility is not ruled out by the different ways the two are described. Robert of Wetherby had been outlawed by July, possibly some time before, whereas Robert Hod was described in the pipe roll merely as a fugitive; that would usually be taken to mean that he was a suspect who had fled, but the confiscation of his chattels could have been noted at a time when he had not yet been outlawed. If Robert of Wetherby's toponym means that he came from Wetherby, he is likely to have been a man of the Percy lordship, for it was a Percy town.[71] His connection with the place may, however, have been remote, and there is no reason why he should not have been in some way subject to the archbishop of York, as Robert Hod was.[72] It is quite within the bounds of possibility that the area in which he was hunted was Barnsdale itself. All that can be said for certain is that the two men shared the same, very common, forename and fell foul of the law in the same, very large, county at about the same time. Robert of Wetherby was probably captured about July; the question of his chattels could have come before Robert of Lexington and his fellow justices for assizes and gaol delivery at the end of that month. Although not 'justices for all pleas', their commission obliged them to take presentments from local juries 'concerning those who are suspected of larcenies, robberies and homicides';[73] and the only surviving plea rolls — from Berkshire, Somerset and Surrey, in Martin of Pattishall's circuit — confirm that the justices dealt with the chattels of fled

---

[68] *RLC* ii. 50: 'ad Robertum de Werreby utlagatum et malefactorem terre nostre querendum et capiendum et decapitandum.'
[69] E 372/69, rot. 9: 'Et pro j cathena ad suspendendum Robertum de Wereby ij s.'
[70] E 372/70, rot. 1: 'Et in custo quem idem Eustachius posuit in Willelmo vinitore et sociis suis assignatis ad insidiandum et capiendum Robertum de Werreby malefactorem xxviij s. per breve regis.' The writ was not enrolled.
[71] *Early Yorkshire Charters, XI*, ed. C. T. Clay (Yorks. Arch. Soc. Rec. ser., Extra ser., ix, 1963), 252 – 4.
[72] Above, and n. 12.
[73] *RLC* ii, 76.

suspects, and of those already dispatched.[74] If the justices followed their planned itinerary they would have been in York on 20 July;[75] a final concord shows that they held another session there on 31 August after visiting Northumberland, Cumberland and Westmorland in the meantime.[76]

From the time of Joseph Hunter in the middle of the nineteenth century, scholars attempting to determine the origins of the legend of Robin Hood have focused particularly on *The Gest of Robyn Hood*.[77] It was the earliest tale or, more accurately, compendium of tales, to be widely disseminated in print. It contains a main theme (of the impoverished knight and his debt to the abbot of St. Mary's York) which does not derive from any known literary analogue, and it offers fruitful ground for the identification of historical originals. If there is any substance at all in the suggestions here advanced, more attention should perhaps be paid to the tale of *Robin Hood and Guy of Gisborne*, which does not form an element of the *Gest* and which itself has no known literary analogue.[78] Although its text is known only from an incomplete version in the Percy Folio, a manuscript of the mid-seventeenth century, its credentials as one of the small canon of medieval Robin Hood tales are impeccable. It formed the basis of a play, part of which survives on a folio which can be precisely dated to 1475 – 6 from accounting matter written on the other side, and which in all probability was performed for the Paston household in the 1470s.[79] In the story Robin is stalked by a yeoman, Guy of Gisborne, whose motive for doing so seems to be the hope of reward; in the play, his antagonist is an unnamed knight, who offers to take Robin for the sheriff in return for 'gold and fee'. The outcome is, of course, that Robin wins and cuts off his opponent's head; in the story, he mutilates it beyond recognition with an Irish knife. He then goes to Barnsdale to help his men, who have been killed or captured by the sheriff of Nottingham and seven score followers. What little we know of the events of 1225 accords well with the general atmosphere of the tale of *Robin Hood and Guy of Gisborne*. It is easy to see how an audience would have had more interest in a tale of an outlaw successfully defying and killing a sheriff and his hireling than a grimly realistic account of a fugitive hunted down and hung up by a chain.[80] Between 1225 and the tales we know lie generations of adaptation, alteration and elaboration, in changing social conditions which may have somewhat removed Robin Hood from the original circumstances in which he found himself and which first made his name well known. What may have survived at the core of the legend were the identities of the chief protagonists, Robin Hood and the sheriff of Nottingham, and the geographical context of their rivalry. We will never know for certain, but we may look for the origins of the legend of Robin Hood in those summer days in Yorkshire in 1225, when the sheriff of Nottingham's men hunted Robert of Wetherby.

---

[74] JUST 1/36, 755 (printed in translation in *Somersetshire Pleas, Civil and Criminal, from the Rolls of the Itinerant Justices, I*, ed. C. E. H. C. Healey and L. C. Landon (Somerset Rec. Soc., xi, 1897), 863).
[75] *RLC* ii. 77.
[76] CP 25/1/262/17, no. 11.
[77] J. Hunter, *The Great Hero of the Ancient Minstrelsy of England: Robin Hood* (London, 1852); Dobson and Taylor, introduction; Maddicott, 'The Birth and Setting'; Holt, *Robin Hood*.
[78] Holt, *Robin Hood*, 74. It is conveniently printed in Dobson and Taylor, 140 – 5.
[79] Dobson and Taylor, 201 – 7; Holt, *Robin Hood*, 30 – 3.
[80] On the audience see, esp., Holt, *Robin Hood*, ch. 6.

Chancellor Ralph de Neville and Plans of Political Reform, 1215 – 1258[1]

D. A. Carpenter

Between 1215 and 1244 a transformation took place in plans of political reform. In 1215 Magna Carta limited the operations of royal government without seeking to control the king's choice of ministers. The lay and ecclesiastical magnates at the parliament of November 1244, by contrast, demanded that *they* should select the king's justiciar and chancellor.[2] At the same time a more radical plan of reform was drawn up, though perhaps not presented to the king. This, the so-called Paper Constitution, foreshadowed the Provisions of Oxford of 1258 by laying down a scheme for conciliar control of the king. Four men, chosen 'by common assent', were to be placed on the king's council and given powers to control certain appointments and supervise aspects of the running of government. Both the justiciar and chancellor were likewise to be chosen 'by all', and could be counted as two of these four elected councillors.[3]

Because there had been no justiciar since 1234, and no chancellor in day-to-day charge of the seal since 1238, what was being demanded in 1244 was, in effect, the restoration of these offices. Under the Angevins, their holders had been appointed by the king and had often become thoroughly unpopular in his service. By 1244, however, the reformers clearly felt that, provided the justiciar and chancellor were chosen 'by all', they could provide a check on the king and a form of open and equitable government. The purpose of this paper is to suggest that, in the formation of such a view, the career of Chancellor Ralph de Neville was of key importance.

In 1244, when the reformers looked back over past justiciars, they can have thought of only one man; that was Hubert de Burgh, who had been appointed justiciar in 1215 and had actually exercised the office from 1219 until his dismissal

---

[1] An early draft of this paper was read by two scholars who died in 1987, C. R. Cheney and E. L. G. Stones. I am also grateful for the comments of Pierre Chaplais and Mrs. Jeanne Stones, and for permission to consult the latter's thesis, written under her maiden name: J. M. B. Fradin, 'Ralph Neville, Bishop of Chichester and Chancellor to Henry III' (Oxford Univ. B. Litt. thesis, 1942). The Stones also allowed me to use their unpublished edition (complete with translations) of Neville's private correspondence. For this correspondence and a valuable discussion of Neville's career, see J. and L. Stones, 'Bishop Ralph Neville, Chancellor to King Henry III and his Correspondence: A Reappraisal', *Archives*, xvi (1984), 227 – 57.

[2] Paris, *CM* iv. 362 – 3.

[3] Paris, *CM* iv. 366 – 8. For the date of the Paper Constitution, see C. R. Cheney, 'The "Paper Constitution" Preserved by Matthew Paris', *EHR* lxv (1950), 213 – 21, which disposes of the argument that it belongs to 1237, for which see N. Denholm-Young, 'The "Paper Constitution" Attributed to 1244', *EHR* lviii (1943), 401 – 23. However, in 1237 the proposals of 1244 were anticipated to the extent that three magnates were added to the king's council: Paris, *CM* iii. 383; see R. C. Stacey, *Politics, Policy and Finance under Henry III 1216 – 1245* (Oxford, 1987), 114 – 15.

in 1232. Hubert, in the course of his career, had made many enemies, but his justiciarship was also remembered with approval, as we shall see. In 1244, however, the Paper Constitution was concerned more with the chancellor than the justiciar. In respect of the justiciar there were merely the regulations, cited above, regarding the method of his appointment. In respect of the chancellor there was also the stipulation that if, for any reason, the king took the seal from him, it should be returned and whatever was sealed in the interval be considered null and void. The further stipulation that 'writs sought against the king and the custom of the kingdom are to be wholly revoked' also dealt with the area of the chancellor's responsibilities. When the reformers looked back over past chancellors, they can likewise have thought of only one man, that was Ralph de Neville, bishop of Chichester. Neville had become keeper of the seal and effective master of the chancery in 1218, and chancellor itself in 1226. He remained in personal control of the seal until 1238; thereafter he retained the title of chancellor and received the emoluments of the office until his death in February 1244.[4]

Neville's career, as keeper of the seal and chancellor, thus spanned the years between Magna Carta and the Paper Constitution. It had several features which made it influential apart from its timescale. Matthew Paris repeatedly asserts that Neville 'received the seal by the common counsel of the kingdom'.[5] Probably, as Powicke surmised, this committal took place at the great council of November 1218, which inaugurated Henry III's first seal and, since the king was a minor, laid down regulations for its use.[6] Neville, therefore, had been appointed in precisely the manner demanded in 1244. He had also, on several occasions, acted in the responsible and independent fashion expected of one thus appointed. Of this the framers of the Paper Constitution were apparently aware, their proposals being influenced by specific incidents in Neville's career.

In 1236, according to Matthew Paris, Neville refused to surrender the seal to the king on the grounds that 'he had received it by common counsel of the kingdom, and therefore could not resign it to anyone without the common assent of the kingdom'.[7] This protestation paralleled almost exactly the statement in the Paper Constitution, in respect of the four elected councillors, that 'as they are chosen by the consent of all, so none of them can be removed without common assent'. Similarly the Constitution insisted that both the justiciar and chancellor could only be replaced 'with the assent of all in solemn assembly'.

Another clause of the Paper Constitution laid down, as we have seen, that if the king, for any reason, took the seal from the chancellor, it should be returned to him, and whatever was sealed in the interval should be considered null and void. This may reflect the events of 1238 when the king, angered by Neville's refusal to withdraw his candidature for the bishopric of Winchester, at last took the seal from

---

[4] J. and L. Stones, 'Bishop Ralph Neville', 228 – 40. Until his death in 1226 the titular chancellor was Richard Marsh, bishop of Durham.

[5] Paris, *CM* iii. 74, 364, 491, 495; *Matthaei Parisiensis Historia Anglorum*, ed. F. Madden (RS, 1866 – 9), ii. 267, 337, 390.

[6] *PR 1216 – 25*, 177; F. M. Powicke, 'The Chancery during the Minority of Henry III', *EHR* xxiii (1908), 227 – 9.

[7] Paris, *CM* iii. 364. Given that Matthew Paris is correct about both the dismissal of Ralph fitzNicholas in 1236, and the changes in the sheriffdoms, I am inclined to accept his testimony here about Neville; but for a different view, see Stacey, 100.

him, while allowing him, as we have said, to remain as titular chancellor and to receive the emoluments of the office.[8] The reformers may also have known of earlier incidents when the king, for a short time, had deprived Neville of the seal in order to authenticate charters of which the latter disapproved, charters which certainly deserved to be nullified, as the Paper Constitution required. In 1234, according to a story which Matthew Paris added to the account of Roger of Wendover, the notorious charter which promised to distribute Richard Marshal's lands in Ireland to his enemies (and thus conspired to bring about his death) was made 'after the seal had been taken from . . . the bishop of Chichester, the chancellor, who did not consent to this fraud'.[9] This episode appears to show Neville performing a role which the 1244 reformers clearly expected of the chancellor — namely, that of preventing the issue of irregular royal letters and charters — the Paper Constitution stipulating that 'writs sought against the king and the custom of the kingdom' (or, if we accept Denholm-Young's emendation, 'the law and the custom of the kingdom') were to be 'completely revoked'.[10]

Most of the information we have used so far about Neville's career has come from Matthew Paris; perhaps Neville was himself the informant although Paris nowhere says so. It is fortunate that there is another incident, this time from 1232, where the evidence of the chancery rolls themselves suggests that Neville opposed the issue of a series of charters which he considered to be improper.

In the months before the fall of Hubert de Burgh at the end of July 1232, Hubert himself and his rival Peter des Rivaux, together with other ministers, extracted charters from the king which confirmed them for life in various offices and custodies.[11] These grants reached a climax during the king's tour of East Anglia in late June and early July, and were supported on 2 July by an oath taken at Burgh, the ancestral home of the justiciar, in which the king swore, on pain of papal excommunication, to observe all the charters which he had granted to Hubert, des Rivaux and other chief ministers. At the same time Hubert, on the king's orders, swore to obstruct the king if he ever sought to violate these charters.

Neville had every reason to feel disquiet about the charters (tabulated on p. 74) issued in late June and early July, and the oaths which accompanied them. The charters of 28 June which conceded to des Rivaux, a foreigner and a clerk, life-custody of the coasts and ports and of all wards and escheats, even though he was to answer for their issues at the exchequer, touched vitally on both the kingdom's security and its system of patronage.[12] These charters were followed by life-grants

---

[8] Paris, *CM* iii. 491, 495, 525; *Ann. Mon.* i. 110; *CPR 1232 – 47*, 231 – 2.

[9] Paris, *CM* iii. 266. By a slip of the pen Paris wrote 'Hugh' rather than 'Ralph', bishop of Chichester. He was probably thinking of Hugh of Pattishall, who became treasurer in 1234: Paris, *CM* iii. 296. The charter rolls for 1233 – 4 do not survive so Paris's story cannot be checked.

[10] Denholm-Young, 'The "Paper Constitution" ', 422, the suggestion being that 'regem' should read 'legem'. The suggestion gains credence from the fact that the parliament of Nov. 1244 complained, according to Matthew Paris, about the issue of writs 'against justice': Paris, *CM* iii. 363. In 1240, however, again according to Paris, complaint was made about the king's desire to grant a charter 'against the crown of the king': Paris, *CM* iii. 629; v. 91.

[11] For much of what follows, see D. A. Carpenter, 'The Fall of Hubert de Burgh', *Journ. British Studies*, xix (1980), 1 – 17.

[12] The port of Dover was excluded from the grant to des Rivaux as being held by Hubert de Burgh. Des Rivaux gained it after Hubert's fall. For the indignation of the magnates when they thought that des Rivaux had been granted Dover castle, see *Ann. Mon.* i. 86.

of the treasurership of the exchequer to Walter Mauclerc, bishop of Carlisle, and of the Tower of London and the castles of Windsor and Odiham to Hubert de Burgh (2 and 7 July). There was, of course, nothing new about life-grants of office,[13] but those conceded by Henry on his East Anglian tour were made when he was surrounded largely by household officials.[14] On 2 July itself no earl was present save Hubert de Burgh, and no bishop save Ralph de Neville. In these circumstances the grants and the oaths could easily be seen as irresponsible acts, totally inconsistent with the king's obligation to uphold the rights of the Crown. This was the view taken by the pope in 1233, when he allowed Henry to nullify the various gifts of 'liberties, possessions, offices and other things', and absolved him from his oath (apparently the oath of Burgh) not to quash them. This was on the grounds that they were contrary to Henry's coronation oath to preserve the rights and honours of the kingdom of England, and had been conceded 'against the foresaid kingdom and to the great prejudice and harm of the royal Crown'.[15] These words foreshadow the demand in the Paper Constitution that letters sought 'against the king' (if that is the correct rendering) should be revoked. They likewise parallel the objection in 1240 of a later keeper of the seal, Master Simon the Norman, that a charter which sought to grant a tax on wool to Thomas of Savoy was 'against the Crown of the king'.[16]

That Neville did make some form of protest over these charters is suggested by their dating clauses. From the beginning of the reign of Richard I an elaborate dating formula, modelled on that employed by the papal chancery, was adopted as the concluding clause for English royal charters. The formula stated that the charter had been 'given by the hand', (*dat[a] per manum*) of the chancellor or some other official, at a specified place and date.[17] Between 1227, when Henry III began to grant charters, and 1238, when Neville was deprived of the great seal, Neville, as

---

[13] Neville himself had been granted the office of chancellor for life in 1227; this charter was confirmed on 14 June 1232 and was buttressed by another specifically granting him custody of the seal for life: *CChR 1226 – 57*, 9, 156. King John had granted the chancery to Walter de Grey for life: *Foedera*, I. i. 93.

[14] The bishop of Norwich attested the charters on 28 June; the earl of Hereford attested the charter of 7 July. All statements about the composition of the court in this article are based on the witness lists to the royal charters enrolled on the charter rolls of 16 Henry III (C 53/26). (All subsequent manuscript references are to documents in the PRO.) The printed calendar omits the witnesses but serves to indicate the days on which charters were enrolled: *CChR 1226 – 57*, 142 – 69.

[15] *Royal Letters*, i. 551. For the coronation oath and the rights of the king, see H. G. Richardson, 'The Coronation in Medieval England', *Traditio* xvi (1960), 151 – 61. Earlier, in June 1232, Neville had given the charters which granted the justiciarship of Ireland for life to Hubert de Burgh, and the custody of the king's wardrobe, chamber and small seal to Peter des Rivaux: *CChR 1226 – 57*, 156 – 7. There was less reason for anxiety here partly because people of more consequence were at court, notably the bishop of Winchester and the earl of Cornwall, and partly because the household offices granted to des Rivaux were peculiarly the king's personal concern.

[16] Paris, *CM* iii. 629; v. 91; for discussion of this episode, see Powicke, *Henry III*, ii. 780 – 2.

[17] For this formula, see R.L. Poole, *Lectures on the History of the Papal Chancery* (Cambridge, 1915), 38 – 9, 48, 55 – 6, 138 – 42; *The Memoranda Roll for the Michaelmas Term 1 John*, ed. H. G. Richardson (Pipe Roll Soc., new ser., xxi, 1943), lx – lxi; V. H. Galbraith, *Studies in the Public Records* (London, 1948), 127 – 30; C. R. Cheney, *English Bishops' Chanceries* (Manchester, 1950), 81 – 90; P. Chaplais, *English Royal Documents* (Oxford, 1971), 14 – 15; J. B. Edwards, 'The English Royal Chamber and Chancery in the Reign of King John' (Cambridge Univ. Ph.D. thesis, 1974), 118 – 32; D. A. Carpenter, 'St. Thomas Cantilupe: His Political Career', in *St. Thomas Cantilupe, Bishop of Hereford: Essays in his Honour*, ed. M. Jancey (Hereford, 1982), 66 – 7.

chancellor, almost invariably gave the charters himself. From 1238, however, the king became the normal giver, charters being 'given by our hand' (*dat[a] per manum nostram*).[18] During Neville's period in charge of the seal, the only occasions when this formula occurred, apart from those mentioned below, were when charters were issued in favour of Neville himself, or were connected in some way with the see of Chichester.[19]

It is, therefore, a remarkable fact that the charters (tabulated on p. 74) which were conceded between 28 June and 7 July to Peter des Rivaux, Walter Mauclerc and Hubert de Burgh, together with the charter embodying the king's oath at Burgh, were all given by the king. They thus form an absolutely unique series in the charter rolls of Neville's time. In each case, apparently, the authorization for the drawing up of the document came not from the chancellor but from the king.[20] This was not, initially at least, because Neville was absent from court for (as the table below shows) the charters given by the king were interlaced down to 3 July with charters (significantly ones of an innocuous nature) given by Neville. Nor was it simply the importance of the charters which caused the king to replace Neville as the giver, for, with the exception perhaps of that containing the king's oath, they were no more important than some given in the past by Neville — for example, the one which granted Hubert de Burgh the justiciarship for life in 1228. The difference was that the charter of 1228 commanded some sort of general consent.[21]

There are, therefore, strong indications that the reason why the king acted as the giver of various charters during his tour of East Anglia was that Neville himself refused to take responsibility for them.[22] When Master Simon the Norman made a similar stand in 1240 he was immediately dismissed.[23] In Neville's case, the immediate reaction to his *démarche* was an attempt to conciliate him. On 28 June, when the king gave the charters in favour of Peter des Rivaux, he also gave a charter to Neville as bishop of Chichester.[24] However, it is possible that Neville subsequently withdrew from court and lost control of the seal. We can approach the

---

[18] L. B. Dibben, 'Chancellor and Keeper of the Seal under Henry III', *EHR* xxviii (1911), 41 – 2, 50 – 1; Chaplais, 14 – 15. In 1230, when Neville stayed behind as regent during the king's expedition to Brittany, his brother, Nicholas de Neville, took over the 'giving' as the chancellor's deputy. In a fair number of enrolled charters between 1227 and 1238 the name of the giver is omitted, the formula being *dat'* etc., followed by the place and date. Whenever it has been possible to check these enrolments against the original charters, or copies of them, the giver has proved to be Neville.

[19] I have only found one certain exception to this statement, the grant to the burgesses of Gloucester on 6 Apr. 1227: *CChR 1226 – 57*, 30.

[20] The evidence for this interpretation of the giving clause cannot be deployed here; but see Edwards, 'Chamber and Chancery under John', 124 – 5.

[21] *CChR 1226 – 57*, 74; there is a photograph of the charter in C. Ellis, *Hubert de Burgh: a Study in Constancy* (London, 1952), between pp. 120 – 1.

[22] Several of the charters given by the king on 28 June in des Rivaux's favour were not of overwhelming importance, e.g. that which conceded him life-custody of Guildford park and Kempton manor, and on 2 July Neville was prepared to give a different version of one of them in a form more favourable to des Rivaux. These charters were given by the king simply because they were dealt with in the same batch as those to which Neville was opposed. All the charters of 28 June in favour of des Rivaux have the same witnesses.

[23] Paris, *CM* iii. 629; v. 91; Powicke, *Henry III*, ii. 780 – 2.

[24] It should be emphasized that it was not the practice, when the king gave a charter in favour of Neville, for him to take the opportunity to give charters in favour of other individuals. In other words, this is not the explanation for the charters of 28 June in favour of des Rivaux being given by the king.

Table

Charters enrolled on Charter Roll 18 Henry III, 27 June – 15 July 1232 (C 53/26, mm.5,4)

Date	Giver	Beneficiary	Contents
27 June	Neville	Hubert de Burgh	quittance of accounts as justiciar of England and Ireland
28 June	king	Peter des Rivaux	six charters granting life-custody of the ports and coast of England, all wards and escheats, the exchange, Jews, and lesser items
1 July	Neville	men of Corfe	quittance of lawing of dogs
2 July	Neville	Peter de Rivaux	land of Gilbert de Laigle in hereditary right
2 July	king	countess of Kent (wife of Hubert de Burgh)	king's oath to maintain her charters
2 July	king	Godfrey of Crowcombe, bishop of Carlisle, Ralph fitzNicholas, Hubert de Burgh, Peter des Rivaux, countess of Kent [sic]; two names erased	note to effect that they have similar charters to that enrolled for the countess of Kent
2 July	king		letter (rather than charter) announcing that Hubert de Burgh has sworn to ensure that the king maintains the charters of Hubert and his wife, Neville, Peter des Rivaux, Ralph fitzNicholas and Godfrey of Crowcombe
2 July	king	bishop of Carlisle	treasurership of the exchequer for life
3 July	Neville	Godfrey of Crowcombe	quittance of military service
5 July	king	Peter des Rivaux	Lydmore castle and Dartmoor forest in hereditary right
?	?	lepers of Thetford	annual fair
7 July	king	Hubert de Burgh	life-custody of the Tower of London, and the castles of Windsor and Odiham
15 July	Neville	Osney abbey	confirmation

evidence here by considering the extent to which Neville was involved in the oaths sworn by the king and justiciar at Burgh on 2 July.

In the printed *Calendar of the Charter Rolls* Neville's name does not appear in the list of those who received charters embodying the king's oath.[25] If, however, we consult the actual roll in the Public Record Office it is clear that two names have been erased from the list. In one case there is no clue to the name removed. But the other name, which stood at the head of the list, was almost certainly that of Neville — the shape and length of the erasure fits exactly with the frequent abbreviation 'R. Cycesīr Ēp̄c', the places where the tails of the 'y' and 'p' have been removed being plainly discernible. What was going on? That Neville was *intended* to be a beneficiary of the settlement there can be no doubt, for his name also appears, in the record of Hubert's oath, as one of those whose charters Hubert swore to ensure the king would uphold. But this does not mean that he consented to his inclusion, any more than did the ministers who were actually absent from court.[26] Hubert, who was almost certainly the moving force behind the oaths, naturally wished to draw the chancellor into the settlement he was attempting to construct. In fact, however, it is pretty plain that Neville had nothing to do with Hubert's oath. That the king acted as giver may not be significant in this instance, for probably Neville could not act since he was one of the beneficiaries.[27] But in the case of the two other beneficiaries present at court, Peter des Rivaux and Godfrey of Crowcombe, who were likewise excluded from acting as witnesses, a unique formula was devised to indicate their involvement — the letter embodying the oath being witnessed 'in [their] presence'. No parallel formula was devised to indicate Neville's attendance.

If, however, Neville was included in the settlement at Burgh without his consent, how was it possible for his name to be recorded at all, as one receiving a charter embodying the king's oath, on the charter rolls, rolls over which, as chancellor, he had control?[28] The answer may be that the records of the oaths of 2 July were enrolled when Neville was absent from court. Neville gave a charter on 3 July and then another on 15 July, by which time the court was back in London. Between these dates only two charters with dating clauses (5 and 7 July) were enrolled. Both were given by the king. It may be that Neville refused to take responsibility for these charters, both of which he might have considered as 'against the Crown'.[29] But equally there is no evidence that Neville was present at all between 4 and 14 July. What may have happened, therefore, is that the oaths of Burgh were enrolled

---

[25] *CChR 1226 – 57*, 164 – 5; C 53/26, m.4. The enrolled charter recorded the king's oath to maintain the charters of Hubert's wife, the countess of Kent. There is then a list of those who received similar charters (*consimilem cartam habet*). The countess had to be included because many of the king's concessions had been made jointly to her and Hubert.

[26] Both Walter Mauclerc and the steward, Ralph fitzNicholas, were absent from court at this time.

[27] For the same reason the king would have given the charter which recorded his oath to uphold Neville's charters, but Neville could have given the charters conceded to the countess of Kent and the other beneficiaries. The charter in favour of the countess of Kent was apparently given by the king on a different occasion on 2 July to that in favour of Walter Mauclerc for the witness lists are different.

[28] For Neville's control over enrolments, see e.g. *CR 1227 – 31*, 118.

[29] At first sight the charter of 5 July, which granted des Rivaux in hereditary right Lydford castle and Dartmoor forest, looks comparatively unimportant. Perhaps the king gave this simply because Neville was now absent from court. On the other hand, Lydford was a royal castle and the grant represented the alienation of a possession of the Crown. The record of this charter was cancelled with the note that des Rivaux had returned it.

in his absence, and that Neville had his name (and that of an ally) removed once he had returned to court and recovered control of the chancery.[30]

An inspection of the charter roll lends support to this hypothesis. That the oaths of Burgh were enrolled in unusual circumstances is implied by the large number of slips found in their texts.[31] That they were enrolled before, rather than after, 15 July, by which time Neville had recovered control of the seal, is suggested by the fact that their enrolment plainly took place some time before that of the charter of 15 July given by Neville.[32] That Neville actually lost control of the chancery may be inferred from the singular nature of the enrolments of two of the charters issued between 4 and 14 July. The charter of 5 July, in favour of Peter des Rivaux, was recorded as given by the king at Thetford, but instead of a list of witnesses there is merely the statement that they were the same as in one of the charters issued to des Rivaux on 28 June. Next on the roll is not a properly written-out charter at all, but simply a bald note to the effect that the Leper hospital of Thetford had received a charter granting it the right to hold a yearly fair. No indication was vouchsafed of the giver, the place, the date or the witnesses. In their different ways these enrolments have no precedent in the charter rolls of Neville's time.[33]

There are, therefore, good reasons for thinking that in 1232 Neville resisted the issue of charters which he considered to be irregular, and that he temporarily lost control of the seal. According to Matthew Paris there was a similar episode in 1234. Such incidents may well have encouraged the belief in 1244 that a chancellor chosen 'by all' would help to prevent the issue of improper royal letters. They may equally have lain behind the stipulation in the Paper Constitution that if the seal was taken from the chancellor it should be returned to him, and that whatever was sealed in the interval should be cancelled. Neville's refusal in 1236 to surrender the seal to the king on the grounds that, appointed by common assent, it was only by common assent that he could be dismissed, was likewise echoed in the Paper Constitution. In 1244, therefore, the memory of Neville's career was a powerful

---

[30] As noted above, the shape of the second erasure affords no clue to the name removed. The most likely candidate is Stephen of Seagrave, with whom Neville had been joint regent in 1230 during the king's absence in Brittany.

[31] In the copy of the charter recording the king's oath to maintain the charters of the countess of Kent (see above, n. 25), the clerk at one point wrote 'foresaid bishop' instead of 'foresaid countess' (an error which he corrected), and superfluously, since her charter was the one written out in full, added the countess's name to the list of those who *consimilem cartam habet*. Although the name of Walter Mauclerc figures on this list, it does not appear, in the letter recording Hubert's oath, as one of those whose charters Hubert swore to make the king uphold.

[32] After the oaths of Burgh there is a gap of 3 cms. before the next enrolled charter, that given by Neville on 3 July in favour of Godfrey of Crowcombe. Both the gap, which is highly unusual, and the hand and ink of the Crowcombe charter make it fairly clear that the latter was enrolled later than the oaths of Burgh. The Crowcombe charter is followed by that given by the king in favour of Mauclerc on 2 July, and then by the charter of 15 July given by Neville. These two charters have the appearance of being written at the same time and later again than the charter of 3 July. I would suggest that they were enrolled after Neville recovered control of the chancery on or shortly before 15 July. There is, incidentally, an erasure 4½ cms. long and ½ cm. deep (sufficient for, say, twenty-five letters) immediately below the record of the oaths of 2 July.

[33] One occasionally finds, in place of the complete record of a charter, the formula *consimilem cartam habet*, as indeed in the oaths of Burgh, but in these cases the implication is that the charter is the same, apart from the different beneficiary, as that given immediately above. That was clearly not the case with the charter conceded to the house of the Lepers at Thetford. (The charter given by the king in favour of Hubert de Burgh on 7 July has no unusual features in its enrolment.)

argument in favour of establishing a chancellor and a justiciar appointed by common counsel. As important, however, in inculcating this lesson, as the specific incidents in Neville's career which we have discussed, must have been the general way in which he discharged his office in the twenty years between 1218 and 1238, when he was in day-to-day charge of the seal. It is worth putting this in a more general context.

At the November parliament of 1244 the demand for the appointment of justiciar and chancellor by common consent was justified, according to Matthew Paris, by the complaint that Magna Carta had been infringed, the money received from aids misspent, and writs 'against justice' conceded thanks to the absence or failure (*defectum*) of the chancellor.[34] There may also have been anxieties provoked by government initiatives in 1244 over the forest, the 'lands of the Normans', serjeanties, distraint for knighthood, and liberties assumed without warrant.[35] More generally, however, the twenty-seven years of peace since the conclusion of the civil war of 1215 – 17 had seen a steady increase in the scope of the king's government, as the burgeoning size of the pipe rolls and curia regis rolls shows. More people than ever before, as litigators and debtors, were coming within the ambit of that government. The consequence was a corresponding increase in the number of petitions coming into the centre demanding justice, favour and the redress of grievances.

It was with such petitions, over many years, that Hubert de Burgh and Ralph de Neville dealt. 'You are justiciar of England, held to dispense justice to everyone', Falkes de Breauté told Hubert in 1219, as the latter commenced his active justiciarship.[36] Hubert's correspondence shows how seriously he took his responsibilities in this area, dealing carefully with a steady flow of letters full of complaints and requests.[37] Neville's responsibility for the issuing of royal letters meant that he coped with a similar type of business. It was he, in the last resort, who decided whether the writs out of course, which many petitioners sought, should or (because they were 'against justice') should not be granted.[38] In 1219, for example, Hubert de Burgh and Peter des Roches, bishop of Winchester informed Neville that, having heard the complaint of Roger fitzJohn, they thought a writ should be made out summoning before the justices of the bench the record of his case in Cornwall. But Neville was to hear Roger's complaint himself, discuss the matter with the judge Martin of Pattishall, and then do what he thought was 'most just and best'.[39] That Neville discharged his responsibilities in an even-handed fashion is suggested, for what they are worth, by the encomiums of Matthew Paris, who described him as 'a solitary column of truth and faith in royal affairs', and who

---

[34] Paris, *CM* iv. 363.

[35] See Stacey, 250 – 2.

[36] *Royal Letters*, i. 5 (where misdated).

[37] An impression of this correspondence may be gained from *Royal Letters*.

[38] These were probably writs out of course which intervened in the judicial process by, for example, preventing cases from going to judgement or inventing *ad hoc* legal procedures; see *DBM* 260 – 3, 272 – 3. For other suggestions, see Denholm-Young, 'The "Paper Constitution" ', 422; Stacey, 216, n. 37.

[39] SC1/6/26. For a letter asking Neville for a judicial writ out of course, see *Royal Letters*, i. 68. For an analysis of Neville's correspondence, much of which deals with his private affairs, see J. and L. Stones, 'Bishop Ralph Neville', 243 – 4.

averred that 'in the midst of the kingdom's many stormy disorders he stood upright, neither bending to right nor to left. He was not like a reed to be blown this way or that by any wind'.[40]

With the disappearance of Burgh and Neville all this came to an end. At the very time when the affairs of more and more people were encompassed by the king's government, so defined and navigable channels of communication with the centre of that government were closing down. After 1234 there was no longer a justiciar specifically charged with 'dispensing justice to everyone'.[41] Four years later there was no longer a chancellor or keeper of the seal, with an independent status, which helped him to oppose the concession of charters 'against the Crown', and to deal fairly with the numerous requests for writs out of course, resisting the issue of those which were 'against justice'. The household officials who kept the seal after 1238 might have had a sense of responsibility, but when Simon the Norman made trouble in 1240 he was immediately dismissed.[42] Equally, with the keepership of the seal now passing quickly from one relatively minor official to another, and sometimes being the responsibility of more than one official at the same time, the process of obtaining writs out of course, for those outside the circle of the court, was much more complex and obscure than in Neville's day.[43]

The measures in the Paper Constitution were essentially designed to open up and control a system of government which, while expanding in scope, had become more enclosed and remote, and for that very reason easier for those on the inside to manipulate and corrupt. The government was to be prized open through the creation of an elective justiciarship and chancellorship, and by the appointment by common consent of four councillors. Two of this group of elected officials (by implication they would frequently be the justiciar and chancellor) were to be always with the king 'so that they may hear the complaints of everyone and can speedily help those suffering injury', precisely the role which Hubert de Burgh had been expected to play as justiciar.[44] Other ministers too, in the first instance, were to be chosen by common consent — two justices of the bench, two barons of the exchequer and at least one justice of the Jews.[45] The aim of the Constitution was thus to exert common control over all the institutions of central government. As the Constitution observed, 'since [the justices of the bench, exchequer and Jews] deal

---

[40] Paris, *CM* iii. 90, 206 – 7; see also 74, 90, 226, 266, 364, 491, 495, 525, 530. However, for Neville's private profit as chancellor, see *Chronicon Petroburgense*, ed. T. Stapleton (Camden Soc., old ser., 1849), 9.

[41] For some perceptive comments on the position of Hubert de Burgh, and the importance of the disappearance of the justiciarship, see W. L. Warren, *The Governance of Norman and Angevin England 1086 – 1272* (London, 1987), 176.

[42] Paris, *CM* iii. 629, asserts that Geoffrey the Templar, who was also involved in keeping the seal, protested with Simon and was likewise dismissed, but Powicke is sceptical about this: Powicke, *Henry III*, ii. 782.

[43] For the keepership of the seal after 1238, see Dibben, 'Chancellor and Keeper of the Seal', 42 – 3. Neville may have been in day-to-day charge of the seal on a few occasions before his death for charters were given by his hand in Nov. and Dec. 1243 but, apart from that, he did not in any real sense act as chancellor in 1242 – 3, as Dibben might seem to imply; see also J. and L. Stones, 'Bishop Ralph Neville', 239.

[44] The reason given by the Paper Constitution for allowing the justiciar and the chancellor to be numbered among the four elected councillors was that both officials needed frequently to be with the king.

[45] After this first election by common assent they were to be chosen by the four elected councillors.

with the affairs of all so everyone should assent to their choice'. There could be no more explicit acknowledgement of the range of English government in the mid-thirteenth century.

The reforms proposed in 1244, therefore, were designed to benefit 'everyone', not just the great magnates. Indeed, those great magnates who were prominent at Henry's court after 1234 were well placed to cope with the situation created by the disappearance of the justiciar and chancellor. In 1244 itself, as Dr. Stacey has argued, the policies which the king had pursued since 1239 may have isolated him from the earls and barons in a way untypical of the rest of his personal rule. That may be part of the background to the Paper Constitution.[46] But even in 1244 the earls of Cornwall and Leicester were prominent councillors, two of the household stewards, John fitzGeoffrey and William de Cantilupe, were great magnates, and the earls of Pembroke, Hereford and Norfolk all attested royal charters. Of course, great magnates with *entrée* to the court might still believe that the king would govern more sensibly and effectively if surrounded by responsible ministers with defined tasks and powers. They might regret in particular the loss of an independent chancellor who could check the king's feckless distribution of patronage and his consequent concession of charters 'against the Crown'. But the groups which had suffered most from the administrative changes since 1234, and had the strongest interest in the reforms in the Paper Constitution, were those with less influence at court, namely barons of local importance, county knights and esquires, freemen and the numerous religious houses whose claims to the chattels and amercements of their men were under challenge at the exchequer. The memoranda roll of 1243 – 4 shows no less than forty ecclesiastics and ecclesiastical institutions in this position; no wonder that the four elected councillors of the Paper Constitution were to be 'conservators of liberties'.[47]

There was nothing surprising in reforms being conceived in 1244 to meet the grievances of these groups. After all, the *quid pro quo* was to be taxation which they, indeed which 'everyone', would have to pay. When the king sought taxation again in the parliaments of the 1240s and 1250s, the demand that he appoint a chancellor and a justiciar by common consent was consequently reiterated.[48] Such plans of reform were not simply the product of some narrow conflict between the king and his 'barons'; they were the price required, by political society beyond the great magnates, for the payment of taxation. In 1258 the great magnates appointed a justiciar and a chancellor both to secure their own control of central government and to meet the grievances of this wider political nation, thus winning support for their regime.[49] The demand for a responsible chancellor was justified in much the same way as it had been in 1244 — as the statement drawn up for presentation to Louis IX in 1264 explained, the absence or failure (*defectum*) of chancellors before 1258 had led both to the concession of writs 'against right and the customary course of the chancery', and to the sealing of 'various excessive and unreasonable

[46] Stacey, 252 – 5; D. A. Carpenter, 'King, Magnates and Society: The Personal Rule of King Henry III', *Speculum*, lx (1985), 57 – 60.
[47] Carpenter, 'King, Magnates and Society', 49 – 50; E 368/15, m.3.
[48] Paris, *CM* v. 5; *Ann. Mon.* i. 336.
[49] In 1258, although the king's keeper of the seal, Henry of Wingham (who was sometimes given the title chancellor), continued in office, he was in effect re-appointed, taking an oath about the custody of the seal 'in the presence of the barons of England': *CR 1256 – 9*, 315.

grants'.[50] Equally, the justiciar in 1258 was to 'uphold right to all persons', much as were the two councillors in 1244 and Hubert de Burgh before that.[51] By 1258, however, the increasing oppression of the sheriffs and justices in eyre, the lawless behaviour of the Lusignans, and their seeming monopoly over royal patronage, had intensified the need for such remedies and broadened their appeal.[52] They were, however, already out of date. The huge weight of petitions produced by the expanding apparatus of thirteenth-century government could no longer be dealt with merely by two officials, however responsible and conscientious. The real answer, grasped by Edward I, was to develop the process of petition to the king's council in parliament.[53]

[50] *DBM* 260 – 3.
[51] *DBM* 102 – 3, 106 – 7.
[52] D. A. Carpenter, 'The Decline of the Curial Sheriff in England, 1194 – 1258', *EHR* xci (1976), 22 – 3, 28, n. 3, 29; J. R. Maddicott, 'Magna Carta and the Local Community 1215 – 1259', *Past and Present*, cii (1984), 47 – 8; H. W. Ridgeway, 'The Politics of the English Royal Court, 1247 – 65, with Special Reference to the Role of the Aliens' (Oxford Univ. D. Phil. thesis, 1983), 266 – 8, 289; D. A. Carpenter, 'What Happened in 1258?', in *War and Government in the Middle Ages: Essays in Honour of J. O. Prestwich*, ed. J. Gillingham and J. C. Holt (Woodbridge, 1984), 113 – 15.
[53] J. R. Maddicott, 'Parliament and the Constituencies, 1272 – 1377', in *The English Parliament in the Middle Ages*, ed. R. G. Davies and J. H. Denton (Manchester, 1981), 62 – 8.

King Henry III and the 'Aliens', 1236 – 1272

Huw Ridgeway

Henry III's favours to Savoyards and Poitevins are well known. Matthew Paris commented waspishly on the number of visitors coming over year after year to England to prey upon the king's generosity; during the Barons' Wars there are voluminous complaints from chroniclers and Montfortians against the 'aliens'. Not surprisingly, in the light of such evidence, Henry's love of foreigners is usually just dismissed as a bizarre expression of his artistic and naïve personality, an easily explained cause of his subjects' discontents.[1] This crude picture has only recently begun to be modified. It has been discovered that Savoyards and Poitevins cannot be lumped together politically: in the crisis of 1258 the former joined the reforming movement, which brought about disgrace and exile for the latter; even before this — and still more afterwards — they experienced differing political fortunes.[2] All the more reason, then, to take another look at this most distinctive phenomenon of Henry's rule. Just how many foreigners did he actually favour, and what reasons lay behind his policy? How did he reward them, and where were they granted lands? And the most intriguing question of all: how were they grafted onto English society with such success for over twenty years before 1258, only to become so unpopular in the course of the next seven years?

Through the influence of Eleanor of Provence, whom Henry married in 1236, and the counts of Savoy, her maternal family, many visitors began to arrive in England from these regions and from others where they held sway: Burgundy and Flanders. The main individuals can be identified from the records, and for the years between 1236 and 1272 we have some 170 names.[3] About two-thirds were clerics and the rest knights, or of knightly status, and some settled permanently in England. They were well received; for instance, thirty-nine obtained lands of varying value from the king and some forty laymen and clerics, all told, were provided with substantial revenues of 100 marks or more per annum. The Poitevin connexion, soon to be so notorious, was smaller.[4] We only see Poitevins in any

---

[1] Powicke, *Henry III*, i. 251, 296 – 7 is a brief, but important, exception. Unless otherwise stated, all manuscript references in this paper are to documents in the PRO.

[2] H. W. Ridgeway, 'The Politics of the English Royal Court, 1247 – 65, with Special Reference to the Role of the Aliens' (Oxford Univ. D.Phil thesis, 1983); id., 'The Lord Edward and the Provisions of Oxford', in *Thirteenth Century England I: Procs. of the Newcastle Upon Tyne Conference, 1985*, ed. P. R. Coss and S. D. Lloyd (Woodbridge, 1986), 89 – 99; D. A. Carpenter, 'What Happened in 1258?', in *War and Government in the Middle Ages: Essays in Honour of J. O. Prestwich*, ed. J. Gillingham and J. C. Holt (Woodbridge, 1984), 106 – 19.

[3] Full references are in Ridgeway, 'The Politics', esp. ch. 1, 6 and appendix.

[4] Ridgeway, 'The Politics', ch. 3, 6 and appendix. At a daily rate of 2*s.*, 50 marks was the average annual payment for knights in royal service, and 100 marks for bannerets.

numbers in England after 1247, when Henry began to give refuge to his half-brothers of the powerful house of Lusignan, sons of the count of La Marche and Isabella, countess of Angoulême. Their influence brought a hundred or so visitors for the remainder of the reign. About two-thirds were laymen, mainly knights (a higher proportion than the Savoyards), and the pattern of the rewards they received from the king was also different: only eight landholders can be traced. But, overall, some twenty-eight Poitevins obtained annual revenues worth 100 marks or more.

One aspect of Henry's generosity is easy enough to understand. Poor soldier though he was, he was recruiting, in the traditional pattern of his ancestors, military allies on a grand scale.[5] This was one of the keys to the influence enjoyed at his court by the aliens: after all, it had been the lack of allies which had contributed so much to the loss of John's continental domains in 1204. It explains why over half the foreign visitors — some fifty Poitevins and 100 Savoyards — never stayed in England for any time but took their money fees and the revenues of their benefices home with them. In the first generation after 1204 Henry had to defend Gascony, vulnerable against the growing power of the king of France, and, of course, he nursed great territorial claims which to the last some of his subjects, even Matthew Paris, thought he should pursue. He also required, in the age-old way, foreign mercenaries to supplement his feudal forces when fighting at home against the Welsh and Scots.[6]

His alliance with Provence and Savoy was part of his moves in the 1230s to construct a coalition in the south against the French king, a policy later continued by Edward I.[7] It is well known that he also made wider use of Savoyards — alongside Englishmen such as John Mansel and Robert Walerand — as his trusted diplomatic agents because the counts of Savoy had unique influence with both warring papal and imperial camps, thanks to their control of the vital mountain passes into Italy. After 1244, when Philip of Savoy, archbishop-elect of Lyons, began to pay host to the refugee Innocent IV, the great devotion of the House of Savoy to the papacy gave Henry a guaranteed *entrée* into the Curia. Although it cost him dearly in the notorious 'Sicilian business', the pope's constant support was otherwise invaluable, not least during struggles with the baronage in the 1260s.[8]

His cultivation of the Lusignans was more narrowly based on his ambitions against Louis IX. He had financed their rebellion against Louis in Poitou as early as 1241–3 and in 1247, when it was rumoured that Louis was planning to march on Gascony, he immediately summoned the Lusignans to his court together with representatives from the Poitevin nobility.[9] After that, they were a useful lever to help keep Louis in check during the long Gascon rebellion of the early 1250s.

[5] B. D. Lyon, 'The Money Fief under the English Kings, 1066–1485', *EHR* lxvi (1951), 161–93.

[6] R. F. Walker, 'The Anglo-Welsh Wars 1217–67' (Oxford Univ. D.Phil. thesis, 1954), 89.

[7] E. L. Cox, *The Eagles of Savoy: The House of Savoy in Thirteenth-Century Europe* (Princeton, 1974), chs. 2–6; F. M. Powicke, *The Thirteenth Century* (2nd edn., Oxford, 1962), 251 and n.

[8] F. Mugnier, 'Les Savoyards en Angleterre au XIIIe siècle', *Mémoires et Documents publiés par la société Savoisienne*, xix (1890), 216–316; M. T. Clanchy, *England and its Rulers 1066–1272* (London, 1983), 230–40. For the important activities of the archbishop of Embrun and William de Chauvent on Henry's behalf at the Curia 1258–66, see *CPR 1258–66*, 37, 51, 155, 221, 566, 658; *CR 1259–61*, 265; *CLR 1260–7*, 80. Ottobuono, the legate appointed to England in 1265, was a relative of the queen: Powicke, *Henry III*, ii. 526 ff.

[9] Paris, *CM* iv. 594, 627–8; Powicke, *Henry III*, i. 188–95.

Perhaps they had political value for Henry as late as in 1258 when his Savoyard diplomats were negotiating the generous Treaty of Paris with Louis.[10] They could in some small way, too, explain why the French king was all the more easily persuaded to stay on Henry's side during the difficult 1260s.[11]

These alliances brought important additions to Henry's armies. The Savoyards furnished contingents for the campaign in Gascony in 1253; they may have brought thirty or more knights.[12] Members of prominent families fought for Henry regularly. They included Peter, son of the count of Geneva, Simon de Joinville from Champagne and members of the Salines family from Burgundy.[13] Perhaps the most useful Savoyard influence lay in Flanders, the traditional recruiting-ground for English kings' mercenaries, where from 1237 to 1244 Thomas of Savoy reigned as count by marriage and where in 1239 Henry's celebrated favourite, William of Savoy, aspired to the archbishopric-principality of Liège.[14] Thomas of Savoy brought his men to Poitou in 1242 and Matthew Paris relates how, in the summer of 1244, when the English baronage were proving obstructive over military and financial aid, Thomas arrived timely in England with the assistance of a force of sixty knights and 100 serjeants against the king of Scots.[15] Even after Thomas's rule ended, links with Flanders were maintained through Queen Eleanor's kinsmen of the influential house of Fiennes of the Pas-de-Calais. For example, when the queen's cousin, Isabella de Fiennes, left England in the course of 1258 she took thirty-six or more rings from the queen 'for the knights and ladies of Flanders'.[16] Mercenaries from Flanders and Picardy helped nip in the bud both the Lord Edward's rebellion in 1260 and opposition to the overthrow of the Provisions of Oxford in 1261 (when we again have a record of the gifts they received from the queen), and in the summer of 1264 it was in Flanders that Queen Eleanor and Peter of Savoy mustered their forces, some of them recruited even from Savoy, for their projected invasion of Montfortian England.[17]

The Poitevins soon proved useful in Gascony which was in easy reach for them. We know — for example, from the surviving terms of the money fee granted by Henry to Guy de Rochford — that some were being paid expressly for supplying knights, when required, to assist the king's authorities in the duchy.[18] In 1252 it was a force from Poitou raised by Geoffrey de Lusignan and William de Chauvigny, lord of Châteauroux, which intervened to save Henry's lieutenant in Gascony from

---

[10] Paris, *CM* v. 388; P. Chaplais, 'The Making of the Treaty of Paris (1259) and the Royal Style', *EHR* lxvii (1952), 235–47, which also highlights the role of Peter of Savoy and the Savoyard archbishop of Tarentaise.

[11] E.g. *CR 1261–4*, 281–2.

[12] *CPR 1247–58*, 269, 274, 307, 314, 320, 322, 326, 359; *CR 1251–3*, 361; *CR 1253–4*, 183, 189, 199, 212, 214, 244, 274; *CLR 1251–60*, 179.

[13] G. W. Watson, 'The Families of Lacy, Geneva, Joinville and la Marche', *The Genealogist*, new ser., xxi (1904), 6–13; *CPR 1247–58*, 231; *CR 1259–61*, 487; *CLR 1240–5*, 316; *CLR 1251–60*, 179, 214.

[14] Cox, 51–81.

[15] Ibid. 116–17; Paris, *CM* iv. 378; vi. 92.

[16] Powicke, *Thirteenth Century*, 545 n.; E 101/349/26, mm.1,2,4.

[17] R. F. Treharne, *The Baronial Plan of Reform 1258–63* (Manchester, 1932), 226–34, 261–71; E 101/349/26, mm.1–8; J. L. Wurstemberger, *Peter der Zweite, Graf von Savoyen* (Zürich, 1858), iv. nos. 644–56.

[18] *CPR 1232–47*, 385.

rebels.[19] When Henry went in person to Gascony in the following year to consolidate his rule, his English feudal force of about 300 knights was supplemented by over 100 Poitevin knights.[20] Poitevins also fought for him in Wales in 1257 – 8, and in 1265 a force, allegedly over 100 of them, landed in Pembroke to help turn the tide finally against Simon de Montfort.[21]

But what of the foreigners settled in England? It has already been mentioned that Henry granted lands to thirty-nine Savoyards: at least a dozen of these estates were to the value of 50 marks per annum, and a further dozen or so were worth sometimes well over 100 marks. The most prominent, after the queen, were Boniface of Savoy, her uncle, archbishop of Canterbury (1244 – 70), his brothers William (1237 – 39) and Peter (1241 – 68) successively lords of Richmond, Peter of Aigueblanche, bishop of Hereford (1240 – 68),[22] Peter of Geneva (1244 – 49) and Geoffrey de Joinville (1252 – 1314) successively lords of Ludlow and Meath;[23] and there were also rich knights such as Eubule of Geneva, Eubule de Montibus, Peter de Chauvent and Imbert de Montferrand.[24] Of the eight Poitevin landowners, large estates were created for Henry's half-brother Aymer, bishop-elect of Winchester (1251 – 60) and his younger brother William de Valence, lord of Pembroke (1247 – 96) and their elder brother Geoffrey de Lusignan;[25] on a smaller, but still significant scale, land was granted to the knights Guy de Rochford, Elias de Rabayn and William de Sancta Ermina.[26]

By introducing such men Henry was, once again, hardly attempting anything new. One thinks of the foreign 'new men' brought into England by Henry I or the 'quasi-imperial' aristocracy favoured by the earlier Angevins or even, it might be said, the model of Henry III's own patron saint, Edward the Confessor, with his Norman followers.[27]

It can be argued that Henry granted aliens land in England with at least some consideration for sound policy, and not solely for reasons of family sentiment. There is something to be said for the view that he hoped that they might assist him to undo some of the damage done by John's reign and his own turbulent minority. By placing kinsmen in certain well-chosen castles and lands he was strengthening his direct influence in the realm and adding, on occasion, to the store of royal land.[28] He could also hope, by bringing three bishoprics into his orbit, to forge something of a new relationship with the Church. He even took pains to effect

---

[19] *Royal Letters*, ii. 76 – 81.

[20] For a full list, see Ridgeway, 'The Politics', 142 – 3, table 3; cf. S. K. Mitchell, *Studies in Taxation under John and Henry III* (New Haven, 1914), 255 n. 7.

[21] *CPR 1247 – 58*, 576 – 7, 586; *CPR 1258 – 66*, 423; E 101/371/8/262.

[22] *DNB*; *GEC, sub. nom.* for general information. For William and Peter of Savoy: *CPR 1232 – 47*, 156; *CChR 1226 – 57*, 259, 293 (Valuations: ibid. 191; *CPR 1258 – 66*, 160). Space prevents inclusion here of a full list, with valuations, of aliens' landholdings. Only the main holdings are mentioned. See Ridgeway, 'The Politics', ch. 6 for details.

[23] Watson, 'The Families', 6 – 13.

[24] Ibid. 8 – 11; *CIPM* i. 890; *CPR 1247 – 58*, 220; C. Moor, *The Knights of Edward I* (Harleian Soc. Publicns., 1929 – 32), i. 192 – 3; iii. 180 – 1.

[25] H. S. Snellgrove, *The Lusignans in England 1247 – 58* (Albuquerque, New Mexico, 1950), 32 – 60.

[26] Moor, iv. 108, 130 – 1; *CPR 1247 – 58*, 172, 178, 220, 292, 394, 398, 533, 552.

[27] Cf. J. Gillingham, *The Angevin Empire* (London, 1984), 61 – 4.

[28] A point highlighted in Watson, 'The Families', 6 – 13. Cf. G. L. Harriss, *King, Parliament and Public Finance in Medieval England to 1369* (Oxford, 1975), 142 – 3.

court policy of aliens + native barons.

marriages between the families of foreign favourites and six English earls, including his brother, Richard of Cornwall, in order to prevent these earls from inter-marrying and constructing independent alliances such as Richard of Cornwall and the Marshals, in particular, had attempted during the minority.[29]

He certainly showed something of a preference for deploying foreigners in potentially treacherous borderlands — in Gascony, Ireland and the Welsh Marches. Few of them, contrary to what is often thought, built up a concentration of land in England itself. Peter of Savoy and the bishop of Hereford, among others, became prominent in Gascon affairs in the 1250s, and in the 1260s two Savoyards became seneschal of Gascony.[30] In Ireland, Henry ensured that William de Valence married one of the Marshal co-heiresses, obtaining the lordship of Wexford; in 1261 the wardship of the heirs of Gerard de Prendergast was divided between Valence and Peter of Savoy, and one co-heiress married Maurice, son of Guy de Rochford.[31] By similar manipulation Henry married a co-heiress of the great Lacy honour of Meath first to Peter of Geneva and then, on Peter's death, to Geoffrey de Joinville; he transferred the custody and marriage of the heiress of Robert de Marisco successively to the Poitevin Fulk de Castro Novo and Eubule of Geneva.[32] The de Burgh family married one of the king's Savoyard kinswomen in 1247.[33] In the 1250s Henry even attempted to give great estates in Ireland to Guy and Geoffrey de Lusignan.[34] It is hardly surprising, then, to find Geoffrey de Joinville as deputy justiciar of Ireland in the 1260s.[35] In the Welsh Marches his policy was, if anything, more noticeable: he established an alien as bishop of Hereford; he put Gloucester castle under the control of agents of Queen Eleanor; the treacherous Marshals were replaced at Pembroke and Goodrich by William de Valence, the Lacys at Ludlow by Savoyards; and for much of the 1250s aliens commanded Montgomery castle, so vital for the middle March.[36] Peter of Savoy's control of Richmond and the Vescy wardship, soon consolidated by a Savoyard marriage with the Vescys, established a royalist presence in the north, as did William de Valence's long wardship of FitzJohn of Warkworth and his absorption of Bertram land in Northumberland.[37] Indeed, it is tempting to echo Dr. Robin Frame's remark that among Henry's potential strengths in 1264 – 5 was the circle of support he now enjoyed, again in

[29] D. A. Carpenter, 'King, Magnates and Society: the Personal Rule of King Henry III, 1234 – 1258', *Speculum*, lx (1985), 59; N. Denholm-Young, *Richard of Cornwall* (Oxford, 1947), 16 – 37.
[30] Ridgeway, 'The Lord Edward', 92; J-P. Trabut-Cussac, *L'Administration Anglaise en Gascogne sous Henry III et Edward I de 1254 à 1307* (Paris, Geneva, 1972), 373 ff. which notes the Savoyard origins of Jean de Grailly (1266 – 7) but not those of Henry de Cusances (1261 – 4). See C. L. Kingsford, 'Sir Otho de Grandison (1238 – 1328)', *TRHS* 3rd ser. iii (1909), 181 – 2.
[31] P. H. Hore, *Ferns and Enniscorthy* (London, 1911), 348 – 9.
[32] Watson, 'The Families', 8 – 11.
[33] *GEC* xii. 171 – 2.
[34] Snellgrove, 48 – 50; *CPR 1247 – 58*, 282.
[35] H. G. Richardson and G. O. Sayles, *The Administration of Medieval Ireland 1172 – 1377* (Dublin, 1963), 77.
[36] *CPR 1232 – 47*, 394; *CPR 1247 – 58*, 89, 368, 457; *CPR 1258 – 66*, 55, 59, 162; *CPR 1266 – 72*, 736; *CR 1253 – 4*, 217; *Flores Historiarum*, ed. H. R. Luard (RS, 1890), ii. 480; Ridgeway, 'The Politics', 22 – 7, 410.
[37] *GEC* xii (pt. 2), 279 – 81; *A History of Northumberland. Issued under the Direction of the Northumberland County History Committee* (Newcastle upon Tyne, London, 1893 – 1940), ix. 247; x. 66 – 8; xii. 449.

such ironic contrast to King John, on and beyond the borders of England: in Ireland, in the north and along the Welsh Marches.[38] How wisely Henry, in the event, used his advantage is another matter, of course.

'Historians have made much play', to borrow Powicke's phrase, 'about the insular objection of the English to foreigners in the thirteenth century'. It would be foolish to deny that 'Down with the aliens!' was a powerful, recurring political slogan throughout the century and at other times,[39] but the evidence that Henry's foreign favourites actually aroused widespread opposition, or even much popular interest, before 1258 is hardly convincing. Matthew Paris, with his unrivalled contacts at the royal court and unconcealed hatred of all foreigners, is the sole detailed narrative source.[40] The other surviving contemporary chroniclers, provincially based, have almost nothing to say before reporting the dramatic exiling of the Poitevins in 1258; and then even the otherwise quite well-informed Tewkesbury and Dunstable annalists were ignorant of the names of major figures such as Guy and Geoffrey de Lusignan and, perhaps, Peter of Savoy.[41] This is probably because Henry's favourites did not travel around much in England and so cannot have been familiar figures before 1258. The evidence is sometimes fragmentary, but it looks as though most spent the bulk of their time in England — if the chancery rolls are to be believed — in or near the royal court. Many were abroad for part of the year; some can occasionally be found at their posts in the border areas. Yet we can guess that they did not visit their estates in person very often because, remarkably, even the greatest did not much use their influence to channel their own, or the king's patronage, into areas where they held land.[42] Only the queen, William de Valence and Aymer, the elect of Winchester, recruited any English knights into their *familiae*.[43] The *familiares* of all the rest, apart from their estate officials, were by and large aliens, the worst example being those of Peter of Savoy.[44] This is what probably made them so peculiarly vulnerable to the 'anti-alien' propaganda of 1258 and thereafter.

Recent research, however, has also, quite rightly, blamed the aliens' unpopularity on the oppressions of their estate officials and lawyers in the localities, to which

---

[38] R. Frame, 'Ireland and the Barons' Wars', in *Thirteenth Century England I*, 164.

[39] *The Song of Lewes*, ed. C. L. Kingsford (Oxford, 1890), 72 – 7; O. H. Richardson, *The National Movement in the Reign of Henry III and its Culmination in the Barons' Wars* (New York, 1897); J. C. Holt, *King John* (Historical Assoc. Pamphlet, 1963), 24 – 7.

[40] R. Vaughan, *Matthew Paris* (Cambridge, 1958), 11 – 20; A. Gransden, *Historical Writing in England c. 550 to c. 1307* (London, 1974), 404 – 38.

[41] *Ann. Mon.* i. 165; iii. 209 – 10.

[42] A full list of the aliens' households is in Ridgeway, 'The Politics', 410 – 46.

[43] William de Valence's principal English knights (before 1265) were not recruited from Pembroke or the Welsh Marches but often from royal service: Geoffrey de Gacelin, Robert de Aguillon, Roger de Leyburn etc. See Moor, ii. 95; L. F. Salzman, 'The Family of Aguillon' (Sussex Archaeological Collections, lxxix, 1938), 45 – 60; A. Lewis, 'Roger Leyburn and the Pacification of England 1265 – 7', *EHR* liv (1939), 194 – 5. For full details of their connexion with Valence: Ridgeway, 'The Politics', 429 – 31. William's administration in Pembroke, however, kept on local knights in office: *A Descriptive Catalogue of Ancient Deeds in the PRO* (London, 1890 – 1915), iii. 416, 434. But there is no evidence that he visited Pembroke before 1265.

[44] All Peter's knights were aliens: Wurstemberger, iv. nos. 377, 532 – 60, 629, 657, 749; E 101/349/ 12, m. 1; E 101/349/26, m. 6; *CLR 1251 – 60*, 249, 357, 507; *CLR 1260 – 7*, 10; *CR 1259 – 61*, 421. Peter appears never to have visited Richmond.

the king was all too prone to turn a blind eye.[45] Nor can it be denied that before 1258 we have several examples of random local attacks on the servants, often vulnerable alien clerks, of both Savoyards and Poitevins.[46] Yet, ironically, nearly all the aliens' estate officials were Englishmen, such as William de Bussay, a Lincolnshire or Cambridgeshire man, the notorious steward shared by William de Valence and Geoffrey de Lusignan.[47] They were no worse, nor better, than the officials of the earl of Gloucester and of other great men who enjoyed the king's favour.[48] And it might be suggested that we cannot always so easily draw lessons for national politics from the unpopularity or popularity of aliens at a local level in any case. Consider what happened in 1258. Aymer de Lusignan, the bishop-elect of Winchester, hated more, perhaps, than any of the Poitevins, was expelled from the realm, whereas Boniface of Savoy, the archbishop of Canterbury, sat on the council of the reformers. Now Aymer most certainly had bitter enemies among the magnates, but the signs are that in his locality he was quite well liked, an exception to the rule. Of course, because King Henry enjoyed staying at Winchester, Aymer could often reside there and build up a local following of knights and clerks.[49] In 1258 the contemporary Winchester annalist bemoaned 'the cruelty and severity' of the barons in exiling Aymer, and when he died suddenly in exile in 1260, and his heart was brought back to be buried at Winchester cathedral, the annalist relates how miracles were wrought at the shrine.[50] But Boniface of Savoy was probably hated in Kent. When the justiciar toured the shire in 1258–9 hearing *querelae*, he received twice as many complaints against the archbishop as there were against Aymer in Hampshire and Surrey.[51] In 1263 local knights raided the archbishop's lands. The same happened in that year to the bishop of Hereford who survived the purge in 1258.[52] Also elected to the council in 1258 was Peter of Savoy; his estate officials were universally high-handed; he put his castle in Pevensey under the command of aliens in the 1260s, and throughout his career his honour of Richmond was even administered by a succession of alien stewards.[53] In comparison, the followers of William de Valence, who was exiled in 1258, were overwhelmingly English.

---

45 Carpenter, 'King, Magnates and Society', 63–70; J. R. Maddicott, 'Magna Carta and the Local Community, 1215–1259', *Past and Present*, cii (1984), 54–61.

46 E 101/349/26, m. 8; *CPR 1247–58*, 114, 156; J. P. Chapuisat, 'Le Chapitre Savoyard de Hereford an XIIIe siècle', *Sociétés Savantes de Savoie: Congrès de Moûtiers 1964* (Chambéry, 1966), 43–51; Paris, *CM* v. 643.

47 Paris, *CM* v. 726, 738–9; *CLR 1251–60*, 44; *CR 1261–4*, 93, 276; *Placitorum in Domo Capitulari Westmonasterii Asservatorum Abbreviatio* (Rec. Comm., 1811), 185; Moor, i. 170–1.

48 Maddicott, 'Magna Carta', 54–61.

49 Paris, *CM* vi. 223; *CPR 1258–66*, 2; Ridgeway, 'The Politics', 438–42.

50 *Ann. Mon.* ii. 97, 99.

51 Against the archbishop, at least thirteen cases (JUST 1/362, mm. 1d, 7, 9, 9d, 11d, 12, 12d; JUST 1/873, mm. 4d, 5: several on some membranes); against Aymer, seven cases, mostly fairly trivial and two dismissed out of hand (JUST 1/873, mm. 1, 7d, 8; JUST 1/1188, mm. 8, 8d, 10d, 11d). After reading these for myself I cannot agree with the analysis of Treharne, 155.

52 Treharne, 301 ff.; Bodleian Library, Oxford, Bodleian MS 91, f. 136; 'The Metrical Chronicle of Robert of Gloucester', in *The Church Historians of England*, ed. J. Stevenson (London, 1853–8), v (part 1), 362.

53 *Hist. of Northumberland*, ix. 249–57; *CPR 1258–66*, 274, 363; *The Historical Works of Gervase of Canterbury*, ed. W. Stubbs (RS, 1879–80), ii. 211; Wurstemberger, iv. no. 749; E. F. Jacob, *Studies in the Period of Baronial Reform and Rebellion 1258–67* (Oxford, 1925), 353–65.

In actual practice, the fate of Henry's favourites was decided at the centre of power, at the court and by *curiales* and the great earls. Here, oddly enough, they were very successful. When in the autumn of 1252 the bishop-elect of Winchester and the archbishop of Canterbury quarrelled in a petty dispute over advowson rights which escalated into a power-struggle at court between the Savoyard and Poitevin factions when Aymer raided the archbishop's estates, the English magnates, rather than ignoring such squabbles, began to take sides. Although neither bishop had long resided in England, Henry III had to ban four earls and their men from taking up arms to help them.[54] Why did the power of the aliens last so long, and over men such as these, for twenty years or more from 1236, only to begin to crumble after 1258? As Dr. David Carpenter has argued, the key lies in abandoning our preconceptions that after the king's minority the earls were always suspicious of favourites, and in appreciating how successfully Henry built a balanced court with place and favours for both English earls and aliens; his security was based as much on amicable good lordship towards the native nobility as on any expansion in his family's power.[55]

I think there are a few more reasons for the aliens' integration. First of all, they were bound into the highest echelons of English society, from the king downward, by marriage. Several owed their estates, in fact, to their respective marriages.[56] Many of these unions, in addition, were happy ones. Queen Eleanor's influence was secure for many years after 1239 when she produced an heir for the king, soon to be followed by several more children. Matthew Paris relates how John de Warenne, earl of Surrey, was stricken by grief at the death of his wife Alice de Lusignan in 1256.[57] In 1265 the Savoyard Agnes de Saluzzo is said to have died of grief on hearing of the imprisonment of her rebellious husband, John de Vescy.[58] Even Joan de Munchensi refused to desert William de Valence in 1258, and soon followed him into exile.[59]

Above all, the fortunes of the aliens rested on the solid foundations of early political success. The Savoyards were lucky to arrive in England in the decade following the king's assumpton of personal power in 1236. The great and rapid 'mortality of the earls', and of magnates, of the king's minority, happened at just that time and left many convenient gaps to fill.[60] Moreover, after intense faction-fighting at court in the 1230s between those who kept Henry III in tutelage — the followers of Hubert de Burgh and Peter des Roches — there are signs that English political society desired a change to stability and peace. The Savoyards, for the most part, used their influence with the king well and helped to provide it.[61] At first,

---

[54] *CR 1251 – 3*, 431; Paris, *CM* v. 348 – 54, 358 – 60; discussed in Ridgeway, 'The Politics', 119 – 33.

[55] Carpenter, 'King, Magnates and Society', 52 – 60.

[56] In addition to William de Valence, Peter of Geneva, Geoffrey de Joinville, Eubule of Geneva and the Rochfords mentioned above, the following (and several more) owed the bulk of their estates to marriage with English heiresses: Eubule de Montibus, Elias de Rabayn, Imbert Pugeys: I. J. Sanders, *English Baronies: A Study of their Origins and Descent, 1086 – 1327* (Oxford, 1960), 88 – 9; *Fees* ii. 1373; *RF* ii. 127, 238; *CIPM* iv. no. 152.

[57] Paris, *CM* v. 551.

[58] *GEC* xii (part 2), 279.

[59] Paris, *CM* v. 726, 730.

[60] Powicke, *Henry III*, i. 140 – 55.

[61] D. A. Carpenter, 'The Decline of the Curial Sheriff in England 1194 – 1258', *EHR* xci (1976), 17 – 21.

Henry clumsily tried to promote them too rapidly, rather as he tolerated the rise of that earlier 'alien', Peter des Roches. In 1236 he broke with the old factions of the minority, created an 'exclusive' council, and put William of Savoy at its head; in 1241, after William's death, he tried to make Peter of Savoy his chief adviser, and invested him with the control of most of the major castles along the south coast.[62] But William was a man of compromise; he quickly won over some of his critics by bringing them into the council and in 1237 he co-operated in the re-issuing of the Charters. The *Flores Historiarum* relates how in 1238 he returned from the Continent to negotiate both the king and himself out of an uprising led by Richard of Cornwall.[63] As for Peter of Savoy, upon the first sign of opposition to his ascendancy in 1241 he publicly resigned his offices and castles, 'prudent and discreet man' that he was in Matthew Paris's surprising judgement, and we soon see him negotiating with the magnates.[64] The Savoyards were lucky, too, that at this point Henry III had plenty of escheated land, which meant that, by and large, he did not have to promote them at anyone else's expense or by arbitrary confiscations.[65] There is no better example of the Savoyards' early discretion, in contrast to the grasping nepotism of Peter des Roches, than when the king in 1241 exercised his right to resume the manor of Dartford (Kent) from the heir to the earldom of Aumâle and gave it to the queen's mother, Beatrice of Savoy, only for it to be restored by the king within weeks to the Aumâles to keep the peace.[66] Perhaps Peter of Savoy's survival in 1241 also owed something to Queen Eleanor's careful intercession with the king that year to secure Henry's recognition of Walter, the new and potentially hostile earl Marshal.[67] Thereafter, she and Peter took pains to cultivate the great men at court, such as Earl Richard of Cornwall, or John Mansel, William de Kilkenny and Henry de Wengham, successively the king's chancellors, and even some of Henry's alien favourites of an earlier generation, such as Earls Simon de Montfort and John du Plessis.[68] It was in their ability to moderate the king's policies and appease their critics that the Savoyards left their most enduring stamp on English political life.

After that, Henry actually introduced foreigners very cautiously. Although between 1241 and 1258 fourteen prominent Savoyard knights, and about a dozen clerks, and a total of at least fifteen Poitevins joined the royal court, they were not all in office at the same time, and numbers grew slowly over the space of fifteen years or more. Very few of them were allowed to wield great administrative

---

[62] Cox, 49 – 51, 59 – 80, 108 – 15.

[63] *Flores Historiarum*, ii. 224; C 53/31 m. 1; Denholm Young, 34 – 5. For a recent assessment of William of Savoy's career, see R. C. Stacey, *Politics, Policy and Finance under Henry III 1216 – 45* (Oxford, 1987), 115 – 24. I cannot, however, accept Stacey's suggestion that there was sustained baronial opposition to William in 1237 – 8. For most of 1237, for example, he actually remained at court by the king's side: C 53/30 mm. 1 – 7.

[64] Paris, *CM* iv. 177 – 8, 187.

[65] Ridgeway, 'The Politics', 185 – 9.

[66] *CChR 1226 – 57*, 186, 261; *CR 1237 – 42*, 335. Cf. D. A. Carpenter, 'The Fall of Hubert de Burgh', *Journ. British Studies*, xix (1980), 14 – 17.

[67] Paris, *CM* iv. 158.

[68] Denholm-Young, 49 – 54; E 101/308/1, mm. 1 – 2; E 101/349/14; E 101/349/26, mm. 1, 3; E 101/349/14; Paris, *CM* v. 508; *Ann. Mon.* ii. 355; BL, Cotton Charter xvii. 6. For Wengham and de Montfort: Ridgeway, 'The Politics', 58 – 9, 66 – 7, 113 – 16, 418. Cf. L. B. Dibben, 'Chancellor and Keeper of the Seal under Henry III', *EHR* xxvii (1912), 39 – 51.

responsibility beyond the households of the king, queen and the Lord Edward or beyond the needs of diplomacy, borderlands and military expeditions (as described above). Within the royal households some held confidential positions, such as keeper of the wardrobe (invariably with English assistants), but many merely specialized in domestic responsibilities, as did Henry's Savoyard stewards, Imbert Pugeys and Eubule de Montibus, or his Poitevin chamberlain, William de Sancta Ermina.[69] Henry did not use aliens in the exchequer or judiciary at all. Few, apart from members of the royal family, are known to have participated formally in council and they were rarely prominent in parliaments.[70] Nor were they active in local administration in England proper: before 1258 only two were sheriffs, Peter of Savoy (briefly in Kent in 1241–2) and the Poitevin, Elias de Rabayn (in Somerset and Dorset 1251–5).[71] In any given year after 1242 the Savoyards held at the most three royal castles, and often none, and the Poitevins on average two or three; to these can be added a handful held by Savoyards for the queen and the Lord Edward and, of course, the aliens' own dozen private castles, just over half in Wales, Ireland and the north.[72] Thus, the aliens hardly dominated Henry's government; they only influenced specialized areas of it. He was also careful, it might be noted, not to create any Savoyard and Poitevin earls.[73] Had it been otherwise, there would surely not have existed political peace during those vital seventeen years of personal rule following 1241.

   That peace was gradually tarnished in the 1250s by the rivalry which arose at Henry's court between the well-established Savoyards and the new Poitevin faction. Matters were not helped by the Savoyards' wide network of friendships with *curiales*, whereas the inexperienced Lusignans behaved indiscreetly and offended courtiers and a handful of the great earls. Tensions reached breaking point in 1258 when the Lusignans began to captivate Henry III's heir, the Lord Edward, and in a great political revolution they and the other Poitevins were toppled and exiled.[74] These events, paradoxically, nearly proved fatal for all the aliens in England. The complex struggles at court do not appear to have been grasped by the provincial chroniclers: they viewed politics from the outside; they saw the 1258 revolution as a reforming movement purging all foreigners from the realm.[75] They avidly absorbed the propaganda circulated against the Lusignans: it was often couched in emotive, general terms denouncing foreigners in language reminiscent of 1215,

---

[69] *Handbook of British Chronology*, ed. F. M. Powicke and E. B. Fryde (2nd edn., London, 1961), 74; T. F. Tout, *Chapters in the Administrative History of Mediaeval England* (Manchester, 1920–33), i. 260–3; v. 232–6; Ridgeway, 'The Lord Edward', 92–3; *CR 1256–9*, 256, 344, 356, 396, 422–3, 438, 444, 450; *CPR 1258–66*, 203, 242, 254, 262; Paris, *CM* v. 702.

[70] Powicke, *Henry III*, i. 296–7; B. Wilkinson, *Studies in the Constitutional History of the Thirteenth and Fourteenth Centuries* (Manchester, 1937), 146; Paris, *CM* iv. 187, 362, 366; v. 5, 325, 373, 602, 634, 676.

[71] *List of Sheriffs for England and Wales to 1831* (PRO Lists and Indexes, ix, London, 1898), 67, 122.

[72] See Ridgeway, 'The Politics', 21–7 for a list. Cf. *DBM* 80–3, 90–1, 112–13 and notes, which show how few aliens were, in reality, deprived of custody of royal castles in the 1258 revolution.

[73] F. R. Lewis, 'William de Valence (*c.* 1230–96)', *Aberystwyth Studies*, xiv (1936), 72–8. Peter of Savoy, too, was never created 'earl' of Richmond: e.g. *CR 1254–6*, 195; *CR 1261–4*, 131; *DBM* 73, 105 etc.

[74] Carpenter, 'What Happened in 1258?', 106–19; Ridgeway, 'The Lord Edward', 89–99.

[75] The only exception was *Ann. Mon.* ii. 355, and here the chronicler (*sub anno* 1263) was probably copying from another source. Cf. Paris, *CM* v. 703.

which re-awakened old fears. For instance, it was alleged that they were not only evil exploiters of wards and heiresses but that they posed a threat to security with their custody of 'nearly all' the king's castles; and that they even had plans to poison the king and baronage and seize power in the realm.[76] Additional damage was done to the aliens by officially highlighting the Poitevins' actual misdeeds because it often aroused resentment against similar conduct by Savoyards, whereas the justiciar's investigations into seigneurial abuses in 1258–9 stirred up a lot of hatred against courtiers in general. Thus, when in 1263 further power-shifts dislodged the Savoyards from court and order broke down with the onset of civil war, the aliens, rather like the Jews, were subject to indiscriminate exile and popular attack.[77] De Montfort and his supporters, for their part, grew to hate and fear them because, as we have seen, the king repeatedly summoned military and diplomatic assistance from foreign allies in order to suppress various types of opposition after 1260. But, as for English provincial society, their xenophobia had begun to be fired in 1258.

My final point, however, is to remark how many aliens survived the turmoil of the years 1258–65. Although Savoyards were on the run after 1263 they soon returned from exile: the archbishop of Canterbury, for instance, in 1266, and even the bishop of Hereford in 1268. A few lines suffered disaster, and a few died out through natural causes in the 1260s but, in all, eleven Savoyard knightly families were established in England for the remainder of the thirteenth century, to which Edward I was to add a handful more.[78] As for the Poitevins, they too returned and by 1272 the families of Lusignan, Craon, Rochford and Rabayn were well-established.[79] I suggest that these men came back not just because Henry III eventually defeated Simon de Montfort; it was because they held land in England, and that was enough to get them accepted. There is a curious hint of this even in 1258 and, here again, we need to look at the magnates. When they turned against the Lusignans, they originally proposed only to exile Guy and Geoffrey whereas Aymer of Winchester and William de Valence, 'who hold lands in England', could choose to remain in custody until the realm had been reformed.[80] Even after they all chose exile, their property — and that of other proscribed Poitevins — was punctiliously kept in store for them, rather than confiscated and dispersed, lest they might return.[81] In 1261, when circumstances permitted William de Valence to

[76] Clanchy, 261–2; *DBM* 77–85, 90–1; *Ann. Mon.* i. 165; ii. 349–50; iii. 209; iv. 118; *The Chronicle of Walter of Guisborough*, ed. H. Rothwell (Camden Soc., lxxxix, 1957), 185; *Annales Cambriae*, ed. J. Williams ab Ithel (RS, 1860), 96. Interestingly, most chroniclers beginning in or after 1263 assume that all the 'aliens' were expelled in 1258: e.g. Thomas Wykes, in *Ann. Mon.* iv. 120; William Rishanger, *Chronica et Annales, regnantibus Henrico tertio et Edwardo primo*, ed. H. T. Riley (RS, 1865), 2, etc.
[77] *DBM* 256–65, 268–79; Powicke, *Henry III*, ii. 437–502; Treharne, 284–328; *Ann. Mon.* i. 177; iii. 225–7; 'Robert of Gloucester', 368; *Gervase of Canterbury*, ii. 224; *Liber Memorandum Ecclesie de Bernewelle*, ed. J. W. Clark (Cambridge, 1907), 151.
[78] Charron, Chauvent, Grailly, Grandison, Joinville (Geneville), Montferrand, Montibus, Montreal, Pugeys, Thurumberd and, of course, Savoy: Moor, *sub. nom.*; *Hist. of Northumberland*, ix. 251ff. For some of Edward I's links with Savoy: Ridgeway, 'The Politics', 35.
[79] Moor, *sub. nom.* One might add Rochechouart: *GEC* iv. 199.
[80] *DBM* 94–5; Paris, *CM* vi. 403. They seem at this point to have forgotten, perhaps conveniently, that Geoffrey de Lusignan held lands; however, they soon took them into safe custody: n. 81, below.
[81] Treharne, 126–30; *CR 1259–61*, 28. Cf. *CPR 1247–58*, 653.

return, one chronicler thought it was 'by assent of the barons', and another remarked that at Dover he accordingly took his oath to the Provisions of Oxford and to abide by the law of the land.[82] He had learnt his political lesson; within a year he was imitating the Savoyards' style and interceding with the king on behalf of his young disaffected kinsman, the new earl of Gloucester.[83] These events are a clue that landholders' solidarity would in the end be more important to many English magnates than the politics of 'nationalism' or reform. They later shrank at the prospect of disinheriting Montfortian rebels; as early as 1258, it would seem, they could not bring themselves to disendow even the hated 'aliens'.[84]

[82] *De Antiquis Legibus Liber*, ed. T. Stapleton (Camden Soc., old ser., 1846), 49; *Flores Historiarum*, ii. 466.
[83] *Gervase of Canterbury*, ii. 216.
[84] C. H. Knowles, 'The Resettlement of England after the Barons' Wars, 1264 – 67', *TRHS* 5th ser. xxxii (1982), 25 – 43.

The Crusade Taxation of 1268 – 1270
and the Development of Parliament*

J. R. Maddicott

The interval between the Lord Edward's assumption of the Cross in June 1268 and his departure for the Latin East in August 1270 was a time of intense parliamentary activity. During these twenty-six months some seven or eight parliaments met, mainly to consider the arrangements for the crusade and its financing. Save perhaps for the opening phase of the reform movement in 1258 – 9, no comparable period of Henry III's reign was so prolific in parliaments. 'Not without weariness and expense', Walter Giffard, archbishop of York, wrote querulously to Cardinal Ottobuono in the spring of 1270, 'were so many parliaments summoned'.[1] Their novelty, however, lay less in their frequency, which merely emphasized that parliament was now the natural forum for the discussion of taxation and other national business, than in the regular summoning of the knights, and probably the burgesses, who represented the commons. It was in these months that taxation, consent and popular representation first came together, in a *conjoncture* which has been surprisingly neglected. The purpose of this paper is to bring forward some unconsidered chronicle evidence for these parliaments, to clarify the obscure circumstances in which a crusading tax was negotiated and finally granted, and, through an analysis of the negotiations over taxation, to delineate the emergent role of the commons. We may then be able to see more clearly the wider significance of this short period for the general history of the English parliament.

Henry III had been personally committed to a crusade ever since he had taken the Cross in 1250. But although it was not until August 1270 that he publicly laid aside that Cross, it was his son Edward who from the start presented himself as the leader of the English crusade.[2] Edward took the Cross at Northampton on 24 June 1268, an action which marked both the culmination of the legateship of Cardinal Ottobuono, who had been promoting the crusade in England for nearly two years, and the beginning of the practical problems confronting the crusade's organizers. The numbers who committed themselves to the Cross at Northampton were large: Wykes gives the figure of 120 knights and barons, and a local chronicle puts the full

---

* I am very grateful to Dr. C. J. Tyerman for reading and commenting on an earlier draft of this paper and to Dr. S. D. Lloyd for his general help and advice.
[1] *The Register of Archbishop Walter Giffard, 1266 – 79*, ed. W. Brown (Surtees Soc., cix, 1904), 157. Compare his similar complaint of 25 Mar. 1271 about the frequency of parliaments: *Historical Papers and Letters from the Northern Registers*, ed. J. Raine (RS, 1873), 36. A list of parliaments for the period is given in the appendix, below 117.
[2] A. J. Forey, 'The Crusading Vows of the English King Henry III', *Durham University Journ.* lxv (1973), 230, 246.

tally at 700.[3] Even if most of these humbler *crucesignati* later redeemed their vows for cash, as seems probable, the noble contingent which eventually departed remained a sizeable one: Edward raised 225 knights by contract before he left, and some 243 protections were issued to those intending to accompany him.[4] The financing of such a force was likely to prove exceptionally difficult.

It had never been the custom to finance crusades from the ordinary revenues of the Crown, and in 1268 this was more than ever impossible. A bitter and destructive civil war, ended only in the previous year with the submission of the earl of Gloucester, had thoroughly disrupted the Crown's revenue-gathering activities and brought Henry's resources to their lowest level.[5] In 1267 his plight had been dramatically shown when he had been forced to pawn the treasures of Edward the Confessor's unfinished shrine at Westminister and to stop the payment of all fees from the exchequer, except to those in his service.[6] Since the Crown's resources cannot have been expected to contribute much, if anything, to the crusade, their exhaustion would have had only marginal effects, had it not also precluded any immediate support from a more traditional source of crusading funds, the Church. In June 1266 Pope Clement IV had recognized Henry's poverty by granting him a tenth on clerical incomes for three years in order to meet his debts and other needs.[7] This levy, collected in many dioceses by royal agents and according to a new and more comprehensive valuation, was deeply resented and still had eighteen months to run at the time of the ceremonies at Northampton. In addition, the clergy were currently burdened by another unpopular tax, the twentieth for the relief of the Disinherited.[8] Because of these and earlier levies Clement IV was unwilling to permit further clerical taxation for a crusade, towards which his own attitude was in any case ambivalent.[9] Although in the event Henry and Edward were able to put pressure on the Church to contribute, it seemed initially that one of the normal sources of crusading revenue would be unavailable.

In these circumstances only the taxation of the laity could provide what was needed. Yet the securing of a general tax was not likely to be easy. There had been no levy on lay moveables since the thirtieth of 1237. Henry's request for a subsidy in the 1240s and 1250s, put forward on at least six occasions,[10] had been repeatedly made the occasion for the presentation of political grievances and then turned down

[3] 'Chronicon Thomae Wykes', in *Ann. Mon.* iv. 218; H. M. Cam and E. F. Jacob, 'Notes on an English Cluniac Chronicle', *EHR* xliv (1929), 104. For the general background see S. D. Lloyd, 'The Lord Edward's Crusade, 1270 – 2: Its Setting and Significance', in *War and Government in the Middle Ages: Essays in Honour of J. O. Prestwich*, ed. J. Gillingham and J. C. Holt (Woodbridge, 1984), 120 – 4.

[4] *Ex inf.* Dr. S. D. Lloyd, and see id., 'The Lord Edward's Crusade', 126; B. Beebe, 'The English Baronage and the Crusade of 1270', *BIHR* xlviii (1975), 143 – 8.

[5] M. Mills, ' "Adventus Vicecomitum" ', 1258 – 72', *EHR* xxxvi (1921), 494 – 6; E. F. Jacob, *Studies in the Period of Baronial Reform and Rebellion, 1258 – 67* (Oxford, 1925), 248 – 75.

[6] *CPR 1266 – 72*, 52, 64 – 5, 135 – 40, 326; *CLR 1260 – 7*, 298.

[7] W. E. Lunt, *Financial Relations of the Papacy with England to 1327* (Cambridge, Mass., 1939), 292 – 310.

[8] *Councils and Synods, II (1265 – 1313)*, ed. F. M. Powicke and C. R. Cheney (Oxford, 1964), ii. 799.

[9] S. D. Lloyd, 'The Crusade of 1270 – 72: A Case Study' (unpublished typescript). I am very grateful to Dr. Lloyd for allowing me to make use of this chapter from his book in advance of publication.

[10] J. R. Maddicott, 'Magna Carta and the Local Community, 1215 – 59', *Past and Present*, cii (1984), 43 – 4.

or ignored. The precedents favoured rejection rather than acceptance of any new attempt to tax. It is true that Henry had since won a war, but in some ways this had created a political and economic climate even less propitious for taxation than that of the years before 1258. The war had impoverished the king's subjects as well as the king. It had left some estates devastated, some towns partly ruined,[11] and very many former rebels heavily in debt for the redemption of their estates under the terms of the Dictum of Kenilworth. Between the conclusion of the war in June 1267 and the inauguration of the crusade a year later, new impositions had already begun to tap lay wealth, though only on a local scale. At the end of 1267 arrangements were put in hand for a new eyre visitation and for a tallage of cities, boroughs and royal demesne lands. When Edward took the Cross the tallage was still being collected, while the eyre, having already sat in three counties, was now active in five others.[12] A costly war, a recent and fragile peace, redemption payments, tallage and eyre, all meant that the exaction of any new tax might prove exceptionally delicate and difficult.

This was the background to Henry's attempts to secure a levy on moveables, which began almost immediately after the crusade had been put in train at Northampton. By the 1260s it was firmly established that such a levy needed the corporate consent of the baronage, but on this occasion the circumstances already discussed must have suggested that it would be prudent to look for consent from a wider circle. Such a move would not, of course, be entirely novel. In 1254 two knights from each shire had been summoned to London to consider Henry's demand for a general aid, and in April 1268, shortly before the meeting at Northampton, townsmen had been summoned from twenty-seven cities and boroughs to take counsel with the king in London, probably in connection with the levying of the tallage.[13] Their summoning points to the growing sensitivity of the government towards the issue of consent. But from June onwards these isolated precedents were to be overtaken and consolidated in what was to become a long campaign to gain the consent of both magnates and commons to the crusading tax which Henry and Edward needed.

Henry first sought a tax at a parliament held at York in September 1268. This parliament, overlooked by modern historians and not listed in the *Handbook of British Chronology*, is described by only one source: the Furness continuator of William of Newburgh's chronicle, that neglected writer who provides so much original information on mid thirteenth-century affairs.[14] For his characteristically precise accounts of the parliaments of this period the Furness chronicler probably drew upon the eyewitness recollections of his abbot, who was normally among

[11] Jacob, 248 – 9; D. Keene, *Survey of Medieval Winchester*. Winchester Studies, II (Oxford, 1985), i. 141, 178.
[12] Powicke, *Henry III*, ii. 563; D. Crook, *Records of the General Eyre* (PRO Handbook, no. 20, London, 1982), 133 – 7.
[13] Maddicott, 'Magna Carta', 46; G. O. Sayles, 'Representatives of Cities and Boroughs in 1268', *EHR* xl (1925), 580 – 5; Powicke, *Henry III*, ii. 563.
[14] 'Continuation' of William of Newburgh, *Historia rerum Anglicanum*, in *Chronicles of the Reigns of Stephen, Henry II and Richard I*, ed. R. Howlett (RS, 1884 – 9), ii. 554. For other independent information provided by this chronicler, see e.g. J. R. Maddicott, 'The Mise of Lewes, 1264', *EHR* xcviii (1983), 593 – 4.

those heads of Cistercian houses summoned to parliament.[15] This suggestion is borne out by his account of the reactions of the Cistercians present in the parliament of October 1268 to the king's demand for a tax,[16] and it points to a means by which other medieval chroniclers may have gathered some of their material. The Furness writer's report of the York parliament is brief enough to be quoted in full, and since a good deal hangs on his precise words the Latin of the printed text is given:

> In Nativitate vero eiusdem sanctae Virginis [8 September] tenuit rex parliamentum apud Eboracum, ubi sicut mandavit, convenerunt ipse et rex Scotiae et reginae utrorumque cum Edwardo et Edmundo et liberis suis. Et omnes fere nobiliores Angliae, cum praelatis ecclesiasticis ibidem aderant, ut de regni utilitate tractarent. Sed, ut patuit in fine, summum negotium regis erat [emungere] bursas praesentium. Ibi etiam dicto tempore desponsavit Henricus de Percy filiam comitis de Warenne. Sed cum ibidem plenarie non convenissent, omnes maiores Angliae se excusaverunt. Jussit rex onmibus, qui affuerunt et qui absentes erant, ut essent Lundoniis die sancti Edwardi [13 October] acturi de negotiis regni.

The chronicler thus records a meeting at York between the English and Scottish royal families, the presence of almost all the nobles, an attempt to raise a tax,[17] the apparent absence of all the *maiores Angliae*, and the summoning of another parliament to meet in London at the Translation of St. Edward. Much of his terse account can be checked and proved accurate. The chancery and exchequer records show that the king was at York from about 7 to 26 September.[18] Just as the chronicler describes, the city was the setting for a family meeting with Alexander III of Scotland and his queen, Margaret, Henry's daughter, which had been arranged before Henry arrived at Northampton in July.[19] The witness lists to royal and private charters, and agreements made there, point to a large assembly, which included the archbishop of York, the bishop-elect of Worcester, the prior of the Hospitallers, the Lord Edward, Edmund his brother, Henry of Almain, Roger de Clifford, Hamo Lestrange, Roger Leyburn, Thomas de Clare, John de Vescy, Adam of Jesmond, Robert de Neville, Robert de Bruce and Guichard Charrun.[20] Most of these men were either Northerners or Marcher followers of Edward.

What, then, are we to make of the distinction which this accurate reporter draws between the *nobiliores*, who were almost all present, and the *maiores Angliae*, who

---

[15] The abbot of Furness was summoned to Montfort's parliament of Jan. 1265: *CR 1264 – 8*, 85; and to Edward I's parliaments in 1295, 1296, 1300, 1301, 1302, 1305 and 1307: *Parliamentary Writs*, ed. F. Palgrave (Rec. Comm., London, 1827 – 34), i. 30, 47, 84, 89, 112, 114, 137, 182. There is no information on those summoned between these dates.

[16] 'Continuation' of William of Newburgh, ii. 555; below, 98.

[17] The key word 'emungere', 'to empty [their purses]', is an editorial interpolation, added to fill a gap in the manuscript, but some such word is clearly intended. It is hard to know what Henry was intending to do with the purses of those present if not to empty them.

[18] *The Itinerary of Henry III*. PRO, Round Room, Press 17/15.

[19] *CLR 1267 – 72*, 41 – 2; *CPR 1266 – 72*, 250 – 1, 259 – 60.

[20] C 53/57, m. 1; *CPR 1266 – 72*, 290, 292, 294.

excused themselves? An initial problem is posed by the state of our text, a fourteenth-century transcript of a lost original, which at this point is both corrupt and badly edited. The manuscript shows no stop after 'excusaverunt' and no capital letter J for 'jussit', thus running together the whole sequence from 'sed cum . . .' to '. . . de negotiis regni'.[21] This, of course, makes a mere jumble, to which sense can best be restored by assuming that some such word as 'quia' originally stood before 'omnes maiores Angliae'. The amended sentence would thus read: 'Sed cum ibidem plenarie non convenissent, [quia] omnes maiores Angliae se excusaverunt, jussit rex omnibus, qui affuerunt et qui absentes erant, ut essent Lundoniis die sancti Edwardi acturi de negotiis regni.'

If this interpretation can be accepted, the chronicler is explaining that because parliament had not met 'fully', the *maiores Angliae* having excused themselves, the king ordered those present and those absent to re-assemble in London at a later date. Whom did he mean by the *maiores Angliae*? We might suspect that this group was synonymous with the nobility but for the fact that our author tells us that almost all the nobles *were* present and all the *maiores* absent. There seems to be no other conclusion than that the *maiores* are the commons (the knights and possibly the burgesses), a conclusion strengthened by a possible use of the word in the same sense by the chronicler Wykes in his description of a later parliament.[22] The *maiores* are not the nobles; and if they are not the commons, it is not easy to find a third identity for them.

One other interpretation of the crucial passage is possible, though not at all probable. (It is mentioned here only because the first interpretation met with a sceptical response in some quarters when this paper was originally delivered and what follows was proposed as an alternative.) The passage should stand as it is printed; the *maiores* are the nobles (certainly the orthodox meaning of the word); they excused themselves, not from attending, for most were already present, but from granting the tax; and they did so on the grounds that some of their number were absent, leaving an 'unfull' parliament. But this seems a far more strained explication of the passage than that put forward above. We know from the records as well as from the chronicle that many nobles were present at York, and they included, moreover, a number of crusaders who would surely have been anxious to see that the king secured his tax. 'Omnes maiores Angliae excusaverunt' seems to stand in a logical relationship to 'qui absentes erant'; and the phrase 'se excusaverunt' is much more likely to be used of an excuse for absence than of a refusal of taxation. The meeting of the next parliament, which as we shall see, was 'full', and which certainly included the knights, supports the view that it was a parliament of this sort which the king had earlier tried to bring together at York.

It seems likely, therefore, that the commons had been summoned to York, that they failed to attend, and that in consequence further discussion was postponed until the October parliament. They can only have been summoned after the decision to crusade had been taken at Northampton at the end of June, giving a relatively short period of notice, and one which spanned the harvest. There may also have been a general reluctance to journey to so distant a part of the kingdom. At the Hilary parliament of 1265, the last known occasion on which knights had been summoned,

21 BL, MS Cotton Cleopatra A.i, f.194v.
22 *Chron. Wykes*, 227; below, 105–6.

it had similarly proved impossible to secure the attendance of those from Shropshire and Staffordshire, and perhaps from other counties.[23] But most notable is the chronicler's implication that the business of the parliament, of which taxation was a central part, could not go forward without the commons. Despite a full showing of magnates, the assembly had not met fully, *plenarie*, without them.

It was a larger assembly which met at Westminster in October 1268. Among the chroniclers, both Arnold fitzThedmar, writing in London, and the continuator of Gervase of Canterbury mention this parliament, but neither does more than describe the trouble which arose during its course when the archbishop of York insisted on carrying his cross in the province of Canterbury.[24] Once again, our main source is the Furness writer. Following immediately from his description of the York parliament, he gives the fullest and most revealing account of what took place at Westminster. This passage is given below in translation, since the precise wording is not critical:

> At the stated time, when there had assembled archbishops, bishops, abbots, priors and other rectors of churches, with earls, barons, knights and innumerable other people, and when the crusade had been preached, the king ordered all who had not taken the Cross to do so. Afterwards he imposed financial exactions on everyone. For he exacted tenths from the beneficed, from a lay tenement for every carucate 20*s*. and for every acre 6*d*. The leaders and faithful men of the kingdom took counsel on these things and asked for a delay until an appropriate time at which they could satisfy the king. The king granted deferments, for some until Christmas, for others until Easter, for others later. The Cistercians indeed answered the king, saying that they could do nothing at all about what the king asked without the general chapter, for which reason the king granted them a respite until the time of the said chapter.[25]

The chronicle thus speaks of a large assembly, including the knights and lower clergy, whose main business was the crusade and the taxation to pay for it. The three main points in his account are corroborated by the record evidence. On 20 September, during the York parliament, Henry had written to Louis IX in response to Louis's request for a meeting at Boulogne. Henry replied that he would certainly come were he not engaged on the matter of the crusade. He had summoned a parliament, 'generale, plenum et sollempne', to meet in London on 13 October, where the crusade was to be discussed with those barons who had taken the Cross, and because of this he asked for a postponement of the proposed meeting until after Christmas.[26] The word 'general' in relation to parliament was here beginning to

---

[23] *CR 1264 – 8*, 98 – 9.

[24] *De Antiquis Legibus Liber: Cronica Maiorum et Vicecomitum Londoniarum*, ed. T. Stapleton (Camden Soc., old ser., 1846), 108; *The Historical Works of Gervase of Canterbury*, ed. W. Stubbs (RS, 1879 – 80), ii. 247 – 8.

[25] 'Continuation' of William of Newburgh, ii. 554 – 5.

[26] *CR 1264 – 8*, 552. The entry for the Oct. parliament in the *Handbook of British Chronology* is based solely on this reference.

acquire its later meaning of a parliament in which representatives were present. Indeed, this seems to be the first instance of a 'general' parliament which is known to have included the commons.[27]

If the Westminster parliament was concerned with the crusade, a series of entries on the dorse of the close rolls proves that it was also concerned with the concomitant taxation. The two most important entries read thus:

> The counties of Hereford, Salop, Stafford and Warwick elect Philip Basset, Roger de Somery, James de Audley, Hamo Lestrange, Gilbert Talbot, Anketin de Martival, together with the counsel of the earls and barons. Roger de Leyburn [*sic*].
> The counties of York, Northumberland, Cumberland, Westmorland and the earldom of Lancashire assent to ('assentiunt in') John de Balliol, Robert de Ros, Eustace de Balliol and Adam of Jesmond, that they may ordain and make arrangements ('ordinent et disponant') in the aforesaid counties concerning the aid granted to the lord king.

All ten of the barons named here appear on a separate list, entered a little later on the roll of some forty-five men, mainly magnates but including six archbishops and bishops and a few clerks and other minor figures, who were 'assigned to ordain concerning the aid throughout the kingdom'.[28]

These entries were noted by Powicke, who assigned them to 'some parliament' held in the autumn of 1268. Although they are not dated, they fall between others dated to 11 and 25 October, and they must therefore relate to proceedings in the parliament of that month. Their interpretation is difficult. They speak as if a tax had already been granted to the king ('de auxilio domino regi concesso'), and they appear to record the election by county representatives of two committees of local barons to make arrangements for its levying in the two groups of counties from which the representatives came. The subsequent list of forty-five barons and other notables, which appears side by side with a list of counties, probably shows the full tally of negotiators who were to be divided among the counties in a similar way. Powicke's first tentative suggestion that 'the baronial element was elected, presumably by their fellow barons', cannot be right: the words of the close roll entries, 'comitatus . . . eligunt' and 'comitatus . . . assentiunt', cannot refer to barons, who would not have been described as 'counties'.[29] Nor could the election of these baronial committees have taken place outside parliament, in the county courts, for the grouping of counties to elect a single committee for each group implies the coming together of county representatives, which would only have taken place in parliament. What we seem to see is something akin to the later process of 'intercommuning', by which, in the parliaments of the mid and late

---

[27] Cf. H. G. Richardson and G. O. Sayles, 'The Early Records of the English Parliaments: The English Parliaments of Edward I', *BIHR* v (1928), 135, n. 4; F. M. Powicke, *The Thirteenth Century* (2nd edn., Oxford, 1962), 343.
[28] *CR 1264 – 8*, 557 – 9; Powicke, *Henry III*, ii. 564 – 5.
[29] Powicke, *Henry III*, ii. 564. He later changed his mind, stating that the whole tally of bishops and magnates listed 'would seem to have been elected by groups of shires': id., *Thirteenth Century*, 222.

fourteenth century, the commons chose certain members of the lords to negotiate with them, usually over taxation and petitions.[30]

The nature of the tax proposed remains still more obscure. Since it is described only as an *auxilium*, it is unlikely to be the twentieth that was eventually conceded in May 1270, for this is always described as such in the records.[31] The very vagueness of the close roll may suggest that although consent had been given to some form of tax, its character and scale remained undetermined, perhaps to be settled by the baronial committees in the localities: rather as, in fourteenth-century France, central assemblies sometimes assented to the necessity for a tax, but left its scope and size to be negotiated locally. A more specific clue lies in the Furness chronicler's remark that the king exacted 'from a lay tenement for every carucate 20s. and for every acre 6d.', for this suggests that the government was contemplating the revival of the carucage, last levied on the laity in 1220 and on the clergy in 1224.[32] Perhaps a land tax, assessed on indestructible hides and carucates, was thought likely to produce a larger yield than a levy on moveables taken in the aftermath of a war which had caused much damage to moveable property.

This whole scheme proved abortive, and there are no further references to it among the chancery or exchequer records. That the close roll records only two county committees, serving only eleven counties, makes it unlikely that others were elected. It is probable that Henry's demands encountered stiff resistance, as the Furness chronicler relates, and very possible that that resistance came chiefly from the knights, and clergy, rather than from the lay magnates. Since the forty-five men listed on the close roll, mainly magnates, are deputed 'to ordain concerning the aid throughout the kingdom', it is a safe assumption that they had consented to it. At least eleven of the thirty-nine laymen on the list had already taken the Cross or would later crusade;[33] they thus had every incentive to press for a grant without which there could be no crusade. Others were royalists who had profited considerably at the expense of the Montfortians after Evesham and whose loyalty and affluence may have made them generous.[34] It is noticeable that the two groups of counties electing committees were ones in which a strong local royalist presence

---

[30] J. G. Edwards, *The Commons in Medieval English Parliaments* (London, 1958), esp. 8 – 9, 18 – 19.

[31] E.g. *CPR 1266 – 72*, 406, 418.

[32] 'Exegit enim a beneficiatis decimas a laico tenemento, pro qualibet carucata xx.s vel pro qualibet acra vi.d.' The meaning of this sentence is not entirely clear. The writer may have intended to refer only to the clergy, who were to pay both a tenth on their spiritualities (mainly falling on the parish clergy) and a carucage on their lay tenements (mainly falling on the bishops and the religious). But it seems more likely that he is describing levies intended both for the clergy and for the laity. We know from the close rolls that taxation of the laity was under discussion; and the phrase which immediately follows in the chronicle, 'consulentibus principibus et fidelibus regni', suggests a debate among the lay magnates, rather than (or perhaps as well as) among the clergy. (I am very grateful to Dr. J. H. Denton for advice on these points.) The rate of the carucage seems extraordinarily high: for comparison, the carucages of 1198, 1200 and 1217 had been taken at 5s., 3s., and 3s. per carucate respectively: S. K. Mitchell, *Taxation in Medieval England* (New Haven, Conn., 1952), 128 – 9, 131, 135. If the conventional reckoning of the carucate at 120 acres is correct, the rate of 1268 would be 2d. per acre, not 6d. as the chronicler has it. Perhaps the copyist has mistakenly transcribed 'iid.' as 'vid.'.

[33] The earl of Gloucester, Roger Leyburn, Henry of Almain, Roger de Clifford, Adam of Jesmond, Eustace de Balliol: Beebe, 'The English Baronage', 142 – 3; James de Audley, Hamo Lestrange, John de Warenne, William de Munchensey and William le Blund: *ex inf.* Dr. S. D. Lloyd.

[34] E.g. the earl of Hereford, Philip Basset, Roger Leyburn, Roger de Clifford: C. H. Knowles, 'The Resettlement of England after the Barons' War, 1264 – 67', *TRHS* 5th ser. xxxii (1982), 26 – 7.

was reflected in the composition of the committee. For example, the four barons chosen for the five northern counties — John de Balliol, Robert de Ros, Eustace de Balliol and Adam of Jesmond — were all prominent supporters of the king in the north-east. Where royalists and crusader magnates were thus concentrated, we might expect them to have been able to put pressure on their counties to co-operate in the negotiating of a tax. In other districts, where such pressure was less marked, county representatives may have been able to avoid electing baronial committees for taxation. From this evidence we cannot be sure of much, yet there may well have been a division of interest between magnates who were prepared to concede a tax and county representatives who were more inclined to resist.

Fruitless though they proved, the parliament of October 1268 and the levies devised during its course throw much new light on the thinking of Henry's government. Representatives were present at a parliament in which taxation was discussed — the first time, so far as we know, that this had happened since the much more famous assembly of 1254. Some of those representatives had played a role, though perhaps reluctantly, in the election of 'taxing committees' from among the baronage — the first occasion in the history of parliament when we can point to any specific action in parliament by the commons. Consultation with these men was clearly thought essential if the tax was to go forward. Yet despite summoning a very large assembly — 'generale, plenum et sollempne', in Henry's own words — the king had been able to secure only consent to the grant of a tax, and not the tax itself. The whole episode points to the constraints on royal power, to which local opinion almost certainly contributed, in the years after Evesham.

For reasons which are unclear, attempts to gain a tax seem to have ceased for more than eight months after the October parliament. Failure on that occasion may have made it seem both prudent and potentially more profitable to wait until the late summer of 1269 before trying again. Since 1232 it had become usual for the assessment and collection of a levy on moveables to take place in September, for it was at that time of the year, after the harvest and before the autumn slaughtering of stock, that the taxable wealth of the country was at its greatest.[35] Having missed the boat in the autumn of 1269, Henry may have judged that the yield of any new tax would be greater if its levying were deferred until the completion of another harvest. Parliaments meanwhile continued to meet, and although there is nothing to suggest that taxation was directly considered during their sessions, measures were put in hand which may have been intended to encourage consent to it at a later date.

These measures were initiated during the Hilary parliament of January 1269. Although no chronicle mentions this assembly, the season was by now a customary one for parliaments, and the witnessing of royal charters by an abnormally large number of bishops, earls and barons in mid-January, together with the revival of the Canterbury-York dispute which had flared up in the October parliament, suggests that custom was followed in 1269.[36] During the course of the parliament, king and council drafted an ordinance intended to restrict the moneylending activities of the

---

[35] Mitchell, 104.

[36] The archbishop of York, the bishops of Winchester, Worcester and St. Davids, the earls of Hereford and Surrey, Henry of Almain, Philip Basset, Roger de Somery, William of Valence, James de Audley and Roger de Clifford were among those witnessing charters on 10 and 15 Jan.: C 53/58, mm. 13–14. For the Canterbury-York dispute, see *De Ant. Leg. Liber*, 108.

Jews. From about 1250 it had become normal for Jews to lend money to landowners in return for the creation of annual rentcharges on their lands. These rentcharges were then often sold by the Jews to magnates and ecclesiastics, and eventually the land itself, the security for the rentcharge, might be transferred to a new owner. Men such as William of Valence, Godfrey Giffard, chancellor from 1267, and the Lord Edward himself, had regularly trafficked in such debts. Their transactions were no more than a variation on an old story: the transfer of land from small landowners to large via the medium of Jewish credit. Now, in January 1269, these practices were curtailed: the future creation of such rentcharges was forbidden; none currently held by the Jews was to be passed on to Christians; and all those remaining in Jewish hands were to be cancelled. At the same time, Jews were prohibited from selling ordinary debts to Christians without the king's permission, and Christians purchasing such debts with that permission were to take them without interest.[37]

This legislation was almost certainly intended to offer relief to small landowners, gentry, knights and minor barons, at the expense both of the Jews and of the magnates who had profited from the difficulties of their inferiors. Such relief was especially necessary at a time when many former Montfortians were borrowing from the Jews in order to meet redemption payments incurred under the Dictum of Kenilworth.[38] According to Wykes, the initiative for it came from Edward and Henry of Almain,[39] both among the leaders of the crusade, who may have had in mind the need to win the backing of the lesser landowners, both for the monarchy in general and for a crusading tax in particular. In a parallel way the much more restrictive Statute of Jewry of 1275 was seen by one chronicler as a *quid pro quo* for the grant of a fifteenth in the same year; and, as we shall see later, the full enforcement of the ordinance of 1269 was part of the price which Henry's government paid for the eventual concession of a tax in 1270.[40] Both in England and in France the persecution of the Jews had become a necessary part of the ideological and moral preparation for a crusade,[41] but this was only a secondary aspect of the legislation of 1269. The new ordinance was the first of a spate of anti-Jewish measures, culminating in the expulsion of 1290, whose primary purpose was to win popular support for the Crown and in particular the support of the gentry for taxation.

Drafted in January, the ordinance was not made public until April, when it was announced during the course of another parliament, briefly noticed in the chronicles.[42] It was not the only sign of a novel responsiveness to provincial feeling at this time. On 24 April, shortly after parliament's conclusion, and perhaps in response to complaints made during its meeting, the king ordered the cancellation

[37] *CPR 1266 – 72*, 376; H. G. Richardson, *The English Jewry under Angevin Kings* (London, 1960), 71 – 3, 104 – 5; C. Roth, *A History of the Jews in England* (3rd edn., Oxford, 1964), 65.
[38] Knowles, 'The Resettlement of England', 34 – 6.
[39] *Chron. Wykes*, 221.
[40] J. R. Maddicott, 'Edward I and the Lessons of Baronial Reform: Local Government, 1258 – 80', in *Thirteenth Century England I: Procs. of the Newcastle upon Tyne Conference, 1985*, ed. P. R. Coss and S. D. Lloyd (Woodbridge, 1986), 17; below, 109 – 10.
[41] See e.g. W. C. Jordan, *Louis IX and the Challenge of the Crusade: A Study in Rulership* (Princeton, 1979), 84 – 6.
[42] *Chron. Wykes*, 221; 'Annales de Wigornia', in *Ann. Mon.* iv. 458.

of the forthcoming Lincoln eyre because seven years had not yet elapsed since the eyre's previous visit to the county. This was a concession both to the reforming principles of the early 1260s, when eyres in several counties had been disrupted because their visits breached the seven-year convention, and to the aspirations of county society which those principles embodied. The attestation of the writ ordering the cancellation of the eyre, 'by the king himself and the whole council', was a mark both of the importance which the government attached to the issue and of its current sensitivity to the mood of the localities.[43]

It was not until a further parliament met in July that the question of taxation was raised again. We know of its meeting only from a letter which Henry wrote from Winchester on 21 June, postponing, on account of his own illness, a parliament which was to have met in London at midsummer. Its meeting was to be deferred until he came to Westminster. There the king arrived about 1 July, staying for the rest of the month.[44] What was done during that time is almost certainly recorded in another letter which he sent to Godfrey Giffard, bishop of Worcester, from Chichester on 7 August. In this letter Henry wrote that the council had decreed that bishops or other churchmen should take the oath of the knights chosen for each county to collect the twentieth granted to the king for the crusade 'by the magnates and other faithful men of our kingdom'. If necessary, the knights should be hurried along ('acceleretis') to take the oath by 8 September, so that they could begin their work by Michaelmas. With the king's letter was enclosed the form of the oath, which embodied detailed instructions for the choosing of local taxers and for the taxation of villages.[45]

At this stage our conclusions about the tax have to be based on the evidence of this letter, which stands alone. Its obvious significance lies in its proving that a tax of a twentieth had been granted, presumably by the July parliament. Had the tax been conceded in April, the arrangements for its assessment and collection could have been made in a more leisurely way. As it was, there was a note of urgency in Henry's instructions, which is to be explained by the short interval between the probable time of the grant, delayed further by the late start of the parliament, and the optimum time for assessment and collection. As we have already noted, Michaelmas was the most profitable time to tax, for it was then that barns and byres were full. These considerations were in turn related to the wider timetable for the crusade. In August 1269 Edward travelled to Paris to discuss with Louis IX and the other crusading leaders the arrangements for their expedition. There it was agreed that Louis should lend Edward 70,000 *livres tournois* for his crusading expenses, and that Edward should appear at Aigues Mortes, in the south of France, for embarkation by 15 August 1270 at the latest.[46] Even before his journey it must have been assumed that the crusade would set out no later than the summer of 1270, already a full two years after the taking of the Cross at Northampton. For the punctual mounting of the crusade it was thus essential to tap the yield of the harvest of 1269, and hence to see that the administrative arrangements for the assessment

[43] *CR 1268 – 72*, 37 – 9; Maddicott, 'Edward I and the Lessons of Baronial Reform', 8.

[44] *CPR 1266 – 72*, 384; *Itinerary of Henry III*.

[45] D. Wilkins, *Concilia Magnae Britanniae et Hiberniae* (London, 1737), ii. 20 – 1 (From Giffard's Register); *Lancashire Lay Subsidies*, ed. J. A. C. Vincent (Lancs. and Cheshire Rec. Soc., xxvii, 1893), 92 – 3; Mitchell, 148 – 9; Powicke, *Henry III*, ii. 565.

[46] *Foedera*, I. i. 481; Lloyd, 'The Lord Edward's Crusade', 124 – 5.

and collection of the tax were put in hand as soon as possible after the July parliament.

These arrangements were to be largely upset by the proceedings of the next parliament, which met in October. With one exception,[47] the chronicles take the view that it was this parliament which granted the twentieth,[48] or that the assessment of the twentieth began about this time.[49] As we have seen, none mentions any grant in July. It is clear from the near unanimity of the chronicles, and especially from the full account given by Wykes, that some form of grant was made in October. But why was it thought necessary to re-open at that time a question which had already been settled in July, as Henry's letter of 7 August indicates? The answer probably lies in the insubstantial nature of the gathering which had conceded the tax in the earlier month. While the Worcester annalist had described the April assembly as a 'magnum parliamentum',[50] that of July was mentioned in no chronicle. The summoning of a midsummer parliament, very probably the third of the year, and following soon after that held in April, may have been unwelcome and may have resulted in a poor attendance, reduced still further by the delay which Henry's illness caused to its assembling. When Henry wrote announcing the postponement of the parliament, his main purpose was to request those coming to stay and await his arrival.[51] The charter witness-lists do not suggest that he had any success in bringing together a large gathering. The seven charters issued in July included among their witnesses only two bishops (Godfrey Giffard of Worcester and Nicholas of Ely, bishop of Winchester, both of them close to the king), no earls, and a handful of other curialist magnates: William of Valence, Henry of Almain, Philip Basset, Roger Mortimer and Roger Leyburn. By contrast, during the parliament of the previous January, also unmentioned in the chronicles, four charters had been witnessed by a total of four bishops, two earls and six barons.[52]

The cumulative evidence strongly suggests that the July parliament was a feeble and badly attended affair. In one sense this may not have mattered much to Henry and Edward. They may, in part, have seen the tax granted by parliament as a means of convincing Louis of their continuing commitment to the crusade, and hence of persuading him that his loan, probably under discussion before he met Edward in August,[53] was a sensible investment. The yield of any tax was likely to fall far short of the cost of a crusade, and the French loan was therefore an essential element in Edward's planning. If the purpose of the tax grant was to some extent diplomatic, the nature of the assembly making it was of little consequence. But in another sense it was of great consequence. Though the consent of the July parliament to a tax was the best that Henry could secure, in circumstances which made it necessary for him to press ahead with all speed, that consent cannot have been regarded as particularly authoritative. It is likely that after parliament's dispersal Henry himself thought it prudent to seek confirmation of the tax, or even consent *de novo*, from a larger

---

[47] *Bartholomaei de Cotton Historia Anglicana*, ed. H. R. Luard (RS, 1859), 143–4; below, 106.
[48] *Chron. Wykes*, 227; *De Ant. Leg. Liber*, 122; 'Annales Londonienses', in *Chronicles of the Reigns of Edward I and Edward II*, ed. W. Stubbs (RS, 1882–3), i. 80.
[49] 'Continuation' of William of Newburgh, ii. 556.
[50] *Ann. Wigorn.* 458.
[51] *CPR 1266–72*, 384.
[52] C 53/58, mm. 9, 13–14.
[53] Edward's journey to France was in prospect during the July parliament: *CR 1268–72*, 71.

meeting, perhaps in response to opposition to a grant made by so meagre a body. One thinks of the eighth granted to Edward I in July 1297, 'by the people standing around him in his chamber', which was later replaced by a tax granted in a properly constituted parliament.[54] If the tax was to be effectively levied, and not merely flaunted before Louis as a token of English sincerity, some broader form of consent was essential.

Such was the reasoning which almost certainly lay behind the Crown's new request for a grant, put to the much fuller and more public parliament which met in October, immediately after the splendid festivities to celebrate the translation of the relics of Edward the Confessor to the king's new church as Westminister. These festivities had been the focus for a very large social gathering of prelates, earls, barons, knights and even burgesses,[55] most of whom had probably also been summoned for the ensuing parliament. Charter witness-lists, in conjunction with the record of the clergy's activity in parliament, point to an impressive ecclesiastical contingent of at least eleven bishops, together with abbots and representatives of the lower clergy;[56] and we have Henry's own word, as well as that of a chronicle, for the presence of the knights.[57] Few parliaments in the reign are likely to have been better attended.

Any consent which Henry could secure from this assembly would carry far more weight than that gained in July. Wykes, our main chronicle source, states unequivocally that such consent was given in the October parliament. His words on the consenting body, however, are not free from ambiguity and deserve to be quoted in full. After the festivities, he says,

> coeperunt nobiles, ut assolent, parliamentationis genere de regis et regni negotiis pertractare; in quo regis astutia, immo ut verius dicam extorsionis cupidinosae nervicia praevalente, annuentibus regni maior-ibus vel contradicere non audentibus, concessum est quod de universis laicorum mobilibus per regnum Angliae sibi vicesima solveretur.[58]

His meaning here may be the seemingly obvious one: the nobles began to discuss the affairs of the kingdom, the king applied pressure for the grant of a tax, the nobles (*maiores*) assented or did not dare to gainsay him, and a twentieth was granted. But there is an alternative interpretation, as Professor McKisack was the first to point out.[59] She saw *nobiles* and *maiores* not as synonyms but as contrasting terms, with the *maiores* complying only reluctantly ('contradicere non audentibus') with what the nobility were willing to concede, and she went on to identify the *maiores* with the *potentiores* of the cities and boroughs, who, according to Wykes,

[54] *Documents Illustrating the Crisis of 1297 – 98 in England*, ed. M. Prestwich (Camden Soc., 4th ser., xxiv, 1980), 8 – 9.

[55] *Chron. Wykes*, 226; 'Annales de Oseneia', in *Ann. Mon.* iv. 227 – 9.

[56] C 53/58, m. 7; *Councils and Synods, II.* ii. 797 – 800.

[57] CR 1268 – 72, 245; *De Ant. Leg. Liber*, 122.

[58] *Chron. Wykes*, 227.

[59] M. McKisack, *The Parliamentary Representation of the English Boroughs during the Middle Ages* (Oxford, 1932), 4.

had been present at the earlier celebrations in the abbey. Wykes is not absolutely clear on the crucial question as to who it was, king or nobles, whom the *maiores* 'did not dare to gainsay'; hence our difficulty. But if Professor McKisack is right in her general view that the *maiores* were not the nobles, it is perhaps more likely that they comprehended the knights, and not just the burgesses, as she thought. We have already seen that there is a strong argument for equating the *maiores* with the commons in the Furness chronicler's account of the parliament of 1268, and we know that the knights and probably the burgesses were not only present at the Westminster parliament of October 1268 but also shared in whatever concession was then made to Henry. The evidence comes from a letter written by Henry in December to the taxers of Dorset, in which the king refers to the tax as 'conceded as much by the magnates and knights as by other laymen'.[60] Although we cannot be certain of how opinions may have divided on Henry's demand for a tax, there is at least a case for arguing that it was resisted more strongly by the commons than by the nobles.

Some resistance there certainly was, and, contrary to what Wykes says, it resulted in the king's demand being only partly met. That the king applied exceptional pressure to get his way, implied by Wykes, is borne out by the other chroniclers. The Furness writer speaks of Henry's extorting from many men the tax that he had been unable to gain in the previous year, and the London annalist says that the twentieth was 'extorted' from the goods of the laity. Most informative of all is the contemporary Norwich chronicler later copied by Bartholomew Cotton, for he rightly notes that resistance to such pressure was to some extent successful: after the Translation of St. Edward 'the king asked for a twentieth on all the goods of the laity of England. His request, however, was not yet conceded, but hung thus in suspense.'[61]

The records prove Cotton correct. No tax was finally conceded until the parliament of April-May 1270, and no money began to come in until July.[62] The apparent inconsistencies, both between different chronicles and between the chronicles and the records, have led to understandable confusion as to what was done in the October parliament. Powicke, for example, following the Norwich chronicler, thought that the king's request 'did not receive a definite answer'.[63] The solution to these problems is found in the chancery rolls, which make it clear that what the king gained in October was consent to the assessment of the tax, but not yet to its collection; it was granted, yet not granted. Between November 1269 and March 1270 a number of writs appear on the patent and close rolls addressed to those appointed to deal with the tax, usually to direct them to make some exemption or to notify them of a new appointee in place of one dead or incapacitated. All these writs speak of those concerned with the tax as assessors, and not collectors.[64] Wykes himself draws a distinction between the assessment or taxing of the grant and its collection ('taxatio pariter et collectio'), though he does not separate the two chronologically. Finally, the hypothesis is put beyond doubt by a series of writs

[60] *CR 1268 – 72*, 245.
[61] 'Continuation' of William of Newburgh, ii. 557; *Ann. Lond.* 80; *Cotton*, 143.
[62] Below, 108 – 11.
[63] Powicke, *Henry III*, ii. 565.
[64] *CR 1268 – 72*, 158; *CPR 1266 – 72*, 398, 399, 406, 477.

issued on 2 April 1270, by which the 'late taxers' of the twentieth in four counties are 'now appointed collectors thereof'.[65] It was only at this stage — in advance of the spring parliament but some five months after the assessment had been authorized — that the collection of the tax began to be put in hand.

The conclusions which follow from this reconstruction of events can be deferred until we have looked at a second aspect of the proceedings in the October parliament: the king's attempt to tax the clergy. Although Henry had sought a levy from the clergy in October 1268, he had failed; nor had the later grant of the twentieth, made in July 1269, applied to any but the laity. By October he may have been more confident that an approach to the clergy would bear fruit. Their members were well represented in parliament, the triennial tenth granted to Henry by the pope in 1266 was coming to an end,[66] and this was an appropriate time to seek its extension. The Bury St. Edmund's chronicler saw Henry's demand as one for a fourth year's tenth,[67] though in fact it was a twentieth that Henry wanted. The clergy and the laity were to be treated on equal terms.

Henry, however, encountered resistance from the clergy which was still more successful, if only temporarily, than that of the laity. It came chiefly from the abbots, priors and representatives of the lower clergy, who, in a series of articles, pleaded the impositions which they had already borne, especially the triennial tenths, as the main reason for their inability to comply with the king's request for a new subsidy. They met separately from the bishops, whom they clearly thought likely to fall in behind the king, for they ended their statement by appealing to Rome and Canterbury against any attempt by the episcopate to impose a tax on them.[68] The Bury chronicler says that the lower clergy appealed against the proposed tax because the bishops were unwilling to do so.[69] Events in the Easter parliament of 1270 were to show that the suspicions of the religious and the lower clergy were well founded; but for the moment they had won. No clerical grant was made, and not even the assessment of clerical property was allowed to proceed.[70]

Henry had thus achieved only a very limited success in the October parliament. He had obtained nothing from the clergy, and consent merely to the assessment of the twentieth, not to its collection, from the laity. It is true that the assessment was to go forward in the autumn and early winter, only a little after the most profitable taxing season of the year. But the eventual collection would become more difficult the longer it was delayed, for the normal rundown in stock and grain resources would make the earlier assessment increasingly unrealistic, and any collection based on it would be all the more likely to produce popular discontent. This eventually proved to be the case.[71] Delay also put the timetable for the crusade in

[65] *Chron. Wykes*, 228; *CPR 1266 – 72*, 418.

[66] Lunt, 307.

[67] *The Chronicle of Bury St. Edmunds, 1212 – 1301*, ed. A. Gransden (London, 1964), 45; cf. *Chron. Wykes*, 227.

[68] *Councils and Synods, II*. ii. 797 – 800; W. E. Lunt, 'The Consent of the English Lower Clergy to Taxation during the Reign of Henry III', in *Persecution and Liberty: Essays in Honor of George Lincoln Burr* (New York, 1931), 160 – 1.

[69] *Chron. Bury St. Edmunds*, 45 – 6.

[70] Wilkins, ii. 21; *CR 1268 – 72*, 245; Lunt, 'Consent', 161.

[71] *Chron. Wykes*, 227 – 8.

renewed jeopardy. As we have seen, Edward had undertaken to join Louis at Aigues Mortes by mid-August 1270, and by the spring of that year he and his father, whose participation in the crusade had not yet been formally abandoned, were planning to leave England in late June.[72] Only if collection followed on rapidly from assessment could such a timetable still be adhered to.

The resistance which Henry encountered was probably rooted in factors already discussed: the impoverishment of the middle ranks of lay and clerical society by war and its aftermath, by levies already imposed, and, in the case of many of the laity, by debt. But there was also a more specific distrust of Henry's intentions. What guarantee was there that any money granted would be spent on a crusade? The bishops showed their suspicions clearly enough when, as a condition of their eventual grant in the parliament of April-May 1270, they insisted that their money should be used for the crusade and not converted to other purposes, and that it should remain under their control until either Henry or Edward departed.[73] After Edward's meeting with Louis IX in August 1269, it must have become clear that Henry's own intended participation in the crusade was no more than a pretence, and any grant of money to him for this purpose may have seemed increasingly hazardous. Some may have remembered that when he had last been granted a subsidy in 1237 he had evaded the strict controls placed on his use of the tax.[74] Yet not all those present in the October parliament took the same view of these issues, and the sources suggest that greater and lesser men, both among the clergy and the laity, held conflicting opinions. If the religious and lower clergy were at odds with the bishops over taxation, so the commons, Wykes seems to imply, were at odds with the nobles. It was the 'proceres et prelatos', he says elsewhere, who consented to the tax:[75] the higher nobility, lay and ecclesiastical, and not the commons or the lower clergy.

The deferment of the collection of the tax marked the strength of the resistance to the tax and the partial victory of the resisters. It must have been intended, though this is nowhere stated, that the collection would follow when some condition imposed on Henry's government had been met; and the planners of the crusade must have continued with their planning on the assumption that this condition, whatever it was, would be met. The definitive grant came in the parliament which assembled on 27 April 1270, though we have already seen that in at least four counties Henry's anxiety to secure immediate cash had led him to order the collection to begin by writs dated 2 April, some weeks in advance of any consent which he could expect to secure from parliament.[76] Like the October parliament, that of April was well attended, not only by bishops, earls and barons, but also by knights and free tenants.[77] Two issues dominated its long and disputacious proceedings: the quarrel between Edward and the earl of Gloucester, which does

---

[72] *Letters from Northern Regs.* 24; *Royal Letters,* ii. 336.

[73] Wilkins, ii. 21.

[74] N. Denholm-Young, 'The "Paper Constitution" Attributed to 1244', in id., *Collected Papers on Medieval Subjects* (new edn., Cardiff, 1969), 146–8.

[75] *Chron. Wykes,* 228.

[76] *Royal Letters,* ii. 336; *Letters from Northern Regs.* 24; *Ann. Wigorn.* 459; *Cotton,* 144; *CPR 1266–72,* 418.

[77] *De Ant. Leg. Liber,* 122.

not concern us, and the granting of the twentieth, together with related arrangements for the crusade.[78]

Although the chronicles provide a tantalisingly inadequate account of the discussions in this parliament, it is clear from their outcome that both laity and clergy came together to impose conditions on a final grant, and that those conditions turned on a demand for the Charters.[79] The tax was granted about 12 May, when Henry wrote to those prelates who had left the assembly early to tell them of the bishops' concession of the twentieth and to ask for payment.[80] On the following day nine bishops met at St. Paul's cross, where they had read out before them both Innocent IV's bull of 1245 confirming the Charters as issued in 1225, and also the sentences which thirteen bishops had published in Westminster Hall in 1253 against all transgressors of the Charters. The nine then excommunicated all those who had contravened the Charters or who had laid violent hands on clerks or clerical goods during the period of rebellion, though time was given to the offenders to make amends.[81] This impressive scene is recorded more briefly by the London annalist, who simply states that the bishops excommunicated all those who broke the peace, contravened ecclesiastical liberties, or infringed the 'customs of England' set out in Magna Carta and the Forest Charter.[82] Now FitzThedmar says that parliament considered 'many articles concerning the customs of England' as well as the quarrel between Edward and Gloucester. Taken together, these two chronicles indicate that the Charters were central to the debates in parliament, and, as Powicke was the first to notice, that the final grant of the tax was conditional on their confirmation, which followed almost immediately after the grant.[83]

The confirmation of the Charters guaranteed what had come to be seen as the liberties both of laity and of clergy, and it would probably be wrong to regard it as a concession to any sectional interest. Yet it is worth remembering that when Henry in 1254 had last had it in mind to consult an assembly of magnates and knights on his need for a tax, his regents had thought that the knights were more likely than the magnates to insist on Magna Carta as the price for any concession.[84] The knights were much more certainly the particular beneficiaries of one other measure which followed the granting of the tax. On 14 May Henry wrote to the exchequer to order the enforcement of the earlier legislation against the creation of rentcharges in favour of the Jews. More specifically, he told the exchequer to call in for cancellation all written instruments creating such rentcharges which had been in the hands of the Jews at Hilary 1269 and which had not been either confirmed by the king or passed on to Christians. The debtors or their heirs were now to be quit of their obligations. As we have seen, this legislation had originally been drafted in the parliament of January 1269 and published in the parliament of the following April,

---

[78] Ibid. 122; *Ann. Oseneia*, 232 – 3; *Ann. Wigorn.* 459. For the Edward-Gloucester dispute, see S. D. Lloyd, 'Gilbert de Clare, Richard of Cornwall and the Lord Edward's Crusade', *Nottingham Medieval Studies*, xxx (1986), esp. 54 – 5.

[79] Cf. Wilkins, ii. 22 – 3.

[80] *Royal Letters*, ii. 336; *Letters from Northern Regs.* 24 – 5.

[81] *De Ant. Leg. Liber*, 122 – 3.

[82] *Ann. Lond.* 81.

[83] Powicke, *Henry III*, ii. 566.

[84] Maddicott, 'Magna Carta', 46.

but it had evidently not been implemented.[85] Now, at a stroke, all who had granted rentcharges to the Jews in order to raise money were relieved of their debts, unless the rentcharges had been confirmed or passed on. Although Henry was not prepared to upset the interests of magnates and prelates — the chief dealers in such debts — by cancelling rentcharges which had come into other hands, his action is likely to have benefited many lesser men, especially perhaps among the indebted ex-Montfortians, who had been forced to grant rentcharges in order to borrow money. That Henry's letter to the exchequer followed only two or three days after the grant of the tax is unlikely to have been a coincidence. Rather, the implementation of the anti-Jewish legislation should almost certainly be seen as a concession made by Henry in the process of gaining consent to the collection of the tax from the parliamentary knights who represented the smaller landowners of the shires.

The grant of May 1270 was made both by the laity and, as already noted, by the bishops, who gave Henry a twentieth of their own property and that of their free tenants and villeins. The religious and the lower clergy continued to resist, as they had done in October 1269, and it was not until the end of the year that they began to fall into line.[86] The clerical grant thus gave Henry most of what he had asked for in the previous parliament. Personal as well as political inducements probably helped him to secure the bishops' consent: on 3 May, while the tax was under discussion, the bishop of Salisbury was granted a yearly fair at Salisbury, and on 7 May the bishop of Worcester was granted the right to hold annual fairs on three of his manors.[87] But much more important, for the bishops as for the laity, was the confirmation of the Charters and the ecclesiastical sanctions which the bishops were now able to bring to bear both on those who infringed them and on others who had encroached on the Church's property rights and privileges. Sentences against both groups of offenders were published not only at St. Paul's cross, but by parish priests in the churches of London and, if Giffard's register for the diocese of Worcester records what was generally done, in all other collegiate and parish churches. Giffard's instructions to his archdeacons for the publication of the sentences were set out with great particularity. Publication was to take place on every Sunday until Pentecost, after the reading of the gospel at mass, and after prayers for the peace and tranquility of the church and kingdom; and the sentences were to be expounded clearly in the vernacular, 'tam literatis quam illiteratis'.[88]

These elaborate arrangements showed the importance which the bishops attached to the concessions gained in parliament and to their publication. They probably had in mind the very similar arrangements made in 1253, when, in return for taxation, the Charters had been confirmed in conditions of special solemnity, sentences published against their infringers, and those sentences then proclaimed by at least one bishop, Robert Grosseteste, bishop of Lincoln, in all the parish churches of his diocese. In 1253, however, the taxes had been ones of limited incidence: an aid on

---

[85] *CR 1268 – 72*, 268; above, 101 – 2. It is not inconceivable that the failure to implement the legislation was due to pressure from the magnates who stood to profit from the continuance of Jewish loans in exchange for rentcharges backed by the security of land.
[86] *Royal Letters*, ii. 236 – 7; *Letters from Northern Regs.* 24 – 5; Lunt, 'Consent', 161 – 2; Powicke, *Henry III*, ii. 567.
[87] *CChR 1257 – 1300*, 139.
[88] Wilkins, ii. 22 – 3.

knights' fees for the knighting of the Lord Edward, and a clerical tenth, both intended to help Henry in Gascony.[89] The tax of 1270 was much more comprehensive: it was a national levy affecting almost everyone, clergy and laity, bond and free, townsmen and country people. Only the very poor are likely to have been exempt.[90] The sentences against those infringing the Charters, published after the assessment of the tax had been completed and during the course of its collection, are likely to have told a large public, if only in a dimly comprehended way, that royal authority was limited, taxes could be bargained for, and redress of grievances set against supply.

Once the collection of the tax had been conceded in May, the uncertainties which had hung over the crusade for almost two years were suddenly resolved. Although the chronicles suggest that further disputes concerning the expedition and its financing were reserved for the arbitration of Richard of Cornwall,[91] these did not hold up the levying of the twentieth. The earlier progress with its assessment meant that the collection could not go forward rapidly. Money began to come in about 1 July, and on 10 July arrangements were made for its reception and storage at the Temple.[92] Shortly afterwards, about 20 July, contracts were drawn up with the eighteen crusading leaders who had agreed to accompany Edward with contingents of knights, and payment was made to them on 26 July. By October 1272 the tax had yielded some £31,500, of which £15,000 had been spent on these preliminary payments and the rest delivered to Edward at the time of his departure for the Holy Land, or during his sojourn there.[93] The drafting of the contracts at so late a date, though doubtless following earlier verbal agreements, and the delay in payment until the proceeds of the tax began to accumulate, shows the indispensability of the twentieth for the mounting of the crusade. It was not the only source of crusading finance, for Edward was also able to draw on the French loan. But without it he would either have had to abandon the attempt to raise forces in England or to have supported them on credit alone. From both these unattractive alternatives he had been freed by the parliamentary consent to taxation which had finally been secured.

The negotiations over taxation between 1268 and 1270 were the most protracted in Henry's reign, and the king's pursuit of a tax met with neither rapid nor total success. His attempts to tax both clergy and laity failed in 1268; in 1269 he secured a grant in July, only to see the wider consent which he sought in October given merely to the assessment of the tax, and not to its collection; his approach to the Church was entirely rejected; and even when the final consent of both laity and bishops was given in May 1270, he had to confirm the Charters and to tolerate the

---

[89] Paris, *CM* v. 376 – 8; Powicke, *Henry III*, ii. 302; Maddicott, 'Magna Carta', 35 – 6.
[90] In 1232 those with less than 40*d*. worth of goods were exempt from taxation: Mitchell, 143. For the fifteenth of 1275 the exemption level was 15*s*., and for the thirtieth of 1283, 6*s*. 8*d*.: 'Annales de Wintonia', in *Ann. Mon.* ii. 121; 'Annales de Dunstaplia', in *Ann. Mon.* iii. 294. The principle was applied regularly from 1290 and had probably been so applied before: J. F. Willard, *Parliamentary Taxes on Personal Property, 1290 – 1334* (Cambridge, Mass., 1934), 87 – 8.
[91] *Ann. Wigorn.* 459; Lloyd, 'The Lord Edward's Crusade', 127, n. 44.
[92] *CLR 1267 – 72*, 132 – 3; *CPR 1266 – 72*, 439; *Royal Letters*, ii. 338.
[93] See the accounts printed in *Lancs. Lay Subsidies*, 104 – 5; and Lloyd, 'The Lord Edward's Crusade', 127.

continuing resistance of the religious and of the lower clergy. His demands were not turned down out of hand, as similar demands had been between 1237 and 1258, but their reception showed that his victorious emergence from the crisis of reform and rebellion had by no means left him politically unshackled. In some ways it had put him under new constraints. The destruction of property, and the loosening of central control resulting from the war, had reduced his local revenues from lands and royal rights, and the need to conciliate hindered any wholehearted attempt at their restoration. Although the county farms remained objectionably high, for example, the counties were not rack-rented, as they had been in the 1240s and 1250s.[94] Nor, after the baronial reforms of abuses in the eyre had been given legal force in the Statute of Marlborough in 1267, is it likely that the eyre was a source of more than moderate profit. These restrictions came at a time when Richard of Cornwall's loans to the Crown were more sparing and less frequent than they had been in Henry's middle years.[95] As a result of the reform movement and its disorderly aftermath, he had become more rather than less dependent for any extraordinary need on the goodwill of his subjects. Despite massive expenditure on building, Gascony and the 'Sicilian business', he had survived for twenty years without a direct tax on the laity. Edward's crusade could hardly be contemplated without one.

The ensuing bargaining over taxation, though it sprang from the Crown's weakness, revealed some of its underlying strengths. In the end Henry got his tax largely at the price of what had become conventional: the confirmation of the Charters and the invocation of ecclesiastical sanctions against those who infringed them. This was the third time in the reign that a levy on moveables had been linked with the Charters; the precedents were those of 1225 and 1237. There was no attempt in 1270 to impose baronial councillors on the king, as in 1237, or to secure baronial consent to the appointment of the great officials, as often in the 1240s and 1250s, still less to demand the wholesale re-ordering of royal government, as in 1258. The projected reforms which Henry's subjects had formerly sought to place against his need for taxation were not resurrected. Nor did they seek remedies for the current revival of abuses in local government, which the Hundred Roll enquiries of 1274-5 were to reveal.[96] In 1270 they returned only to the Charters, a restraint on kingship that was neither novel nor adventurous.

In part, of course, such conservatism merely reflected the collapse of the radical cause. After the battle of Evesham, the two-year long disturbances which followed, and the partial codification of the baronial provisions in the Statute of Marlborough, reform was a dead letter. Local grievances certainly remained, which Edward, as king, was to seek to rectify, but they found no political outlet. To an equal extent the absence of political conflict reflected changes in the composition both of the nobility and of the episcopate since 1258. The active leaders of magnate society in the late 1260s were all members of the royal family: the Lord Edward, his cousin Henry of Almain, his brother Edmund, his uncle William of Valence. The connections of this family group reached well down into the baronage. Edward numbered among his close friends perhaps half a dozen major barons (Thomas de

[94] Maddicott, 'Edward I and the Lessons of Baronial Reform', 6–7.
[95] N. Denholm-Young, *Richard of Cornwall* (Oxford, 1947), 157–61.
[96] Maddicott, 'Edward I and the Lessons of Baronial Reform', 6–7.

Clare, Roger Leyburn, Payn de Chaworth, Roger Clifford, Hamo Lestrange, Roger Mortimer), and Edmund undertook to lead on crusade a contingent of some ninety-nine men who are likely to have included some barons as well as many knights.[97] Of the earls, more obscure figures at this time, it is worth noting that John de Warenne, earl of Surrey, and William de Beauchamp, earl of Warwick, were both party to the conspiracy led by Edward and Edmund which came together in 1269 to strip Robert de Ferrers, former earl of Derby, of his lands.[98] Most of the Crown's magnate opponents of the early 1260s were either dead, like Simon de Montfort, Hugh Despenser, and Humphrey de Bohun; ruined, like Robert de Ferrers; or reconciled, like John de Vescy. The only dissident of consequence was Gloucester, and his opposition was intermittent and rooted in grievances rather than principles. If Henry was impoverished, he nevertheless stood firm on the support of the higher nobility.

The episcopate was similarly loyal. The rump of Mortfortian bishops, of whom Walter Cantilupe, bishop of Worcester, was the moral leader, had been dispersed by the action of the legate in 1266. Cantilupe himself was dead; and in the absence of Boniface of Savoy, archbishop of Canterbury, who withdrew to his native land in November 1268,[99] leadership of the clergy passed to Walter Giffard of York and, to some extent, his brother Godfrey Giffard of Worcester, successive chancellors from 1265 to 1268 and strongly royalist. If not submissive in their dealings with the king, the bishops were at least complaisant.[100] The period after Evesham saw none of the clerical *gravamina* against royal encroachments on ecclesiastical liberties which had characterized the decades before 1258; and it was the episcopate, alone among the clergy, who agreed to taxation in the parliament of April – May 1270.

It was not surprising, therefore, that bargaining over taxation produced no new reforming codes or initiatives. None could have been expected in the aftermath of a civil war and in a country effectively led by a royalist nobility. But this does not mean that the constraints on the Crown's freedom of action in the late 1260s were wholly financial rather than political. It has been a central argument of this essay that in these years the Crown faced for the first time the need to consult the commons in parliament — certainly the knights and probably the burgesses — on matters of taxation. In the absence of any writs ordering elections or of returns of members, it is, of course, difficult to be sure of much. We do not know the name of a single man who sat for either a county or a borough. Yet taken together the scraps of evidence in the chronicles and chancery records for the attendance of the commons are mutually consistent and extend impressively across the whole period. They were summoned to the York parliament of September 1268, but their failure to appear caused the postponement of business, almost certainly concerning taxation, until the next parliament. In that parliament, in October 1268, they were present when at least two groups of county representatives came together to elect baronial committees for taxation. They were present, too, at the parliament of October 1269, when, together with the magnates, they granted the assessment, but not the collection, of the twentieth. Finally, they were present in the parliament of

---

[97] Lloyd, 'The Lord Edward's Crusade', 127 and n. 38.
[98] *CR 1268 – 72*, 122 – 6; Powicke, *Henry III*, ii. 525 – 6.
[99] Powicke, *Henry III*, ii. 576.
[100] Cf. *Chron. Wykes*, 219.

April – May 1270, when the collection of the tax was at last agreed to. Of their presence or absence at the three other parliaments of the period, in January, April and July 1269, we know nothing; but, even allowing for this lacuna, no previous sequence of parliaments had produced so sustained a record of attendance by the commons.

When we try to gauge their importance in these assemblies, the evidence is apt to seem still thinner and more ambiguous. Most commentators on Edward I's parliaments (discussion has never extended back into Henry III's reign) have taken the view that the function of the commons was simply to assent to what had been previously authorized by the magnates. 'Initially', writes Dr. Harriss, 'the representatives had been summoned merely to ratify the magnates' acceptance of the plea of necessity . . . the role of these early representatives was probably very circumscribed . . . consent implied no uninhibited right of refusal . . . their assent was probably largely formal'.[101] The history of the negotiating of the twentieth ought to make us pause before accepting these judgements. We should even contemplate the possibility that the commons were already exercising a real influence on decisions in parliament, that in consenting to taxation they did more than endorse the decisions of their superiors, and that in consequence the government was concerned to placate them. If the Furness chronicler is right, the York parliament of 1268 was not assembled *plenarie* without the *maiores*, and despite a full showing of *nobiliores* important business was deferred to the next parliament. There, the commons were drawn into arrangements for taxation when county representatives chose groups of barons to manage the taxation of their localities. When this scheme fell through, possibly because of opposition from some of those representatives, legislation followed within a few months for the benefit of those who had made over rentcharges to the Jews in exchange for loans. The order for the implementation of that legislation in May 1270, immediately after the concession of the tax, confirms the view that this was a deliberate offer of relief to the smaller landowners represented in the commons, and one made in the process of bargaining over the grant.

The influence of the commons was probably in large part negative and may have been exercised in opposition to that of the magnates. It is clear that taxation was strongly opposed throughout the period: Henry failed to secure it in October 1268, partly succeeded in October 1269, and was fully successful (at least in his approach to the laity) only in May 1270. The centre of resistance to his campaign is not likely to have been among the higher nobility, dominated as they were by perhaps fifteen to twenty men who were unshakeably royalist, either by blood or by connection. It is inconceivable that these men, most of whom were committed to the crusade, should have opposed the levy on which their venture partly depended. To judge from the number of magnates who received summonses to parliament in the 1290s, when lists of those summoned begin to survive, this upper group may have comprised perhaps one-quarter or one-third of those summoned.[102] We cannot

---

[101] G. L. Harriss, *King, Parliament and Public Finance in Medieval England to 1369* (Oxford, 1975), 42, 52 – 3; cf. Mitchell, 224 – 8, for similar views. Mitchell's arguments about the subordinate role of the commons in 1283 are very unconvincing.

[102] For the numbers of those summoned in the 1290s, see J. Enoch Powell and K. Wallis, *The House of Lords in the Middle Ages* (London, 1968), 219 – 31.

determine the extent to which they were able to influence the lesser baronage, men whose views, and even names, remain almost wholly obscure. But throughout the thirteenth and fourteenth centuries the major division of wealth, power and political influence in gentle society was probably not between nobles and knights, but between the greater nobility on the one hand and the lesser nobility and the knights on the other. It is quite possible that this division may have been reflected in the discussions concerning taxation between 1268 and 1270, when the lesser barons and knights — provincial in their interests, set apart from the court, economically vulnerable, and open to exploitation from above via debts to the Jews — may have remained closer to each other than to the Lord Edward and his friends.

Both the chronicles and the records suggest that political differences between the commons and the nobility found expression in parliament. In October 1268 a large group of nobles was prepared to co-operate in raising a tax, but apparently only two groups of county representatives elected the 'taxing committees' on which the scheme depended, and it was never carried forward. The possible conflict of interest at that time may have re-emerged a year later, when, on one interpretation of Wykes's evidence, the *maiores* of the commons only grudgingly assented to a tax grant backed by the nobles. Acceptance of this interpretation would seem to reinforce the conventional view of the relative role of magnates and commons in matters of taxation: authorization of the grant by the magnates; formal assent by the commons. Yet Wykes's account is a misleading one, for he fails to note that only the assessment, and not the collection, of the tax was granted: a compromise which seems to have recognized the reluctance of the commons to proceed. Although the evidence is too exiguous for anything approaching certainty, its cumulative weight suggests that it was the commons, conceivably in alliance with the lesser baronage, whose recalcitrance delayed the grant for so long: just as in 1254 the earls and barons had been willing conditionally to grant an aid to the king, but the knights had been thought unlikely to do so until Henry had confirmed Magna Carta.[103] They had long been the mainspring of political life in their localities; now they were beginning to emerge as an independent force at the centre, with a political will that might by overridden but could not be ignored.

Between the grant finally made in 1270, and both the previous grant of a direct tax in 1237 and the previous attendance of knights at a central assembly concerned with taxation in 1254, lay the great divide of 1258 – 65: a period when the grievances of local society had come to the forefront of politics, when the involvement of knights in local government had deepened, and when Simon de Montfort had thrice sought the backing of local representatives in parliament. The baronial reform movement, despite its apparent failure, had brought a change in the political climate which was acknowledged by the renewed summoning of representatives to parliament between 1268 and 1270. It was probably Edward who most clearly recognized and sought to profit from the change. In the long term, the coming of the commons to parliament should be seen against the general background of his attempts to restore stability to a kingdom which he would soon inherit, comparable in aim with the generous settlement which he offered to the Cinque Ports in 1266 and with his personal reconciliation with former Montfortians such as Adam Gurdon and John de Vescy. In the short term, his immediate

---

[103] Maddicott, 'Magna Carta', 46.

objective, the crusade, partly depended on the grant of a tax for which the consent of the commons was now judged essential. The anti-Jewish legislation, which he and his fellow crusader Henry of Almain initiated, should be seen as a means to winning that consent. If the summoning of representatives rested on Mortfortian precedents, themselves a recognition of social change, it was also a studied contribution to political stability and an expedient necessary to achieve the end on which Edward had set his heart.

Consolidating and expanding on precedent, the parliaments of 1268 – 70 themselves created a still more significant precedent for the future. In retrospect it is clear that they forged what was to become an unbreakable link between direct taxation and the consent of the commons. After 1270 the Crown never again secured a grant of direct taxation without going to an assembly in which the commons were represented. Even in 1283, when the Welsh war made it impossible to call together a parliament to consider taxation, it was still thought necessary to summon representatives to the two separate assemblies which met at York and Northampton.[104] When Edward secured a grant in July 1297, not from parliament but from an irregular meeting of his supporters in his chamber, his breach of the political convention which he had helped to establish nearly thirty years earlier caused an outcry.[105] It was a convention which owed much to a long process of political and social evolution going back to 1215 and before. But it owed more to a particular and local combination of circumstances — to the recent activities of Simon de Mortfort, to the need for stability after civil war, to the economic difficulties facing the Crown and the knightly class, and, by no means least, to Edward's resolve to launch a crusade: an enterprise whose consequences were to be ephemeral for the history of the Holy Land but portentous for the history of England.

---

[104] Mitchell, 225 – 6.
[105] *Documents Illustrating the Crisis of 1297– 98*, 8 – 9.

Appendix

Meetings of Parliament, Sept. 1268 – April 1270

Those parliaments marked with an asterisk are new additions to the list given in *Handbook of British Chronology*, ed. E. B. Fryde, D. E. Greenway, S. Porter and I. Roy (3rd edn., London, 1986), 544. The list of sources is intended to be comprehensive and adds to those listed in the *Handbook of British Chronology*.

Date and Place	Summoned and Attending	Source
*1268, 8 Sept. York	Magnates; commons summoned, but failed to appear	'Continuation of William of Newburgh, ii. 554.
1268, 13 Oct. Westminster	Prelates, magnates, lower clergy, knights	Ibid. 554 – 5; *De Ant. Leg. Liber*, 108; *Gervase of Canterbury*, ii. 247 – 8; *CR 1264 – 8*, 553.
*1269, Jan. Westminster	Prelates and magnates only (so far as is known)	*De Ant. Leg. Liber*, 108; C 53/58, mm. 13 – 14.
1269, 7 Apr. Westminster	Magnates only (so far as is known)	*Chron. Wykes*, 221; *Ann. Wigorn.* 458.
1269, July Westminster	Magnates and prelates only (so far as is known)	*CPR 1266 – 72*, 384; Wilkins, ii. 20.
1269, 13 Oct. Westminster	Prelates, magnates, lower clergy, knights, burgesses	*Chron. Wykes*, 226 – 7; *De Ant. Leg. Liber*, 122; *Cotton*, 143 – 4; *CPR 1266 – 72*, 245.
1270, 27 Apr.	Prelates, magnates, knights	*Cotton*, 143 – 4; *De Ant. Leg. Liber*, 122 – 3; *Ann. Oseneia*, 232 – 3; *Ann. Winton.* 108; *Royal Letters*, ii. 336.

Crusader Knights and the Land Market in the Thirteenth Century

Simon Lloyd

All crusaders, regardless of their rank and position in society, faced the same broad challenges as they prepared for their great adventure. They needed to take care for the state of their souls, for they were pilgrims and penitents, as well as holy warriors, engaged in an extremely hazardous enterprise from which they might not return; they needed to settle their affairs satisfactorily and to arrange for the safeguarding and administering of their personal and family interests for the duration of the crusade; and they needed to raise the liquid cash required to meet expenses incurred before departure and anticipated thereafter. By the mid-thirteenth century, if not considerably earlier, the practical arrangements stemming from these requirements had crystallized into sets of measures commonly taken and appropriate to the immediate circumstances, profession and place within society of individual crusaders. They were located within a juridical and institutional framework that generally acknowledged the precepts of that coherent body of spiritual and material privileges accorded to crusaders in canon law, and automatically available upon assumption of the Cross: privileges which were designed to free the crusader from any obstacle which might hinder or prevent the fulfilment of his vow, whilst also enabling him, judicially and financially, to accomplish his passage the more easily.[1] In short, the crusade had become institutionalized to a degree which justifies our talking in terms of certain *rites de passage*[2], as it were (appropriate to crusaders of particular social classes, marked by fairly precise patterns of behaviour, and recognized in law), which had emerged in the course of time since the First Crusade. Joinville's famous account of the preparations he made for his departure with Louis IX in 1248 provides a picture, albeit partial and idealised, of the type and range of measures commonly taken by

---

[1] See J. A. Brundage, *Medieval Canon Law and the Crusader* (Madison, London, 1969), esp. chs. 5, 6. This paper is an expanded and recast version of part of ch. 5 of my book, *English Society and the Crusade, 1216 – 1307* (Oxford, 1988). Unless otherwise stated, all manuscript references in this paper are to documents in the PRO.

[2] I use the term loosely, but following his vow, taken in liturgical ceremony (and until its fulfilment, or his death on crusade), the crusader was in some sense a liminal being. In another sense, many of the preparatory measures commonly taken by crusaders bear close comparison to the dispositions made by men preparing for death.

men of his elevated position and status.[3] There is, regrettably, no English equivalent to Joinville's account, but the evidence suggests that it gives a reasonably true reflection of certain of the measures taken by English crusaders of his class at the time — the knights and lords with whom this study is specifically concerned.

It was through the measures taken to meet their various pressing needs that crusaders exerted probably their greatest impact upon society and economy. More particularly, it was in their urgent pursuit of coin that they entered the land market through the sale, pledge or lease of their property. The knights, especially, required large quantities of cash to hand, and fast, since the onus of crusade financing rested primarily upon the knights as a function of the way in which crusading forces were organized around them. For many the thirst for cash was virtually unquenchable as they sought to balance the expenditure on men, supplies, equipment and transport. Sums might be cobbled together from a variety of sources and through various expedients: perhaps a grant from the papal crusading subsidy, though this was a murky business in which the smaller fry tended to lose out; perhaps a grant from a greater crusader lord, if the knight contracted to serve with him on crusade; loans or gifts from kinsmen, friends or lords; advances against annual fees; renunciation of rights, or reparation of injury, to a religious house in return for prayers and a pouch of silver; confirmation, for a sum, to rights or properties held of the crusader; the securing of satisfaction for unpaid debts; sales of particular privileges in the crusader's gift; or the sale of disposable assets, such as timber. The possibilities, if not endless, were certainly many, but the sums accruing from such sources, welcome though they were, went only some way towards meeting costs.[4] For most, it was the disposal of land which provided the most certain way of raising sums of the magnitude required.

How much land, in aggregate, came on to the market in this way it is impossible to calculate, although the sheer number of transactions for which there is evidence indicates that it was considerable. But the level of English participation in the crusades of the thirteenth century, at least those to the Holy Land, makes it certain that each expedition prompted a notable, if temporary, surge of activity in the land

---

[3] Jean de Joinville, *Histoire de Saint Louis*, ed. J. Natalis de Wailly (2nd edn., Paris, 1872), 62 – 4, 68 – 70. This has come to be regarded as a classic statement of a crusader's preparations in the thirteenth century, but Jean relates only what he chose to record some sixty years after the event. Some of his other acts are known, but we remain fundamentally dependent upon his octogenarian reminiscences. Above all, he was at pains to underline the moral and spiritual concerns of himself as a departing crusader, and the impulse to certain practical acts necessary to achieve that state of purity regarded as a vital condition for the safety of his soul and crusade success. He accordingly stressed the measures he took to free himself of encumbrances which might have courted disaster in a holy enterprise, providing only sparse coverage of purely practical measures. His account provides an invaluable glimpse of the mentality of a departing crusader, but it cannot be considered as a rounded description of a crusader's preparations.

[4] Thus Lord Edward paid 100 marks to each knight he contracted in 1270, but, even allowing for the transport provided, this could have gone only a little way towards the likely costs of each knight and his entourage. As a measure, prices for horses at Acre in 1271 – 2 reached as high as 50 marks: E 101/350/ 5, m. 1; C 62/49, mm. 4, 6; C 62/51, mm. 8, 10, 11.

market.[5] The impact of crusaders upon that market is not to be considered solely in quantitative terms, however. To gain a rounded picture we need to consider the effects of their transactions at the local and regional level, locating them firmly within the social, economic and political contexts in which they occurred, and with close reference to the motives of those who chose to do business with the crusader in question.

Many clearly regarded the prospect of a crusade as a golden opportunity to cash in on a local crusader's needs by snapping up one or more of his properties, prized for one reason or another, as we shall see. For others, the news that a neighbour had taken the Cross precipitated anxieties and dilemmas: to bid or not to bid for his property, that was the question. Either course might be attended by considerable risks of a financial or political complexion. It is quite plain that a crusade did not always present a favourable opportunity for rapacious institutions or acquisitive individuals, as is sometimes supposed.[6] The matter was frequently a great deal more complicated than that.

I

Crusaders tended to avoid alienating their lands permanently through sale if they could. Any temptation to sell up was tempered by their sense of duty to family and lineage, and most, of course, had every intention of returning home again. They preferred to raise the money they needed through loans, normally secured upon their estate, but some were either driven to sell, or otherwise decided — or were persuaded — to take this course. Since the resulting transactions led to permanent changes in the tenurial structure and the patterns of local and regional power, it is appropriate to consider these first.

The remarkable tale of the sales of Hugh fitzHenry is particularly revealing of the contexts within which such transactions occurred. It is also exceptionally well documented and worth bringing to attention regardless of its crusading connections.

---

[5] The stature of the crusade leaders, and the partial listings that can be made, suggest the scale of English participation. Five earls led those participating in the Fifth Crusade. 'L'Estoire de Eracles empereur . . .', in *Recueil des Historiens des Croisades: Historiens Occidentaux*, ed. Académie des Inscriptions et Belles-Lettres (Paris, 1844 – 95), ii. 342 – 3, says Ranulf of Chester alone maintained 100 knights in the host at Damietta. 'Chronica Albrici monachi Trium Fontium', in *Monumenta Germaniae historica . . . Scriptores*, ed. G. Pertz *et al.* (Hanover and elsewhere, 1826 – 34), xxiii. 948, says Richard of Cornwall's crusade (1240 – 1) comprised *c.* 800 knights, entirely credible if we include the forces sailing with Simon de Montfort, William de Forz, William Longespee and other leaders. Longespee, according to Paris, *CM* v. 76, led 200 knights to Egypt in 1249 – 50. Lord Edward contracted for a minimum of 225 knights in England in 1270: S. D. Lloyd, 'The Lord Edward's Crusade, 1270 – 2: Its Setting and Significance', in *War and Government in the Middle Ages: Essays in Honour of J. O. Prestwich*, ed. J. B. Gillingham and J. C. Holt (Woodbridge, 1984), 126.

[6] As e.g. by G. Constable, 'The Financing of the Crusades in the Twelfth Century', in *Outremer: Studies in the History of the Crusading Kingdom of Jerusalem*, ed. B. Z. Kedar, H. E. Mayer and R. C. Smail (Jerusalem, 1982), 75 and sources cited.

Hugh, a knight of Berkshire, took the Cross in or before 1247, joining the Templars at some point thereafter.[7] He determined to sell his estate even though he had a son, Henry.[8] His one hide in Hill in Leamington Hastings (Warwickshire), held of Abingdon abbey and rated as 1/6 knight's fee, was sold to Robert Hastang for 24 marks, the transaction completed by final concord of 3 February 1248.[9] In north Oxfordshire he held 1/2 fee of the honour of Wallingford.[10] By final concord of 23 June 1247 Hugh recognized the property, a carucate in Alkerton and two virgates in neighbouring Balscott, to be the right of Master Simon de Walton, who gave him 300 marks.[11] These properties were 'outliers'; the core of Hugh's holdings lay in Berkshire, and it was from their sale that he did best.[12] Abingdon abbey, the lord of Hugh's fee, eventually purchased the estate, but since the convent consequently found itself in serious financial embarrassment, the detailed account of the transaction was entered in one of the abbey's letter-books at the end of the thirteenth century as a cautionary tale which future generations of monks should heed.[13]

Hugh's one knight's fee[14] comprised, we are told, two carucates and a virgate in Abingdon[15] (together with a spacious house there, moated and defensible), a hide in Dry Sandford, eight virgates in East Drayton, and one virgate in 'Babhanger' (see map on p. 127).[16] (In addition, but excluded from the sale, was 'terra de Hulle',

---

[7] This information occurs in the detailed letter-book account of Hugh's sales to Abingdon abbey: BL, Cotton Julius A. ix, fos. 166 – 7; printed, but with misreadings and omissions, in R. Hill, *Ecclesiastical Letter-Books of the Thirteenth-Century* (privately printed, no date), 269 – 72, and briefly discussed on p. 36.

[8] MS Cotton Julius A. ix, f. 166 reveals that he initially intended to sell precisely to raise cash for his expedition. One of the deeds of his sales to Abingdon, copied in one of the abbey's cartularies, named Henry as his son: Bodleian Library, Oxford, MS Lyell 15, f. 133v. I am indebted to Dr. Albinia de la Mare for her help in connection with this MS.

[9] *Warwickshire Feet of Fines*, ed. E. Stokes *et al.* (Dugdale Soc., xi, xv, xviii, 1932 – 43), no. 679; further, *Fees* ii. 1278. The abbot acknowledged Hugh's right in 1245 – 6, probably a preliminary to the sale: *Warwicks. Feet of Fines*, no. 625. Hugh's hide, with that held by William de Curly, comprised the Abingdon estate in Hill. Significantly, Robert Hastang, having secured Hugh's holding, married William's coheiress and united the two parts of the abbey's estate in his own hands: *VCH Warwickshire*, vi. 152.

[10] *Fees* ii. 823.

[11] *Feet of Fines for Oxfordshire, 1195 – 1291*, ed. H. E. Salter (Oxford Rec. Soc., xli, 1930), 141. On 27 May 1247 Hugh, for 11 marks, secured Michael de Wroxstane's quitclaim to the Balscott property, plainly in preparation for its sale to Simon: ibid. 141. Simon, notable curialist, justice, and future bishop of Norwich, was active in the land market. More particularly, he already held land in Balscott and neighbouring Tysoe (Warwicks.) before this purchase: *VCH Oxfordshire*, ix. 177.

[12] On at least one occasion Hugh was identified as 'of Abingdon': *Fees* ii. 823.

[13] MS Cotton Julius A. ix, fos. 166 – 7. The instructive purpose of the tale is made quite explicit.

[14] See *Fees* ii. 845, 848; *VCH Berkshire*, iv. 342. The letter-book reveals that Hugh also enjoyed liberty of waif and stray, observing that it was in repentance for his savage exploitation of this right that he took the Cross. From the letter-book, not surprisingly, Hugh emerges as an unpleasant character, but little is known of him. I have been unable to establish that he duly became a Templar. His ancestors were among the original post-Conquest tenants of Abingdon. See esp. *Fees* ii. 1278.

[15] Confirmed by CP 25(1), 8/16, no. 1; largely transcribed in MS Lyell 15, f. 134r – v.

[16] I have been unable to identify 'Babhanger'. Hugh held ½ mark rent in Abingdon: MS Lyell 15, fos. 133v, 134r. He was also in possession of a tenement there in 1248: *The Roll and Writ File of the Berkshire Eyre of 1248*, ed. M. T. Clanchy (Selden Soc., xc, 1972 – 3), 35, no. 66. It is not apparent that either of these was held of the abbey.

most probably a constituent part of Hugh's fee.[17]) It was an attractive estate, as the letter-book account is at pains to stress: fairly compact, centred on Abingdon, lucrative and well-appointed. When news reached the royal court that Hugh had put it on the market, several nobles eagerly sought to purchase, notably Richard of Cornwall. The monks were worried; the spectre of so great a magnate ensconced on their fee, at the very heart of their territorial interests, was understandably alarming. Indeed, Hugh's house 'contra Burustret' (Bath St., Abingdon) must have been within 400 yards of the abbey.[18] In their view there was a grave risk to themselves and future generations of monks, especially through the subversion of their liberties and local influence. The obvious response was to buy out Hugh themselves; only then could they feel safe. But there was insufficient cash to hand and a substantial number of the brethren argued against purchase, largely in fear of the financial consequences. They were overruled in the conventual discussions, however, the greater part of the obedientiaries being swayed by the political argument for purchase. Abbot John de Blosmeville gave his consent,[19] and the monks despatched as their proctor to negotiate with Hugh one Nicholas of Headington, a man 'exceedingly skilled and circumspect in secular affairs'.[20] The deal hammered out must have taken the monks' breath away: they were to purchase for little short of 1000 marks, Hugh insisting that he be paid in the new coin struck only in 1247. The cash was to be delivered by Easter 1248, 300 marks to be paid by Michaelmas 1247 when the convent should take livery of the estate. (The kitchener was to be bound to supply the cash, duly weighed and counted.) As security, the kitchener's vill of Shippon was to pass to Hugh until Easter 1248, but if the convent then defaulted in its final payment the vill would remain in perpetuity to Hugh or his assigns. In addition, the convent was to find a chaplain to celebrate for Hugh's soul for ten years, and to institute two corrodies, for Hugh and his son, for the rest of Hugh's life.[21] Hugh was certainly driving a hard bargain.

There were further unhappy murmurings within the convent over these terms, but the transaction went ahead and Prior Walter duly arrived with other brothers at Hugh's house in Abingdon on Michaelmas Day 1247 to take seisin. But Hugh 'had prepared a great party ('magnum convivium') for several knights and magnates in his house that day.' This was interpreted as a ruse, Hugh seeking to delay livery by claiming that the demands of hospitality prevented him from handing over seisin

---

[17] MS Lyell 15, fos. 133v, 134r. 'Hulle' is a lost place-name, but may refer to Inkpen Hill — much further away, some five miles from Kintbury. See M. Gelling, *The Place-Names of Berkshire* (English Place-Name Soc., xlix – li, 1973 – 6), ii. 310. If so, the connection with Abingdon abbey is indicated by the fact that Pagan fitzHenry, Hugh's ancestor in the fee, had interests there in 1166: *The Red Book of the Exchequer*, ed. H. Hall (RS, 1896), i. 306.

[18] See Gelling, ii. 434; and map in M. Biddle, G. Lambrick and J. N. L. Myres, 'The Early History of Abingdon, Berkshire, and Its Abbey', *Medieval Archaeology*, xii (1968), 28.

[19] *Chronicle of the Monastery of Abingdon, 1218 – 1304*, ed. J. O. Halliwell (Berkshire Ashmolean Soc., 1844), 6.

[20] He may have been that Nicholas of Headington who was active in the abbess of Lacock's service around this time, acting as her attorney and probably retained as her legal adviser. See esp. *Lacock Abbey Charters*, ed. K. H. Rogers (Wiltshire Rec. Soc., xxxiv, 1978), nos. 6, 268, 273, 301 – 2, 375, 416 – 17.

[21] The one corrody was probably in part compensation for Henry's lost inheritance. In addition, in the deeds conveying his property in Berks. to the convent, Hugh reserved 'terra de Hulle' and his ½ mark rent in Abingdon to the inheritance of Henry: MS Lyell 15, fos. 133v, 134r.

until the morrow. It could be that Hugh was simply throwing a farewell party, but the monks, clearly suspecting that he was about to back out, perhaps to arrange another deal, despatched their proctor Nicholas to expostulate with Hugh. All day they argued, Nicholas countering Hugh's 'lies and falsehoods' and probably threatening legal action as well. Around Vespers, with his guests arriving for dinner and a great crowd gathering outside to hear and see what was happening, Hugh at length conceded and handed over seisin, making his way with his household and his 300 marks to his new temporary home of Shippon, just one mile from Abingdon. The party had to be cancelled, and the assembled company, naturally disappointed, were seemingly dispersed with some difficulty by the monks. Following this scare the abbot and convent wisely determined to procure a final concord in the royal court 'to their greater security', but this only added to the considerable costs. That concord, made before the justices in eyre at Gloucester, reveals that Hugh acknowledged his property in Abingdon to be the right of the abbot for 800 marks of silver.[22] Considering the costs incurred in the provision of a chantry and two corrodies, the fees of Nicholas of Headington, the journey to Gloucester for the final concord, conveyance charges and other overheads unknown, the total price for Hugh's fee in Abingdon and Berkshire, as the letter-book indicates, was probably not far short of 1000 marks.

In raising the cash the monks got into serious difficulties. They were obliged to mortgage some of their lands and rents, and they borrowed what they could from their friends. So tight was the squeeze that they even had to turn down a request for a loan from their daughter-house of Colne.[23] The pressure came at a bad time anyway in the convent's affairs for considerable expenditure had been necessitated by the extensive building programme at the abbey under Abbot John and his predecessors.[24] Special internal arrangements had to be made to handle the affair. Hugh's estates, along with the debt, were initially made over to the kitchener,[25] but the burden was too much and had to be shared, notwithstanding the marked development towards departmental autonomy at Abingdon which had led, just three years earlier in 1245, to the regulation that no office was to bear the burdens of another. Each obedience was now obliged to make regular payments against the debt, and only by cutting back on the normal expenditure of each;[26] the monks were in for a very lean time. No wonder, then, that the affair of Hugh fitzHenry's estate was entered in the letter-book many years later. Its crippling effects and its painful memory remained fresh and needling.

Hugh's various sales suggest a great deal concerning the context in which crusaders' transactions need to be firmly located, and they suggest something of the

---

[22] Dated fifteen days after Easter 1248: CP 25(1), 8/16, no. 1; substantially copied in MS Lyell 15, f. 134r – v. One of the conveyance deeds, however, states that the abbot and convent gave him 800 marks for *all* his property in Berks., excluding the ½ mark rent and 'terra de Hulle': ibid. f. 133v. A much later list of Abbot John's acquisitions states that 800 marks was the price for all Hugh's lands in Abingdon and Berks.: H. E. Salter, 'A Chronicle Roll of the Abbots of Abingdon', *EHR* xxvi (1911), 731.

[23] MS Cotton Julius A. ix, f. 159.

[24] See Biddle, Lambrick and Myers, 'The Early History of Abingdon', 48, 50. Abbot John was also accused of rapacity and maladministration in connection with the abbey's financial position. See G. Lambrick, 'Abingdon Abbey Administration', *Journ. of Ecclesiastical History*, xvii (1966), esp. 172 – 3.

[25] This was anticipated at the time the transaction was completed. See the copies of Hugh's deeds in MS Lyell 15, fos. 133v – 134r. Unfortunately these are not dated.

[26] Lambrick, 'Abingdon Abbey', 172 – 3. The letter-book also mentions this exceptional arrangement.

potential scale of their consequences. Most obviously, they underline the buoyancy of the English land market in the thirteenth century, suggesting that as a general rule crusaders found little difficulty in finding a buyer, even if the asking price, as in the case of Hugh's Berkshire lands, was seemingly high. It was, as is well known, predominantly a seller's market, and crusaders, as others, could expect to do well when disposing of their land.[27] Part of the explanation for Hugh's ability to drive a hard bargain for his Berkshire estates lies in the fact that there were keen prospective buyers other than the monks. Richard of Cornwall alone is named, but the letter-book explicitly states that others were interested, pinpointing those of the curial connection.[28] The entire tale suggests strongly that Hugh, open to bid and counterbid, was playing off potential purchasers, with Earl Richard and the monks as the front runners. But allowance must be made for considerations other than those concerning supply and demand for land alone.

   Local political and tenurial circumstances go a long way towards explaining why Earl Richard and the Abingdon monks should have been the leading bidders. Richard, of course, was an active land-speculator and shrewd businessman with a vast income at his disposal, but in this particular case his appetite was surely whetted by his tenure of the neighbouring honours of Wallingford and St. Valery, and his other landed interests in Oxfordshire, Berkshire and Buckinghamshire (see map on p. 127). These included Harwell, just four miles from Hugh's property in East Drayton.[29] Plainly, Hugh's estates would nicely expand Richard's regional holdings. But Hugh's properties were held of Abingdon abbey, and at Abingdon, as at many other houses, a policy of recovering fees became well-established in the thirteenth century.[30] Under Abbot John de Blosmeville (1241 – 56) himself, Abingdon recovered not only Hugh's fee, by far the largest purchase, but the manor of Sunningwell, properties in Abingdon and other holdings as well.[31] A variety of motives lay behind these acquisitions, but in the case of Hugh's property we find unambiguous evidence of what may be suspected in many other contemporary transactions: purchase dictated by the fear of encroachment by outsiders on the fee of a monastic overlord.[32] Indeed, that fear in this case seems to have driven the monks in some desperation to complete the sale. This, surely, is why they threw in

[27] Further below, 135 – 6.

[28] Simon de Walton was probably one to mind: above, 122.

[29] See N. Denholm-Young, *Richard of Cornwall* (Oxford, 1947), Appendix ii, 162 – 70 for his holdings. For Richard's dealings, see briefly S. Raban, 'The Land Market and the Aristocracy in the Thirteenth Century', in *Tradition and Change: Essays in Honour of Marjorie Chibnall*, ed. D. Greenaway *et al.* (Cambridge, 1985), 244 – 6.

[30] See e.g. B. Harvey, *Westminster Abbey and Its Estates in the Middle Ages* (Oxford, 1977), ch. 6, esp. 164 – 7; S. Raban, *The Estates of Thorney and Crowland* (Cambridge, 1977), esp. 62 – 5; E. King, *Peterborough Abbey, 1086 – 1310: A Study in the Land Market* (Cambridge, 1973), esp. 53 – 4, 66 – 9; J. A. Raftis, *The Estates of Ramsey Abbey: A Study in Economic Growth and Organization* (Toronto, 1957), ch. 4.

[31] Salter, 'A Chronicle Roll', 731. The monks may have enjoyed, or hoped for, first refusal since they were the lord of Hugh's fee. See esp. on this point of refusal, Harvey, 165 – 6; P. A. Brand, 'The Control of Mortmain Alienation in England, 1200 – 1300', in *Legal Records and the Historian*, ed. J. H. Baker (London, 1978), esp. 29 – 34. So far as crusaders specifically are concerned, *Quantum predecessores I* established in 1145 that they were first expected to approach their feudal lords and kinsmen when alienating land to raise cash. See Brundage, 176 – 7.

[32] See esp. S. Raban, *Mortmain Legislation and the English Church, 1279 – 1500* (Cambridge, 1982), esp. 147 – 8.

the offer of two corrodies and a chantry — as sweeteners to tip the balance of Hugh's thinking in their favour — and why, too, they were prepared to go to Gloucester to secure the crucial final concord with Hugh, even though Justice Thirkelby was at Reading and Wallingford only a few weeks later.[33]

The argument that prevailed in the initial conventual discussions was to the effect that the monks had no choice but to buy Hugh's lands, considering their location and the immense regional power and influence of Richard of Cornwall, even though it was patently a very risky financial venture. There is no suggestion that they were hoping to profit through speculation, or wished to purchase for any other economic motive. (Nor is there any indication that Hugh was economically vulnerable.) Their fundamental concern undoubtedly lurks behind the letter-book's observation that it was Richard whom 'all the English [or at least the monks] feared more than his own king'. For them the stakes were terribly high, and that potent symbol of Earl Richard's regional power, Wallingford castle, lay uncomfortably close to them. No less a cause for concern was Richard's possession (from 1244) of the consolidated bloc of the Chiltern hundreds of Binfield, Ewelme, Langtree, Lewknor, and Pirton, across the Thames in south Oxfordshire. The earl's influence in local society and government had been steadily growing from the late 1220s; by 1247 – 8 it was immense, and the prospect of its further expansion can only have disturbed the monks profoundly. Never before, it seems, had they been confronted by such a powerful figure so near to them. They purchased Hugh's estates because it was politically expedient or necessary to do so, and Hugh profited from their deep anxieties. It is not without significance that the monks were apparently uninterested in securing his holdings further away in north Oxfordshire and more distant Warwickshire, even though his hide in Hill was of their own fee.

If the purchaser felt no pressing need to buy up a crusader's property by virtue of local politics, he nevertheless bought for precise reasons. Most commonly, he saw the opportunity to expand or fill out his interests in the locality concerned. Master Simon de Walton's purchase of Hugh fitzHenry's holding in Balscott is one of many examples.[34] Since Simon thereby became lord of the manor it may also be that the curial cleric's desire to improve his general social standing was involved in this instance. It was a personal consideration that certainly played a part in the landed investments of many merchants and bourgeoisie, and a crusader's cash needs could provide an opening for such men.[35] Again, consolidation of local interests was often involved. For example, that London mercer on the make, Philip le Taylor, began to acquire property beyond the city walls in 1259.[36] He already held a stake in the neighbouring Crayford and Erith areas of Kent when he purchased the manor and church of Crayford, and leased that of Erith, from the crusader John de St. John in 1270.[37] Another Londoner, John le Ferun, was more interested in properties in

[33] Thirkelby was at Reading and Wallingford in July 1248, and at Gloucester 3 May – 4 June. See D. Crook, *Records of the General Eyre* (PRO Handbook, no. 20. London, 1982), 106 – 10. For the use of corrodies by the Westminster monks in their transactions, see Harvey, 193.

[34] Above, 122.

[35] See e.g. Harvey, 190, concerning Londoners; E. Miller, 'Rulers of Thirteenth Century Towns: the Cases of York and Newcastle upon Tyne', in *Thirteenth Century England I: Procs. of the Newcastle upon Tyne Conference, 1985*, ed. P. R. Coss and S. D. Lloyd (Woodbridge, 1986), 135 – 41.

[36] See G. A. Williams, *Medieval London. From Commune to Capital* (London, 1963), 59, 332 – 3.

[37] Williams, 59, 332 – 3; and specifically *CPR 1266 – 72*, 464; *CR (Suppl.) 1244 – 66*, 44; *CIMisc.* i. 227. For his Kentish property at his death, see further *Select Cases in the Exchequer of Pleas (1236 – 1304)*, ed. H. Jenkinson and B. Formoy (Selden Soc., xlviii, 1931), 155.

• *Blackthorn*
(*Richard of Cornwall*)

• *Yarnton*
(*Richard of Cornwall*)   • *Beckley* (*Richard of Cornwall*)

Princes Risborough
(*Richard of Cornwall*)
•

• *Oxford*

Dry Sandford
(*fitzHenry*)
•

Shippon •   *Abingdon*
(*Abingdon*)

• *Watlington* (*Richard of Cornwall*)

Drayton
(*fitzHenry*)

• *Benson* (*Richard of Cornwall*)

Marlow
(*Richard of Cornwall*)

• *Harwell*
(*Richard of Cornwall*)

Wallingford (*Richard of Cornwall*)

Henley
(*Richard*
of *Cornwall*) •

East Ilsley   *Compton*
(*Thomas* •   (*Sifrewast*)
de *Clare*)

•
Checkendon
(*Thomas de Clare*)

Aldworth
(*Sifrewast*)
•

Hampstead Norreys
(*Sifrewast*)

River Thames

*The sales of Hugh fitzHenry
and Nicholas de Sifrewast*
(*possession at time of sale indicated*)

0   5   10   15 km
0   5   10 mi

Essex. His purchase of the manor of Elmdon for £200 in late 1269 from the crusader Robert de Munteny expanded his interests in the county.[38] John de Gisors provides another illuminating example. Patrician, vintner and royal merchant, who would lead the royalist Londoners in the Montfortian period, he purchased and speculated actively in the land market around London from the 1230s. Ralph de Thony, in search of cash for his crusade, farmed his manor of Walthamstow to John for six years in 1239. It was one of three manors John acquired in Essex.[39]

In the case of Richard Hotot's purchase of Clapton (Northamptonshire) local and personal factors of a different complexion were involved, for Clapton had been part of the ancestral Hotot estate, fragmented in the years 1175 – 90, which Richard was determined to reconstitute. Between 1213 and his death, *c.* 1250, he spent 413 marks acquiring the different fragments. 170 marks went on Clapton, purchased from Hugh de Ringstone in 1242. Hugh had previously bought the holding for 100 marks in 1240 from his brother Ralph, who accompanied Richard of Cornwall's crusade. In 1248 Richard Hotot finally attained his goal by purchasing the remaining portion of the original estate for 160 marks. The especial point of interest from our perspective is that a crusader's need for cash initiated further transactions which allowed one man to realise his dream, and Richard's preparedness to pay 170 marks for a property which two years earlier had sold for 100 marks indicates his determination in the matter.[40]

In none of the cases considered above is there any suggestion that the crusader concerned was experiencing anything more than short-lived liquidity problems arising out of a crusading intention. But Nicholas de Sifrewast, knight of Oxfordshire and Berkshire, and sheriff of those counties (1265 – 7), was one whose affairs probably were in crisis before he took the Cross for Lord Edward's crusade. There are definite signs of difficulties. In 1239 his father, William, leased the manor of Aldworth (Berkshire) for twenty years, and since we also know that William was indebted to a Jew in 1255, it looks as if Nicholas inherited some financial problems on the death of his father shortly after.[41] In 1257 Nicholas himself leased Hampstead Norreys (Berkshire) for eight years.[42] Men did not usually lease their patrimonies as a matter of course, and Hampstead Norreys — Hampstead Syfrewaste as it was then known — was apparently the *caput* of the family estates.[43] It is perhaps further indicative of his situation that in 1272 – 3 Nicholas found himself hard pressed to pay back to the king debts outstanding from his period of shrieval office.[44] For Nicholas, then, the prospect of the 1270 crusade may well have prompted him to sell up and enter the service of Thomas de Clare, that service to include crusading with his new lord as one of Thomas's bachelors. In

[38] KB 26/191, m. 6d (enrolment of the deed). Robert regained Elmdon, enfeoffing his son with it before his death in 1287: *CIPM* ii. 386. For John's further interests in Essex, acquired before his death in 1273, see *CCR 1272 – 9*, 26, 50 – 1; *CIPM* ii. 278 – 9, 510; *CFR 1272 – 1307*, 7.

[39] For the lease, see *CRR 1237 – 42*, no. 167; for John, see Williams, 68 – 70, 325 – 6.

[40] For the details of this intriguing tale, and comment, see 'Estate Records of the Hotot Family', ed. E. King, in *A Northamptonshire Miscellany*, ed. E. King (Northamptonshire Rec. Soc., xxxii, 1983), 8 – 9, 44 – 6; id., *Peterborough Abbey*, 47 – 8.

[41] *CChR 1226 – 57*, 245; *VCH Berkshire*, iv. 3; *CR 1254 – 6*, 102.

[42] *CPR 1247 – 58*, 546; *VCH Berkshire*, iv. 73.

[43] It later passed to the Ferrers and then Norris families: *VCH Berkshire*, iv. 74.

[44] E 368/45, mm. 6, 6d.; E 159/47, m. 12d.

1269 – 70 the two entered into a complex agreement whereby Nicholas made over to Thomas most of his paternal inheritance in Berkshire but receiving some of it back for life.[45] Thomas's territorial ambitions help to explain why he and Nicholas came together, for in the late 1260s and early 1270s Thomas was developing an interest in the Thames valley. In particular, West Drayton and East Ilsley (Berkshire) came into his hands on the fall of the Montfortian Gilbert de Elsfield; he was still in possession in 1276.[46] Thereby, Thomas and Nicholas became neighbours, for East Ilsley is only some five miles from Hampstead Norreys, four miles from Aldworth and two from Compton, also held by Nicholas (see map on p. 127). If Nicholas was indeed in difficulties, then here was a splendid opportunity for Thomas to step in and consolidate his new local interests. Nicholas, on the other hand, had secured a powerful patron whose star was then in the ascendant, both nationally and locally. The arrangement looks to have been admirably suited to the immediate circumstances and likely prospects of both parties.

II

Thus far we have been largely concerned with sales of property, but the evidence suggests that crusaders avoided selling up permanently if they could, certainly their entire estates. That such a drastic act was considered unusual, at least at this social level, is indicated by Henry III's observation, when granting 400 marks of wards, marriages and escheats to Robert Charles in 1270, that he had been moved to pity on hearing that Robert had sold 'all his land' to accomplish his crusade.[47] Crusaders naturally preferred to borrow, meeting a short-term need by a short-term expedient. It was, then, in the short term that they exercised the greatest impact on the land market and the tenurial structure as they strove to raise cash.

Forms of gage and lease were the devices chiefly employed. Mortgage was apparently the most common form of pledge used by twelfth-century crusaders, but it looks as if the vifgage was altogether more typically employed by crusaders in the thirteenth century, in England at any rate.[48] Part of the explanation may be that only a few potential mortgagees could raise the cash in one sum at short notice without risking financial difficulties for themselves; if they could, then outright purchase would have been a better investment from their point of view.[49] Equally, mortgage must often have appeared unattractive to the crusader since, following his

---

[45] For the details, see Lloyd, 'The Lord Edward's Crusade', 130 – 1.

[46] *CCR 1272 – 9*, 270; *VCH Berkshire*, iv. 342.

[47] *CPR 1266 – 72*, 434 – 5. In 1276 Edward I duly granted Robert £40 per annum of land for sixteen years, on his surrendering Henry III's letters patent: *CPR 1272 – 81*, 170. Robert certainly went on crusade: C 62/51, m. 10. Henry III's particular concern for Robert is partly explained by his family's services to the royal house.

[48] The thirteenth-century crusader utilized that device appearing most appropriate in the particular circumstances. This is quite apparent from the terms of royal licences to alienate. For the twelfth century, see esp. Constable, 'The Financing of the Crusades', 72 – 3. The subject of financing through gage and lease requires further study. I am indebted to Dr. Paul Brand for his help and suggestions.

[49] But see Raban, *Mortmain Legislation*, 109 – 11, on the possible advantages of lease as a prelude to full ownership.

expenditure on crusade, he then needed to raise the cash to redeem his pledge when out of possession of the property in question, risking possible forfeiture if he could not. In contrast to mortgage, vifgage was more appealing because the principal was repaid from the revenues of the property whilst it was in the gagee's hands. It may well be that the developing land-hunger in thirteenth-century England frequently led to a situation in which crusaders, as suppliers of land, could secure the more favourable terms of the vifgage.

So far as leases are concerned, it would appear at first sight that such transactions scarcely met the crusader's need to secure lump sums quickly, but it is probable that in many instances the lease in fact disguised a loan, as Maitland long ago observed.[50] Too much should not be made of formal distinctions, especially since it was not uncommon in leases for an initial premium to be paid as well as a regular rent. In any event, much would depend upon the respective circumstances and bargaining positions of borrower and creditor. Typical of the sort of arrangement which often resulted was that agreed in May 1235 between Philip Daubeny, preparing for his third and last crusade, and Bishop Jocelin of Bath and Wells. Philip pledged his manor of South Petherton (Somerset) to Jocelin for £280, but even the bishop of one of the wealthiest English sees could or would not find the sum at once. He made an initial payment of £120, and bound himself to pay £40 per annum for four years from Easter 1239. He paid a further £40 for all the corn sown in the manor in 1235, and £19 10s. for rent of the manor in the current term along with its stock. Jocelin would receive all profits and issues until the end of the seven-year term, but if he received more than £280 he was to apply the surplus to support of the Holy Land or other pious uses. This looks to have been a considered compromise, combining elements of lease and vifgage, in which the crusader's need for ready cash was tempered by the circumstances of the creditor. Typically, one or other of the parties secured royal confirmation of the transaction.[51]

With transactions of these kinds, as well as outright sale, much of the interest lies in explaining why a crusader disposed of one property but not another, and why the investor concerned was interested in securing that particular estate.[52] There was a marked tendency to dispose of acquisitions or 'outliers' rather than the patrimony: a wife's marriage portion, estates granted in wardship or otherwise *de ballio*, or holdings which had come to the family only recently.[53] Reminiscent of the monastic benefactions of many, it is a pattern to be expected of a society in which men tenaciously clung to their patrimonies if they could. Philip Daubeny may be cited by way of general illustration. In 1235 he received royal licence to alienate four manors held of the king, each *terra Normannorum* and each a recent acquisition, but he is not known to have raised cash from his other estates.[54] Study of the local

---

[50] F. Pollock and F. W. Maitland, *The History of English Law Before the Time of Edward I* (2nd edn., Cambridge, 1898), esp. ii. 112.

[51] *CChR 1226–57*, 203. Jocelin later demised the manor to his steward, William de Wethamstead, for the term; should William die, the dean and chapter of Wells were to have it for the remainder of the term: *CChR 1226–57*, 226. This suggests active speculation.

[52] Judging from royal licences to alienate, only a very few considered alienating all their properties, and even then these were probably precautionary general licences against possible future need.

[53] Limiting clauses would have prevented alienation of some properties.

[54] *CPR 1232–47*, 74, 93. Significantly, Philip had already utilized these manors, in different ways, for his crusades of 1221 and 1228: *PR 1216–25*, 287; *PR 1225–32*, 175.

tenurial context of each of these manors reveals that it was alienated to a creditor already with some interest in the area. South Petherton, as we have seen, was snapped up by Bishp Jocelin of Bath and Wells.[55] Chewton (also Somerset) was leased by Hugh de Vivona, whose landed power was concentrated in the county.[56] Bampton (Oxfordshire) went to the abbot of Cirencester.[57] Wighton (Norfolk) was demised to Richard of Cornwall, whose East Anglian interests were centred not so far away on Eye.[58]

It is also apparent that, in many cases, this tendency to prefer the disposal of acquisitions in the matter of crusade financing is but one manifestation of a wider policy on the part of the family concerned. The manor of Wrockwardine (Shropshire), for example, remained to the Crown until 1231 after Robert de Bellême forfeited it in 1102. In 1200 it was farmed to Hamo Lestrange, and then in 1203 to John II of Knockin, his brother. In 1228 John became tenant for life, but in 1231 it was granted in fee to his son, John III. By 1255 John had enfeoffed his son Hamo, who, shortly before departure on crusade in 1271, granted it to his younger brother Robert, probably in consideration of a sum.[59] Hamo's grant fits well within the wider pattern of the Lestranges' usage of Wrockwardine.

The local and personal factors considered above help to explain why ecclesiastical corporations, *curiales*, merchants, and local knights and magnates were chiefly the purchasers, lessees or gagees of crusaders' properties.[60] Otherwise, crusaders' kin appear often to have stepped in — which had the advantage of keeping the property in the family whilst providing the crusading member with badly needed cash — or a crusader might come to an arrangement with his associates or friends. John Lovel, for example, was licenced in May 1270 to lease for ten years his manors of Elcombe (Wiltshire), Summerfield ('Suthmere'), Docking and Titchwell (all Norfolk), held in chief, to raise cash for his crusade.[61] In February 1271 Henry III confirmed the lease to William de Calne, Martin of Summerfield and Master Henry Lovel.[62] Previously, in September 1270, John had appointed Martin and Henry as his attorneys for the crusade, testifying to their close relationship, and John had already granted land in Docking to Martin in 1268 – 9.[63] Master Henry was a kinsman of John, and both men probably knew William de Calne well, for all three appear as being of the curial connection. In

---

[55] Philip was granted the manor by 1223, receiving it in fee in 1231: *RLC* i. 534, 541b, 554; *CChR 1226 – 57*, 142. He used it first to support his nephew Ralph, and initially was licensed to pledge it to him in Feb. 1235, before alienating it to Bishop Jocelin: *CPR 1232 – 47*, 93; *CR 1234 – 7*, 25.

[56] *CPR 1232 – 47*, 106. On Philip's death, it seems, Hugh was granted it *de ballio*: *CChR 1226 – 57*, 211. For Philip's previous interest in the manor, see esp. *RLC* i. 550b; *PR 1216 – 25*, 287; *Fees* i. 377.

[57] *CR 1234 – 7*, 68, 390; *Fees* i. 614. Philip was granted it in 1227: *CChR 1226 – 57*, 54.

[58] *CR 1234 – 7*, 385; *Fees* i. 591. Philip was granted it in 1227: *CChR 1226 – 57*, 57; *Fees* i. 388, 402.

[59] *VCH Shropshire*, xi. 310.

[60] According to Constable, 'The Financing of the Crusades', 74, 'the vast majority [of crusaders] turned to religious houses, which were the principal institutions of credit in the eleventh and twelfth centuries.' This impression may be distorted by the lop-sided survival of certain types of evidence, but economic and social developments did lead to a different pattern of credit financing in the thirteenth century.

[61] *CPR 1266 – 72*, 425. For his holdings there, see *Fees* i. 591; ii. 718, 730, 912.

[62] *CPR 1266 – 72*, 514.

[63] *CR 1268 – 72*, 281; *RH* i. 464.

addition, William was a knight of Wiltshire, in which county lay John's manor of Elcombe.[64]

In the light of these various considerations it is not surprising that the Jews, a traditional source of capital, apparently played only a minor role in crusade financing. But there were other reasons. It is well known that in the course of the thirteenth century, especially from the 1240s, their capacity to act in the land market was seriously affected by savage royal taxation and repressive legislation, before their expulsion from England in 1290. More specifically, at times of crusade, we find the king earmarking block sums to subsidise the expeditions of his kinsmen. The Jews were 'persuaded' to grant 3000 marks towards Richard of Cornwall's crusade in January 1237, for example; by November, Henry was ordering distraint of those who had not paid.[65] Again, Lord Edward was granted 6000 marks from the Jews in 1270 for his expedition.[66] The Crown's, or rather perhaps Henry III's, attitude in this regard is neatly expressed by the king's declaration in May 1269 that the Jews be free from tallage for three years, unless Henry or his sons should meanwhile go to the Holy Land.[67] Under such immediate pressures, on top of other royal demands, it is probable that many Jews were unable to meet the needs of lesser mortals at times of royal crusade.[68] Allowance must also be made for the impact of virulent anti-semitism, which contributed to legislation restricting the nature of Jewish moneylending activities, which underpinned the expulsion of Jews from certain towns and even entire counties — inevitably militating against transactions with local crusaders — and which perhaps led some crusaders, on principle, to rule out Jews as a source of cash through financial transaction.[69] In any event, they must frequently have been excluded by limiting clauses which prevented the conveyance of certain properties to Jews or others.[70] Moreover, they probably became a less attractive proposition with the development

---

[64] For William, see esp. *CPR 1258 – 66*, 291, 490; *CIMisc*. i. 186, 281; *CPR 1247 – 58*, 433; *CPR 1266 – 72*, 378 – 9; *CIPM* ii. 32. John had for long been associated, like other members of his family, with Henry III and Edward. His career can be pursued through the various chancery enrolments.

[65] *CPR 1232 – 47*, 173; *CR 1234 – 7*, 410; *CR 1237 – 42*, 4.

[66] *CPR 1266 – 72*, 545 – 6.

[67] *CPR 1266 – 72*, 345.

[68] The almost complete silence in the records on this score would suggest that they were not. Since unredeemed pledges leave most trace in the records, it may be that the Jews, at least in the first half of the century, played a larger role than now appears, their crusader clients duly redeeming their pledges. For the financial pressures upon the Jews at the time of the 1240 – 1 crusade, see now R. C. Stacey, *Politics, Policy and Finance under Henry III 1216 – 1245* (Oxford, 1987), 143 – 7. The stimulus, which has not been explained, for the extraordinary 1/3 demanded of them in 1239 was very probably Richard of Cornwall's crusade, for anti-Jewish feeling and attendant financial demands had become an integral part of the background to crusade preparation by this time.

[69] Particular mention should be made of the 1269 ordinance, which forbade the practice whereby Jews lent money in return for an annual rentcharge on the borrower's land, and the statute of 1275 which explicitly prohibited usury. See esp. H. G. Richardson, *The English Jewry under Angevin Kings* (London, 1960), 71 – 3, 104 – 7. For local expulsions before 1290, see C. Roth, *A History of Jews in England* (3rd edn., Oxford, 1964), 58.

[70] A lord might certainly intervene to prevent the entry to a fee of an individual *non grata* in his eyes. See Raban, *Mortmain Legislation*, esp. 12 – 13; Brand, 'The Control of Mortmain Alienation', esp. 32 – 3. The 1270 crusader, William le Graunt, for example, granted the manor of W. Allington (Leics.) for life in 1268, was prohibited from alienating the whole or part of it to hinder its reversion to the grantors: *Final Concords of the County of Lincoln, 1244 – 1722*, ed. C. W. Foster (Lincoln Rec. Soc., xvii, 1920), 226.

of the more sophisticated international banking system and the rise of the merchant bankers, especially those of Italy. From the 1240s and 1250s these bankers came to play an increasing role in the financial world, and with their local branches in both the West and the Latin East many English crusaders saw the advantages of making over some of their properties or revenues to them against loans.[71] The financing of Lord Edward's own crusade would come to depend crucially upon the facilities provided especially by the Riccardi of Lucca.[72]

III

However much cash a crusader might raise himself, or receive from other sources, he could still find himself hard pressed during a crusade and upon his return. There are some spectacular examples of immediate poverty resulting. For instance, Matthew Paris records that Guy de Lusignan arrived back in England from Egypt around Christmas 1250 in such straits that he travelled on foot and turned out of his way to beg hospitality from the abbot of Faversham. He requested the abbot to provide him and his few companions with horses to take them to London, declaring on oath that he would return the mounts. According to Paris, he did not; the despicable Poitevin returned neither thanks nor horses to his host: 'thus this shameless guest may be compared to a snake in the bosom or a mouse in the cheese'.[73] Not for the first time Guy was able to sponge off his half-brother: within days Henry III was arranging emergency relief for Guy, including four manors in wardship.[74]

Guy's immediate plight was real enough, but there is no indication that it was anything more than short-term. How different was the predicament of Thomas de Fenwick, knight of north Tynedale, upon his return from Lord Edward's crusade. Shortly before his departure Thomas leased his manors of Fenwick and Matfen for six years to Richard de Middleton, but we learn in October 1272 that Thomas and his men had lately ejected William, Richard's son and heir, from Fenwick.[75] Perhaps, after the heat and sickness of Acre, Thomas wanted his home back for recuperation, but other evidence reveals that he was in financial difficulties. In 1274, for 70 marks borrowed from Alan de Swinburn, a neighbour, he conveyed to the lender four of his men, their chattels and land, in Great Heaton. In the same year he conveyed a further two carucates to Alan for £100 which, in those telling

---

[71] Guy de Lusignan is an early example, employing his annual fee from Henry III to raise money in this way: *CPR 1247–58*, 5; *CR 1247–51*, 218.

[72] See esp. R. W. Kaeuper, *Bankers to the Crown: The Riccardi of Lucca and Edward I* (Princeton, 1973), esp. 78–82, and more generally on their wider role in England, 1–35. Their role in crusade financing, as other ventures, was probably much greater than appears, for there survive no recognizances of debt from certain clients known otherwise to have had significant dealings with them: ibid. 31, and n.

[73] Paris, *CM* v. 204. The sheriff of Kent received 20 marks in compensation for the assistance he gave to Guy on landing, partly confirming Paris's tale: *CR 1247–51*, 326.

[74] *CPR 1247–58*, 83, 84.

[75] *CPR 1266–72*, 683.

words, 'he has given me in my great necessity'. Ultimately, by final concord in Michaelmas Term 1275, he acknowledged Alan's right to the entire manor and its appurtenances.[76] Shortly afterwards Thomas died, his property by now mostly sold or leased.[77] There is seemingly no indication that he faced financial crisis before his crusade.

Many more probably found themselves obliged to act like Thomas. There are plenty of recorded debts, some considerable, owed by returned crusaders and it is tempting to see many property transactions occurring in the immediate aftermath of a crusade as being directly consequent. But we need to be on guard lest we assume too much from chronological coincidence, for rarely can it be positively demonstrated that the motive for alienation was indeed the need to raise cash to pay off debts incurred specifically through crusading.[78] A case in point is provided by the well-documented sales of the knight Berengar le Moyne to Ramsey abbey, the lord of most of his estates. In 1276 Abbot William of Godmanchester bought up Berengar's manors of Barnwell, Hemington and Crowthorpe, and his fee in Littlethorpe (Huntingdonshire) for 2500 marks. A further 750 marks was spent on his holdings in Niddingworth, Holywell and Ramsey itself.[79] Since Berengar accompanied Lord Edward on crusade in 1270, it is tempting to think that he sold up partly or wholly because of debts that he had incurred thereby.[80] But there is no evidence to this effect. Moreover, the magnitude of the sums involved, coupled with the fact that Berengar secured an annuity of 100 marks and lease for life of the abbey's manor of Chatteris, does not suggest that he was disadvantaged in the business, nor that he was economically vulnerable and necessarily constrained to sell. It is more likely, perhaps, considering the broader economic policies of the abbots of Ramsey in the later thirteenth century, that their eagerness to invest in land, and to recover their own fee, led to Berengar's being made an offer which it was difficult to refuse.[81] The terms of their transactions might well indicate that it was the abbot who was eager to buy, rather than Berengar to sell. Perhaps, too, Abbot William had to compete with other bidders, in a fashion reminiscent of the case of Abingdon and Hugh fitzHenry (discussed above). It would certainly be rash to assume from the evidence available that the need to pay off any debts stemming from his crusade was the decisive, or only, reason for Berengar to sell at this time.

It looks further as if the exercise of royal patronage, as in the case of Guy de Lusignan (discussed above), or other support from kinsmen, friends or lords frequently helped many indebted crusaders over the worst. This would help to explain why alienation of property by returned crusaders did not occur as frequently, or to the extent, as may have been expected. Alexander de Balliol, for

---

[76] J. Hodgson, *A History of Northumberland* (Newcastle upon Tyne, 1820 – 58), II. i. 212 – 13; III. ii. 1 – 3; National Register of Archives, *Swinburne (Capheaton MSS)*, Part I (1962), 88, 92.

[77] *Northumbrian Pleas from De Banco Rolls 1 – 19*, ed. A. H. Thompson (Surtees Soc., clviii, 1950), 80 – 1.

[78] S. Painter, *Studies in the History of the English Feudal Barony* (Baltimore, 1943), 84, appears correct in his observations relating to this matter.

[79] *Chronicon Abbatiae Rameseiensis*, ed. W. O. Macray (RS, 1886), esp. i. 107 – 8; ii. 339 – 40, 345 – 6; app. i (p. 344); app. ii (p. 348); and see Raftis, 109, 237.

[80] He received a crusader's protection in July 1270: *CPR 1266 – 72*, 440; and in 1280 acknowledged receipt of 50 marks 'on his return from the Holy Land', part of 200 marks delivered for safe-keeping to the abbot: *Descriptive Catalogue of Ancient Deeds in the PRO* (London, 1890 – 1915), iii. no. A.5163.

[81] See Raftis, ch. 4.

example, after crusading with Lord Edward, had returned from the Latin East by February 1272. His elder brother Hugh had meanwhile died in 1271, leaving Alexander as his heir. In February 1272 Henry III, responding to Alexander's urgent request that he be put in seisin of his lands, regretted that this could not be done immediately since the inquisition and extent of Hugh's lands had not yet been completed, but he obliged him to the extent of instructing that the inquisition be completed speedily, that the escheator answer to Alexander for all the issues of his lands, and that Alexander be allowed to sow and cultivate his estates before livery.[82] Within a month Alexander was seised, and Henry graciously pardoned his relief fine.[83] Alexander was obviously feeling the pinch and Henry responded so far as custom and procedure allowed. That Alexander was married to Eleanor of Geneva, a close relation of the queen, doubtless had some bearing upon Henry's actions, but probably more important was the lobbying which Lord Edward is said, in the royal letters, to have done on Alexander's behalf.

Alexander's finances remained precarious. In 1275 he owed 200 marks each to William de Valence and Master Roger de Seyton, in 1276 a debt of £80 3s. 8d. to two Florentine merchants, and in 1278 a further 110 marks.[84] In 1278 he also found himself pressed to pay £300 still owing from the relief fine of his brother Hugh.[85] It is not surprising, then, that he leased his manor of Whittonstall and other properties, nor that he alienated the rent of his mill at Bywell, on the Tyne, before July 1275.[86] But Alexander and his family were fortunate because Edward I partly came to the rescue on his death in 1278 by granting very reasonable terms for the payment of his debts to the Crown, his friends Otto de Grandson and the Lord Edmund apparently using their influence with the king.[87] No extensive sale or lease of assets, it appears, was even necessary, and the records do not suggest that his son, John, was in any great difficulty after Alexander's death. Finally, it should be stressed that Hugh, whom Alexander succeeded, was already in great debt to the king when he died in 1271.[88] It is a salutary warning that we should never assume that a crusader's debts upon his return were necessarily a sole consequence of his crusading, nor that any subsequent property transactions were prompted by his expenditure on crusade. Plainly, the notion that returned crusaders, saddled with debt, were commonly obliged to sell up needs to be corrected.

IV

The significance of the crusades for the overall level of activity in the thirteenth-century English land market should not be exaggerated if, as we have been led to

---

[82] *CPR 1266 – 72*, 628; *CIPM* i. 270, for the inquisition.
[83] *CR 1268 – 72*, 472.
[84] *CCR 1272 – 9*, 248, 251, 431; *CDS* ii. 26.
[85] *CDS* ii. 26.
[86] Hodgson, VI. 52 n.; *CCR 1272 – 9*, 200.
[87] *CFR 1272 – 1307*, 105, 106. In 1277 he was allowed temporary respite for payment of those debts: *CCR 1272 – 9*, 379.
[88] See esp. *RF* ii. 532 – 3.

believe, it was generally a buoyant one. But there can be no doubt that at times of crusade the supply side of that market was eased as crusaders strove to raise funds. Guibert of Nogent, writing of the First Crusade, indicates that prices in northern France then fell spectacularly as so much property became available in the stampede to sell: men sold 'at a lower price than if [they] were captive in a harsh prison and needed to be ransomed quickly'.[89] Guibert may have exaggerated, but his comments, presumably based upon his knowledge of conditions in the Laonnais and neighbouring areas, reflect the fact that north French recruitment to the First Crusade was high, and that, without entering into the complexities of the matter, the situation had not yet reached the point where demand for land had outstripped supply. In those circumstances many crusaders would inevitably have been disappointed by the sums their property could command. Very different was the situation in thirteenth-century England with its fast developing land-hunger. Crusaders there knew well that they could expect to do nicely, even if they were at a disadvantage because of their need to complete transactions speedily. In connection with properties in the richer and more populous parts of the realm, at least, it was always likely that a number of prospective bidders would be waiting in the wings. Whether such a happy circumstance, from the crusader's point of view, obtained elsewhere is uncertain. But if it did not, then for many the financial pressures of a crusade can only have been that much more severe, for the costs of transport and the prices charged on campaign for foodstuffs, horses and other necessaries did not, so far as we know, make allowance for the microeconomic factors at work in crusaders' homelands. Further research might, possibly, provide an answer to this question. The implications could be important, not only for our understanding of the nature and dynamics of the English land market, but also for our understanding of crusaders' fund raising and, possibly, the regional variations in the pattern of crusader recruitment.

---

[89] Guibert of Nogent, 'Gesta Dei per Francos', *Rec. Hist. des Croisades: Hist. Occ.* iv. 140 – 1; see also Orderic Vitalis, *Historia Ecclesiastica*, ed. M. Chibnall (Oxford, 1969 – 80), v. 16, who was familiar with the situation in Normandy.

The English Episcopate, the State and the Jews: the Evidence of the Thirteenth-Century Conciliar Decrees

J. A. Watt

'For about a century and a half', wrote Maitland, 'the Jews were an important element in English History.'[1] The subsequent writing of our national history has never quite perhaps done justice to that importance. But since Maitland wrote, the history of the Jewish experience in Europe has transcended mere national histories. The phenomenon of anti-semitism has made it necessary, in the words of Gavin Langmuir, 'to change the subject of the treatment of the Jews from an issue of sectarian history to a central problem for medieval historians as such'.[2] In studying this subject, obviously the role of the Church and the influence of religious ideas is of central importance, and it is with a detail of this role and influence that this paper is concerned.

One can readily agree with Langmuir that 'the most obvious factor affecting the status of medieval Jews was the doctrine and law of the Church and the actions of individual churchmen',[3] while at the same time recognizing that the detailed studies of that doctrine and law are for the most part still to do. Likewise we can agree with H. G. Richardson about 'the impotence of ecclesiastical authorities to legislate for the Jewry in defiance of the civil power',[4] while recognizing that the relationship between the doctrine and law of the Church and the State monopoly of control over the Jewish community has not been fully worked out. This short paper is, then, an investigation into an aspect of these two problems.

The first part of the enquiry is, for the most part, a relatively straightforward matter, for the basic source material — the councils and synods of thirteenth-century England — has been supremely well edited and presented by C. R. Cheney.[5] The second part, an assessment of the interaction of that law and doctrine on royal policies towards the Jews and on the life of the Jewish community in England, is an altogether more complex and debatable matter. For present purposes, operating within the tight limits of a conference paper, it must suffice to deal adequately with just the first part of the enquiry, namely how the English bishops regarded the Jews and what they construed should be their policy towards them.

---

[1] F. M. Pollock and F. W. Maitland, *The History of English Law before the Time of Edward I* (new edn., Cambridge, 1968), i. 469. Excellent overview: P. Hyams, 'The Jewish Minority in Medieval England 1066 – 1290', *Journ. of Jewish Studies*, xxv (1974), 270 – 93.

[2] G. I. Langmuir, 'The Jews and the Archives of Angevin England: Reflections on Medieval Anti-Semitism', *Traditio*, xix (1963), 244.

[3] Langmuir, 'Jews and the Archives of Angevin England', 193.

[4] H. G. Richardson, *The English Jewry under Angevin Kings* (London, 1960), 187.

[5] *Councils and Synods with other Documents relating to the English Church: II. Part I (1205 – 1265), Part II (1265 – 1313)*, ed. F. M. Powicke and C. R. Cheney (Oxford, 1964). [Hereafter, *CS*]

The number of conciliar and synodal decrees relating to Jews which has survived is not large. It would not seem that the relations of Christians and Jews was a source of major concern so far as episcopal legislators were concerned. At any rate, the issue was far from the forefront of their minds: of the thirty-six sets of canons published by Professor Cheney for the period between 1205 and 1290, when the Jews were expelled, only eleven contain relevant material. Some of it is pure repetition, as with the decrees of Worcester diocese of 1219, 1229 and 1240; in some, the reference to Jews is quite incidental as, for example, the canon which forbids the alienation of church property to laymen, Christian or Jewish, or the ban on consulting sorcerers, including Jewish ones. In none can the treatment be said to be extensive.

It is also limited in diocesan range: only six dioceses and two Canterbury provincial sets have Jewish material. There is nothing of York provenance; nor did the issue of Christian-Jewish relations apparently receive a mention at some of the more influential and important legislative occasions: Bishop Robert Grosseteste's council of 1239, for example, or the legatine councils of Cardinal Otto and Cardinal Ottobuono in 1237 and 1268 respectively. Nevertheless, the issue was raised sufficiently often and, on analysis, proves sufficiently coherent and integrated, to permit the conclusion that it may be regarded as a representative minimum statement of the episcopate's main concerns in the regulation of Christian-Jewish relations.

The legislation must be read in its appropriate canonistic perspective. It emerges from a background in the traditional juridical understanding of the relationship of Christian and Jew as it had become standardized in Gratian's *Decretum*,[6] and it had been updated in more recent papal legislation of which the decrees of the two general councils, Lateran III (1179) and Lateran IV (1215), had a place of particular importance. With the promulgation of the Gregorian *Decretales* in 1234, the old and new law received its authoritative blend. This legislation with its attendant canonist commentary was available to all,[7] whether themselves trained in the schools or not, and it is to be taken for granted that it was known, to a greater or lesser extent, to all episcopal legislators. Yet the English legislation is not a mere reiteration of the general law of the Church: it has been selected and adapted for English needs, and there are elements — and probably omissions — that are distinctively English. In only one case — that of the Exeter decrees issued by Bishop Peter Quinel in 1287 — does one have the impression that the legislation is no more than a reissue of the conventional canon law regulations, smacking more of the schools than of the particular diocesan scene.[8] Elsewhere, the impression is that the general rules have been shaped to the needs of the local situation.

Those needs are pastoral: what is considered to be necessary for the preservation of the faith and morals of the Christian flock. Looked at from another angle, they are of course anti-Jewish and may well show, as H. G. Richardson thought, 'the implacable hostility of the Church towards the Jews'.[9] But the purpose of the

---

[6] Gratian did not allocate a specific *locus* for canons regulating Christian-Jewish relations. They occur incidentally to the coverage of other topics, e.g. in D.45 (on the conduct of bishops towards their subjects; D.54 (on serfdom); C.17, q.4 (on sacrilege); C.28, q.1 (on marriage); *De cons.* D.4 (on baptism).

[7] In the *glossa ordinaria* on *Decretales* 5.6 (*De Iudeis et Sarracenis et servis eorum*).

[8] *CS* II. ii. 1044 – 5.

[9] Richardson, 192.

legislation is to safeguard Christians from what were thought to be, rightly or wrongly, the dangers arising from the presence of a religion which, though tolerated, was considered false and therefore, in contemporary terms, potentially corrupting. 'Saepe malorum consortia etiam bonos corrumpunt': often the fellowship of evil persons corrupts even the good. The dictum comes from Gratian's *Decretum*;[10] its citation in an English episcopal canon in the context of Christian-Jewish relations is an important clue to the motivation informing much of this legislation.[11]

For it is fear of Jewish proselytism which lies behind the one regulation which is virtually common to each set of canons. This was the ban on Christian women acting as servants in Jewish households, especially if this meant living-in.[12] They were forbidden, too, to act as midwives at Jewish births or as wet-nurses to Jewish boys. The rule had been promulgated by Alexander III at Lateran III and had been consolidated by a particularly trenchant decretal of Innocent III.[13] Alexander III's canon makes it clear what lay behind the restriction: '[Jews] through prolonged relationship and continual intimacy easily dispose the minds of uneducated people to their superstition and faithlessness.'[14]

Fear of conversion to Judaism was not the only danger churchmen saw in Jewish employment of Christian women as wet-nurses, midwives and servants. There was the further risk of inter-marriage and illicit sex. Bishop Giles of Bridport in his Salisbury council of 1257 accused Jews in his diocese of acting 'to the scandal of the Christian faith and in contempt of their own law' by having sexual intercourse with married as well as single Christian women. The guilty women were to be excommunicated, the guilty Jews deprived of contact with Christians, who would be excommunicated if they ignored the boycott. The bishop instructed that the rule about distinctive dress ('distinctio habitus') should be meticulously observed because of the dangers to morals consequent on its non-observance.[15] The phrase

---

[10] C.28, q.1, C.12 (Council of Toledo IV). There are variants on the same theme in the canonist literature: *Glossa Ordinaria*: 'Nota quod familiaritas malorum vitanda est, ne boni corrumpantur ab eis' (*Casus ad Decretales* 5.6.8.).

[11] Exeter II (1287), c.49: *CS* II. ii. 1044.

[12] Worcester I (1219), c.6: *CS* I. i. 55; Worcester II (1229), c.44: *CS* II. i. 178; Worcester III (1240), c.91: *CS* II. i. 318; Oxford (1222), c.46: *CS* II. i. 120; Chichester I (1245 x 1252), c.71: *CS* II. i. 466; Salisbury IV (1257), c.27: *CS* II. i. 560; London (1280 x 1290?), c.115: *CS* II. i. 658.

[13] *Decretales*, 5.6.7, 13.

[14] 'Quoniam Iudeorum mores et nostri in nullo concordant, et ipsi de facili ab continuam conversationem et assiduam familiaritatem ad suam superstitionem et perfidiam simplicium animos inclinarent': *Decretales*, 5.6.8. The *Glossa Ordinaria* added, s.v. *in nullo concordant*: 'Et in habitu etiam differre debent a christianis, ut possint melius euitari.'

[15] 'Licet in conciliis Lateranensi [Lat. III, 1179] ac Oxoniensi [Canterbury province, 1222] prohibitum sit expresse ne iudei mancipia habeant christiana, plerique tamen iudei nostre diocesis, ut dicitur, huiusmodi prohibitione contempta, nutrices, obstetrices, et alia mancipia christiana dampnabiliter presumunt in suis obsequiis retinere. Nec huiusmodi transgressione contenti in graviorem prorurumpunt audaciam, ut non solum cum christianis solutis sed in nostre fidei scandalum et in sue legis contemptum cum mulieribus commisceant coniugatis. Unde presentis synodi approbatione statuimus ut mulieres, tam solute quam coniugate, super huiusmodi crimen confesse vel convicte nominatim excommunicationis sententia percellantur, et donec ad arbitrium nostrum vel officialium nostrorum satisfecerint artius evitentur. Iudeis vero super hoc convictis vel confessis, donec competenter hoc emendaverint, omnis christiana communis per censuram ecclesiasticam denegatur. Quod vero circa distinctionem habitus cautum est, propter pericula que ex habitus confusione contingunt, omni diligentia statuimus observandum': *CS* II. i. 560 – 1.

'distinctio habitus' makes it clear that he was referring to C.68 of Lateran IV which, with the aim of preventing sexual unions of Christian women with Jews or Moslems, sought to generalise the practice, apparently already in being in some parts of Christendom, of Jews and Moslems adopting differentiating clothing. The language of the Salisbury decree is unusual in following C.68 so literally. For in the West generally and in England specifically, Innocent III's injunction had been implemented in the form of a sign or badge worn on the clothing. In a decree of 30 March 1218 Henry III's regency government had ordered the Jews to wear on the breast of their outside garment two white tablets (a *signum* frequently associated with the *synagoga*: Moses's tablets of the Law) of linen or parchment, so that by such a sign Jews might be distinguished from Christians.[16] Archbishop Stephen Langton's Oxford council of 1222 adopted what was essentially the same *tabula*, specifying that it should be of a different colour from the clothing being worn, and defining its size as two inches in breadth and four inches in length. This became pretty well the standard form and most canons refer to the need for it to be worn. Jewish historians have habitually and understandably expressed strong views about the imposition of what they regard as 'the badge of shame', seeing the underlying intention to have been the infliction of humiliation and degradation.[17] There can be no doubt that thirteenth-century Jews objected to the *tabula* and were prepared to pay for dispensations from the obligation to wear it, in England as elsewhere.[18] But the English episcopal legislation, as indeed the commentary of the canonist schools, reveals no evidence of any intention other than that of preventing sexual relations between Christians and Jews.

A third regulation highlighted in the English canons and, like the issues of Christian servants in Jewish households and the wearing of distinctive dress, also prominent in the law of the universal Church, concerned the building of new synagogues. It had for centuries been the principle that since Jewish worship was tolerated, Jews should be allowed their synagogues unmolested. Even in Gregory I's time it was possible for the pope to say that Jews had enjoyed freedom of worship 'per longa retro tempora', and that text was in Gratian's *Decretum*.[19] But if they were to be allowed their synagogues without disturbance, Gregory had written elsewhere, they were not to be allowed to build new ones. Pope Gregory offered no explanation for this restriction; he simply referred to the 'legalis diffinitio' which had ordained it. His reference was to a law of Theodosius II, reissued in Justinian's *Codex*, now an authoritative text for medieval canon lawyers. Gregory I's text had been reissued in the *Compilatio Ia* of the twelfth century and it had found a place in the Gregorian *Decretales*.[20] Further, Alexander III had reiterated the prohibition against new synagogues, refining the restriction to include a veto on any substantial

---

[16] Full text: *CS* II. i. 121, n.1.

[17] Best analysis: G. Kisch, 'The Yellow Badge in History', *Historia Judaica*, iv (1942), 95 – 144. With the emphasis on intended degradation and humiliation: e.g. S. Grayzel, *The Church and the Jews in the Thirteenth Century* (Philadelphia, 1933), 59 – 70; L. Poliakov, *The History of Anti-Semitism from the Time of Christ to the Court Jews* (New York, 1965), 65. Synan has suggested that judgements that the introduction of the *tabula* was 'a device to humiliate, or to degrade the Jew require qualification': E. A. Synan, *The Popes and the Jews in the Middle Ages* (New York, London, 1965). 104.

[18] Richardson, 179, and, about the same time in Castile, Grayzel, no. 38.

[19] D.45, c.3.

[20] *Decretales*, 5.6.3.

rebuilding or even enrichment of an existing synagogue.[21] Stephen Langton supplied his own explanation of this 800-year example of Christian intolerance, which was to become the law of England in 1253. The archbishop forbade the construction of new synagogues on the grounds that many Jewish acts of wickedness ('enormia') had demonstrated that they were ungrateful for their privileged position in Christian society. Hence Christian severity.[22]

The same prelate promulgated another rule which manifested hostility, and he was not the only one so to do. Archbishop Langton put it this way: 'Jews shall not in future presume in any way to enter churches and lest they have an excuse for entering, we strictly forbid any properties of theirs to be stored in churches.'[23] This was a restriction which seems to have been particular to England. Certainly it is not to be found either in Gratian, or in current decretal legislation, or in the standard canonist commentaries. The rationale behind this prohibition seems to have been this: to allow a Jew into a church was to risk his expressing contempt for the Christian religion — the stereotype of the Jew as eager blasphemer, which can be found in canonist writing.[24]

In his anxiety to make the point that it was the State, and not the Church, that had the ultimate control of the destinies of the English Jewry, H. G. Richardson had no high opinion of the importance and relevance of the episcopal statutes. He was dismissive about their status even as ecclesiastical law, thought them 'perfunctory', and argued that 'much of the content of diocesan statutes was never meant to be more than a pious gesture'.[25] This judgement on the bishops' motivation misunderstands why they saw fit to legislate on the matter of Jewish-Christian relations. The Jews were plainly seen as a potential source of danger: to the faith, by proselytism and insult, to morals, and in the areas of sex and avarice. (Attitudes to usury will be considered later in this paper.) We may well question whether these fears were well-grounded and whether they merited a programme of protective measures. We may regret that English bishops never saw fit to imitate the papacy and issue the relevant canon law on the protection of Jews from the attacks of Christians, for it is clear that Jews were in greater need of protection from Christians than *vice versa*. These reservations about the need for, and the quality of, the statutes do not, however, affect the assessment of the underlying motive. It was not mere pious gesture. The regulations formed part of that *cura animarum* which was the primary business of the ecclesiastical statutes. Its direct solicitude was with the souls of Christians and there was nothing perfunctory about that.

---

[21] *Decretales*, 5.6.7.

[22] 'Et quoniam supra iuris statuta non habent a nobis foveri, ut pote qui per multa enormia hiis diebus commissa probantur multipliciter nobis ingrati, prohibemus ne de novo construant synagogas . . .': *CS* II. i. 120. The theme of the Jewish ingratitude may well derive from Innocent III (*Decretales*, 5.6.13, itself a response to complaints against Jews made by the archbishop of Sens and the bishop of Paris).

[23] 'Ecclesias etiam de cetero nullatenus intrare presumant, et ne occasionem habeant ingrediendi, inhibemus districte ne deposita eorum in ecclesiis conserventur; et si contra presumptum fuerit, per episcopum corrigatur': *CS* II. i. 121. The canon had been anticipated in Worcester I (1219), c.6: *CS* II. i. 55, and was reiterated in Worcester II and III, London II: *CS* II. i. 178, 318, 652.

[24] Cf. text and commentary, *Decretales*, 5.6.1, 4.15.16. In the commentary on Alexander III's instruction that Jews should be confined to their houses on Good Friday, the *Glossa Ordinaria* asserted: 'Consueuerunt enim tunc deridere christianos in contumeliam creatoris . . . cum enim fidem nostram contemnant.'

[25] Richardson, 189.

There were, however, indirect effects of this concern for the English Jewry. Richardson was undoubtedly right to stress, when trying to assess the importance of this legislation, the Crown's attitude to these effects. The Jews were, to all intents and purposes, the king's serfs who, in 'Bracton's' words, 'could have nothing that is his own for whatever he acquires, he acquires, not for himself, but for the king'.[26] Hence, anything that touched the king's Jews might call for royal permission. Bishops might threaten excommunication against women who went into service in Jewish households; they might forbid their priests to let Jews store their goods in churches; they might rule for their subjects' consciences that to invest money with Jews in the hope of gain (*pro spe lucri*) was gravely sinful. But they had no spiritual hold on 'those who are outside' — 'de his qui foris sunt non iudicat ecclesia ut poenam spiritualem infligat' was standard doctrine.[27] So if Jews were to be compelled to wear the *tabula*, or were to be prevented from building new synagogues, excommunication and other canonical penalties had no place. The sanction had to be indirect. Innocent III had popularized the principle, in the legislation of Lateran IV, that where Jews had to be coerced by the ecclesiastical power, the appropriate means was to deny them contact with Christians.[28] In other words, they were to be boycotted. Those Christians who continued to do business with them, or to sell them food, would be excommunicated. Such a drastic intervention into the lives of Jews was not acceptable to the Crown and was forbidden.[29] Nor were ecclesiastical judges allowed to bring cases of debt involving Jews into their courts.[30] The clergy continued to complain occasionally about the secular power preventing the boycott and even to legislate, as in the Council of Lambeth of 1261, that judges who ordered the lifting of the boycott were to be excommunicated.[31] There is nothing in the history of Church-State relations in thirteenth-century England to suggest that such threats could be implemented. It was made abundantly clear that the king's Jews had only one master.

To say this is not to imply that the Church was challenging this position. There was no real conflict of policy between Church and State. That there were adjustments to the boundary between the two jurisdictions should not be allowed to conceal the basic identity of views between them. The civil law enforced most of the regulations which formed the subject matter of the ecclesiastical statutes: John's confirmation of the charters of the Jews in 1201 made it unlawful for them to receive or buy ecclesiastical objects;[32] it was the Crown which ordered the wearing of the *tabula* in 1218,[33] and which, in 1234, ordered sheriffs in Norfolk and Suffolk to proclaim in the towns of these counties a prohibition on Christian women nursing Jewish children or serving Jews in their homes in any other capacity.[34] And it was

---

[26] Pollock and Maitland, i. 468.

[27] Cf. *Glossa Ordinaria ad Decretales*, 5.65, asking the question: 'Quid ad nos de his qui foris sunt?' Ten cases were listed in which the church coerced Jews. The gloss concluded: 'quandoque tamen indirecte excommunicat eos, quia excommunicat christianos ne cum eis aliquod commercium habeant'. In another context this indirect excommunication was referred to as 'subtractio communionis christianorum': *Glossa Ordinaria*, 5.19.2.

[28] *Decretales*, 5.6.16.

[29] As e.g. in 1222, 1235: *CS* II. i. 120, n. 2.

[30] *CS* II. i. 55, n. 1.

[31] *CS* II. i. 679.

[32] *Rotuli Chartarum in Turri Londinensi asservati*, ed. T. D. Hardy (London, 1835), 93.

[33] *CS* II. i. 121, n. 1.

[34] *CS* II. i. 55, n. 1.

royal piety that made over to the Crown the whole area of Jewish converts' aid. Henry III's foundation of the *domus conversorum* in 1232 brought to the Crown not only the material care of converts from Judaism,[35] but also a jurisdiction in areas which might have been thought to belong more properly to the clergy. Such at least seems the conclusion to be drawn from the decision by the Crown in 1236 that the children of a converted Jew, who wished for them to become Christian too, should be allowed to choose for themselves whether they followed their father into Christianity or remained 'in errore suo'.[36] That it was Edward I who issued the instruction that Jews should attend conversion sermons was entirely in accord with the logic which the royal establishment of the *domus conversorum* had developed.[37] The Crown's involvement in, or rather monopoly of, matters concerning the *conversi* would explain the otherwise surprising omission of any reference to converting Jews in the episcopal statutes.

The essential complementarity of Church and State in Jewish affairs was to be most obviously demonstrated in the so-called 'Statute concerning the Jews' issued in January 1253. This decree is to be seen not so much as making 'a marked change in the attitude of the king towards the Jews'[38] — from hostility to episcopal attitudes to accepting them — as a comprehensively specific declaration of an existing policy of Church-State co-operation.

The *provisio* of 1253 has thirteen clauses.[39] Two of them (C.1 and C.12) define the special relationship of Jews to the king (they were bound to his particular service) and his control over where they lived. A third clause (C.13) defined the penalty for breaking the regulations now being issued as forfeiture of property — a sanction which promised to be swifter and more effective than boycott backed by excommunication. Of the remaining ten clauses five can be related directly to issues which had figured in the ecclesiastical statutes. The other five can be related to their background in general canon law and ecclesiastical theory. The detail can be quickly summarized. C.4, which had come to the English episcopal legislation from Lateran IV, ordered Jews to answer to the rector of the parish in which they lived for all parochial dues owed on their houses.[40] C.5 forbade the nursing of Jewish boys, the employment by Jews of any Christian as servant, and prohibited Christians from living in Jewish households. (These regulations were a stock element of the English conciliar canons.) It also went further than any episcopal decree in forbidding Christians even to eat with Jews, a prohibition well known in canonist writing.[41] Cls. 8 and 9 enforced the wearing of the *tabula* and the ban on intimacy between Christians and Jews. C.10 forbade Jews to loiter in churches. When C.12 forbade Jews to settle in any town other than the ones in which they were already settled without special licence of the king, the decree was implicitly

---

[35] M. Adler, *Jews of Medieval England* (London, 1939), VI 'The History of the Domus Conversorum', 279 – 306.

[36] *CR 1234 – 7*, 358.

[37] Adler, 300.

[38] Richardson, 180.

[39] *CS* II. i. 473 – 4.

[40] Lateran IV c.68 = *Decretales*, 5.6.15; Oxford, c.46: *CS* II. i. 121; Exeter II, c.49: *CS* II. ii. 1045.

[41] E.g. in the commentaries of the leading thirteenth-century canonist, Hostiensis: '. . . nec christiani cum eis comedant'. *Summa*, 5.6 *Et in quibus Iudei graventur*. '. . . . cum (Iudeis) non licet comedere'. *Apparatus ad Decretales*, 5.6.10 *s.v. canonicas*.

controlling the establishment of new synagogues. Two clauses referred explicitly to this type of royal control which commended itself to episcopal opinion. C.2 prohibited the establishment of Jewish schools, which were associated with synagogues, in any town other than those in which they had been established in King John's time. C.3 instructed Jews to celebrate their synagogue services in low voices so that they could not be heard by Christians. (Complaints against the unacceptable level of Jewish voices at their celebrations are known in thirteenth-century France, and on at least one occasion Innocent III had urged Philip Augustus to restrain them from so doing.)[42] In 1276, Edward I was to close a synagogue in London because the Friars *de penitentia*, whose church was nearby, had complained of being disturbed.[43] Other prohibitions included in the statute, while not known to have figured in the legislation of English councils and synods, were part of the common stock of Christendom's control over Christian relationships with Jews. The veto (C.7) on public debate with Jews figures frequently elsewhere. No doubt it was to be understood along lines to be articulated by Aquinas: it was forbidden 'because it is dangerous to debate in public about the faith in the presence of simple folk whose faith is all the firmer for not having heard anything against what they believe'.[44] Also known outside England was the prohibition (C.6) on Jews eating meat in Lent.[45] Presumably it was thought that by so doing, when Christians were abstaining, it might be interpreted that they were mocking or tempting Christians. Finally, C.11, an instruction that no Jew should in any way obstruct the conversion of another Jew, was an inevitable concomitant of royal involvement in Jewish conversion.

The *provisio* of 1253 and the establishment of the *domus conversorum* of 1232 constitute the two most striking manifestations of the rapport that existed between Church and State in the regulation of Jewish-Christian relationships. This rapport was not seriously disturbed by occasional ecclesiastical grumbles about the alleged shortcomings of the State in the way it operated aspects of the common policy. The *gravamen* of 1257 and the resultant Canterbury provincial legislation of 1261, already mentioned, was one example of this temporary disaccord. Another was the complaints of John Peckham in the parliament of 1285, which show the archbishop's impatience with defects in the procedure for the caption of converts whose lapse back into Judaism he had 'signified' to the royal curia.[46] In the same compilation of *gravamina* the bishops complained that the Crown had failed to protect Christians from usurious extortions by Jews, and asked that the king compel the restitution of all that had been extracted from Christians by usury. That they were looking for the complete abolition of Jewish money-lending is shown by their demand that the king should force Jews to earn their living by working with their hands and in trade.[47]

---

[42] Grayzel, no. 14 (16 Jan. 1205).

[43] D. L. Douie, *Archbishop Pecham* (Oxford, 1952), 324–5.

[44] *Summa Theologiae* 2a, 2ae, 10, 7 (Blackfriars edn., vol. xxxii, 58).

[45] Councils at Avignon (1209) and Narbonne (1227). Grayzel, 304, 316.

[46] *CS* II. ii. 961 (*resp. ad xvi art.*). Good coverage of Peckham and the Jews in Douie, 308–9, 323–30. The background to the complaint 'contra iudeos apostatos' has been skilfully clarified by F. D. Logan, 'Thirteenth Century London Jews and Conversion to Christianity', *BIHR* xlv (1972), 214–29.

[47] 'Cogat etiam (regia clementia) eos vivere de labore manuum suarum vel industria mercature . . . et sub pena horribili nec nostris labiis nominanda eos studeat ab omnibus mutuis usurariis cohercere . . .': *CS* II. ii. 962 (*resp. ad xvii art.*).

The bishops were not here asking for the adoption of any new policy, for ten years earlier Edward I, in the *Statutum de Judeismo*, had forbidden the practice of usury by Jews and instructed them to turn to farming or commerce as alternative, acceptable ways of earning a living. The complaint was against its non-implementation: 'we marvel', the prelates declared, 'because the royal court does not know how the Jewish evil [of usury] can be curbed'.[48] They suggested fierce penalties (leaving it for the lay power to specify them), prohibition of all secret dealings between Christians and Jews, and rigorous enforcement of the wearing of the Jewish *signum*. The complaint got a sympathetic response from the government, perhaps not surprisingly since there were years when the State and the royal family were subjecting the Jews to extreme pressure and needed little encouragement to keep it up. The fact that the complaint was made draws attention to another important dimension of the rapport between ecclesiastical and royal attitudes to the Jews.

It is, I think, possible to draw a distinction in ecclesiastical attitudes to the practice of usury. Lateran IV had forbidden Jews to exact 'heavy and immoderate usuries'.[49] It had not prohibited usury in any absolute sense and had thereby condoned, implicitly, the practice of moderate usury.[50] This Innocentian doctrine was consistently adopted by the papacy thereafter, tempering doctrinal extremes to the realities of contemporary economic and social life. In the schools, however, attitudes were more rigorous. Aquinas argued that Christians were not permitted to profit from monies which Jews had raised by usury. Hence rulers, knowing that Jews had no other source of income but money-lending, were not allowed to retain what had been extorted *per usurariam pravitatem*; they were bound to make restitution.[51] The profit of money-lending, profit made by Jews and received by Christians either in the way of business or as a gift, was to be equated with money received from a robber as a simoniac. It could not therefore be accepted; it if were, restitution must be made before the sin could be forgiven. This was the teaching, representative of its type, offered by the moral theologian, Robert of Flamborough, in his discussion of how the matter should be handled in the confessional.[52]

---

[48] '. . . mirantur prelati quia nescit curia regia qualiter possit iudaica malitia refrenari; nec certe unquam sciet quamdiu permittat iudeos per contractus usurarios involvere christianos et nobilium maneria adquirere per voraginem usurarum; quia hoc est favere iudeis in suis criminibus contra christianos': *CS* II. ii. 961 – 2.

[49] Lateran IV, c.67 (=*Decretales*, 5.20.18). *Constitutiones Concilii quarti Lateranensis una cum Commentariis glossatorum*, ed. A. García y García (Vatican City, 1981), 106.

[50] I am here accepting, in general terms, the argument of K. R. Stow, 'Papal and Royal Attitudes to Jewish Lending in the Thirteenth Century', *Association for Jewish Studies Review*, vi (1981), 161 – 83.

[51] 'Super hoc ergo sic respondendum videtur, quod cum ea quae Iudaei per usuras ab aliis extorserunt non possint licite retinere, consequens est ut, si etiam vos haec acceperitis ab eis, non possetis licite retinere, nisi forsan essent talia quae a vobis vel antecessoribus vestris hactenus extorsissent. Si qua vero habent quae extorserunt ab aliis, haec ab eis exacta illis debetis restituere quibus Iudaei restituere tenebantur.' 'De regimine Iudaeorum', in *Opuscula Philosophica*, ed. R. M. Spiazzi (Marietti edn., Milan, Rome, 1954), 728, p. 250.

[52] Robert's presumption was that the Jew had come by his money unjustly: '. . . quia judaeus eas per usuram rapuerat'. Hence he equated the Jew with the robber: '. . . a judaeo vel alio foeneratore'. The confessor was to give this advice to one who confessed to taking illicit gifts: 'Si aliquid habuisti a judaeo vel fure vel praedone vel raptore vel foeneratore vel simonaico, redde. Immo plus dico: si aliquid habuisti ex empto vel dono a judaeo vel alio foeneratore vel aliis similibus quos superius enumeravi, non potes illud retinere; de illicite acquisitis dico.' *Robert of Flamborough Canon-Penitentiary of Saint Victor at Paris, Liber Poenitentialis*, ed. J. J. F. Firth (Toronto, 1971), 184, 185.

This rigorous view was not confined to the professors. Robert Grosseteste advised the countess of Winchester in the early 1230s that rulers who accepted usurious profit were living on the proceeds of robbers and, as it were, consenting to sin, themselves sinning grievously.[53] Peckham was to warn Queen Eleanor of Castile along similar lines: 'pernez vus garde ke usure est peche mortel'.[54] (The 1285 *gravamen*, discussed above, may well have had her in mind.) Grosseteste had pushed the logic to its conclusion: Jews should be most strictly forbidden to practice usury. Instead they should be made to provide for themselves by working with their own hands, not by exploiting Christians.[55] Aquinas was to offer the same advice to the sister of Louis IX, Margaret of Brabant.[56] Peckham was of the same mind.[57] But between Grosseteste and Peckham the rigorous stance about usury and its practical consequence, the prohibition of money-lending by Jews, had made an important advance. From being the attitude of the schools and reforming bishops, it had become the official policy of Christendom's leading royal exemplar. King Louis IX thought it his duty to protect his subjects from Jewish oppression and to disengage his government from involvement with money immorally obtained. In 1235 he had ordered that the Jews of the royal domain should live by work of their own hands. In 1254, on his return from crusade, he promulgated the same order in an *Ordonnance* for the whole kingdom.[58] In 1275 Edward I fell into line, and the bishops were determined to hold him to it.

H. G. Richardson thought Edward's piety was that of Louis IX,[59] and more recently it has been suggested that 'Edward's piety should not be dismissed lightly'.[60] Edward himself predictably was to claim religious motivation. When he

---

[53] 'Sciant itaque principes qui eos fovent vel eis favent in usuris a christianis, se esse reos peccati eorum, ut sic futuros participes poenae eorum. Quia sicut dicit beatus Paulus: *Non solum qui talia agunt, sed qui agentibus consentiunt, morte digni sunt* (Rom. 1.32). Et sicut dicunt sancti expositores omnes, reputantur consentientes, qui cum possint impedire, et non impediunt. Principes quoque qui de usuris, quas Judaei a Christianis extorserunt, aliquid accipiunt, de rapina vivunt, et sanguinem eorum quos tueri deberent, sine misericordia comedunt, bibunt': *Roberti Grosseteste Episcopi Lincolniensis Epistolae*, ed. H. R. Luard (RS, 1861), v. 36.

[54] 'Ovekes co, pur Dieu, madame, quaunt vuz recevez terre ou manoir, encuru par usure de Juis, pernez vus garde . . .': *Registrum epistolarum Iohannis Peckham, archiepiscopi Cantuariensis*, ed. C. T. Martin (RS, 1884 – 5), ii. 619 (Sept. 1283). Douie, 328. In Dec. 1286 Peckham was still trying to persuade her not to acquire lands which Jews had extorted from Christians by usury: *Reg. Peckham*, iii. 937 – 8.

[55] 'Debentque principes qui eos tenent captivos, ne occidantur defendere, et insimul, ne christianos usuris opprimant, severissime prohibere; et ut de licitis manuum suarum laboribus victum sibi acquirant, providere': *Roberti Grosseteste Epistolae*, v. 34.

[56] 'Melius enim esset ut Iudaeos laborare compellerent ad proprium victum lucrandum, sicut in partibus Italiae faciunt, quam quod otiosi viventes solis usuris ditentur, et sic eorum domini suis reditibus defraudentur': *De reg. Iud.* 730, p. 250.

[57] 'Coget etiam (regia clementia) eos vivere de labore manuum suarum vel industria mercature . . .': *CS* II. ii. 962.

[58] Excellent account of Louis IX's anti-usury campaign in R. Chazan, *Medieval Jewry in Northern France. A Political and Social History* (Baltimore, London, 1973). See esp. 103 – 24.

[59] Richardson, 225.

[60] M. Prestwich, 'The Piety of Edward I', in *England in the Thirteenth Century. Procs. of the 1984 Harlaxton Symposium*, ed. W. M. Ormrod (Grantham, 1985), 120.

expelled the Jews in 1290, he asserted that he did so to save Christians from further oppression by Jewish usury, and 'ob honorem Crucifixi'.[61] But in finding a place for royal piety in the fashioning of royal policy we should not concede it pride of place. It is difficult to resist the conclusion that moral and pious arguments were being used to rationalize more mundane purposes of royal finance.[62]

---

[61] Text in *Select Pleas, Starrs and other Records from the Rolls of the Exchequer of the Jews (1220 – 1284)*, ed. J. M. Rigg (Selden Soc., xv for 1901, 1902), xl – xli. Edward had taken the Cross in 1287; in 1290 he still hoped to depart for the Holy Land in 1293. Most probably, this gave additional poignancy and weight to his assertion 'ob honorem Crucifixi'. I am grateful to Dr. S. D. Lloyd for this suggestion.

[62] For an examination of how contemporary sources showed awareness of manipulation of the Jews for royal political and financial ends, S. Menache, 'The King, the Church and the Jews: Some Considerations on the Expulsions from England and France', *Journ. of Medieval History*, xiii (1987), 223 – 36.

Forest Law and the Peasantry in the Later Thirteenth Century

Jean Birrell

Discussing the position of the subject in the royal forest in a long and wide-ranging article published in 1910, Margaret Bazeley concluded that forest law was, all in all, 'even at its worst, perhaps not much more harsh than the ordinary law could be'. But she also pointed to its expense and its arbitrariness as major problems for forest dwellers. 'Fines', she said, 'if not always heavy, were numerous and imposed at every turn', and a peasant 'might get off lightly or die in prison'.[1]

Miss Bazeley was writing about the Forest of Dean, but the questions she raised about the effects of forest law have a much wider interest. This paper aims to examine some of these issues, but for a wider group of royal forests, and by concentrating on the consequence of forest law for one section of the population — the peasantry. How and to what extent did forest law affect them? Was forest law in the thirteenth century a serious obstacle to their access to the various resources (woods, game, potential arable and pastures) it contained? How significant was the financial burden it imposed, especially in the light of the many other demands on the peasantry from landlord and State towards the end of the thirteenth century? Was the 'arbitrariness' of forest law any greater or worse than that experienced in other aspects of life? Or was forest law, as some historians have tended to assume, a matter of little relevance to the peasantry — something, rather, which primarily affected lords of estates within the forest? It is the conclusion of one recent historian of the royal forest that 'throughout the Middle Ages the royal forest was an issue of the upper landholding classes', on whom 'the heaviest burden . . . fell', and that it is 'not to be identified as an issue of the lower classes'.[2]

It will be argued here that forest law did constitute a significant impediment to the activities of peasants living within the forest. The woodland of the royal forests provided a living, or part of a living, for the local peasantry on a scale that is perhaps still not fully appreciated, perhaps because it escapes many of the records conventionally used to study peasant economy. To take one obvious example, the forest provided wood and timber not just for direct use on the holding, crucial though that was, but also for sale to an expanding market — local towns, for example. There is an unusually explicit statement of this in the records of the 1272 eyre for Wychwood (Oxfordshire). The tenants of certain villages within this

---

[1] M. L. Bazeley, 'The Forest of Dean in its Relations with the Crown during the Twelfth and Thirteenth Centuries', *Trans. Bristol and Gloucestershire Archaeological Soc.* xxxiii (1910), 276. Unless otherwise stated, all manuscript references in this paper are to documents in the PRO.
[2] C. R. Young, *The Royal Forests of Medieval England* (Leicester, 1979), 171.

forest, we are told, were making on average two trips each week from the forest to Oxford and other markets to sell cartloads of wood. Eighty tenants in Combe, Stonesfield and Wootton, it is claimed, were between them responsible for well over 8000 cartloads a year, and similar, though smaller figures were quoted for other villages.[3] In addition, there were 'innumerable' cottars in some villages, and in others 'many', who were 'continually' entering the forest and extracting an 'infinite' amount of wood, both by horse and cart, and on their backs. We may treat the actual figures with some scepticism, but they clearly point to a flourishing local activity. Cutting and selling wood and timber, however, was contrary to forest law, and liable to be either impeded by the forest officers, or financially penalised, or both. And the constraints that forest law imposed on woodcutting were paralleled by constraints on other uses of the forest, to which I will return. Overall, this financial burden was heavy, and it affected large numbers of people. Furthermore, while it is possible to see forest law at this period as simply a licensing system, with the amercements imposed not so much as penalties for offences as licences to operate, such an approach risks seriously underestimating the weight of the amercements, the cumbersomeness of the procedures, and the large number of additional persons perforce involved, and often financially penalised — in the pledging system, for example. There are also indications that the forest peasantry were subject not just to the imposition of forest law, but also to harassment by forest officers on such a scale as to form a significant additional burden on them, and that this added another dimension to the consequences and unpopularity of forest law.

The main outlines of forest law are well known. The law protected 'the vert and the venison', that is the deer and their habitat or cover. Thus, not only was hunting the deer an offence, but so, too, was 'waste' or, to put it another way, exploitation of the woods within the forest.[4] Various pre-existing rights to take wood or pasture animals within the forest were protected, at least in theory. It was activities going beyond these, in particular for commercial or industrial use, which were prohibited. And, of course, what rights existed, and who possessed them, and where they should be exercised, were matters by no means always undisputed. The Forest Charter of 1217 attempted to curtail some of the worst features of forest law and the abuses committed by foresters, but it left the system basically intact.[5]

The Forest Charter also put some limits on the area subject to forest law. Nevertheless, though much reduced from its former size, the royal forest was still enormous in the thirteenth century.[6] Individual forests were numerous and large, by no means all wooded or wild, and they often contained many settlements within their boundaries. The Forest of Feckenham (Worcestershire), for example, was about 240 square miles in area and had about eighty villages and hamlets within it. The Forest of Cannock (Staffordshire) covered about 230 square miles and included

---

[3] E 32/137, m. 6. For peasant activities in forest regions, see J. Birrell, 'Peasant Craftsmen in the Medieval Forest', *Agricultural History Review*, xvii (1969), 91 – 107.

[4] The best discussion of forest law remains that of G. J. Turner in his introduction to *Select Pleas of the Forest (1209 – 1334)* (Selden Soc., xiii for 1899, 1901).

[5] Young, 67ff. For common rights, see J. Birrell, 'Common Rights in the Medieval Forest: Disputes and Conflicts in the Thirteenth Century', *Past and Present*, cxvii (1987), 22 – 47.

[6] M. L. Bazeley, 'The Extent of the English Forest in the Thirteenth Century', *TRHS* 4th ser. iv (1921), 140 – 72.

some forty settlements.[7] It needs to be emphasized, however, that actual bounds are only part of the story. As Miss Bazeley long ago showed, the forest was riddled with exemptions of one sort or another, and, in any case, forest law was not always uniformly enforced everywhere. Henry III continued the practice of his predecessors of granting privileges within the forest to great subjects, creating further complications on the ground. In particular, lords often held their woods within the forest quit of the regard; that is, they were not liable for vert offences. But however eroded, the area subject to forest law remained large, and contained, in a country in which woodland was often in short supply, a significant proportion of the remaining large tracts of woodland.

The records of the forest eyres, the chief record of the workings of forest law, survive in any number only from the second half of the thirteenth century. The records of earlier eyres have rarely survived, and few eyres were held in the fourteenth century, or even after the late 1280s. For many forests, however, we have the records of the two, three or four eyres held between mid-century and 1290. I shall be concentrating here on those for the Forests of Cannock, Wychwood (Oxfordshire), Feckenham (Worcestershire) and Dean (Gloucestershire), which together make up a fairly representative section of the big Midland forests.[8]

Eyre rolls are very long and interesting documents full of information about many aspects of medieval life, from the composition and conduct of aristocratic hunting parties, to the type of crops sown and the frequency of cropping on newly-cleared assart land. However, although the procedures of forest courts were extensively discussed by an earlier generation of historians, notably by G. J. Turner, they have been little treated since, and they are conspicuously missing from some recent discussions of medieval English law courts. Not all aspects of the procedure are clear, but by the second half of the thirteenth century the eyre roll is primarily a record of the penalities imposed at the eyre, largely cash amercements. It also reveals incidentally, in more or less detail, much of the many and diverse operations of forest law in the periods between eyres. Unfortunately, few of the intermediate records have survived except in their abbreviated recapitulations in the eyre rolls. Particularly regrettable is the loss of so many of the records of the swanimotes and attachment courts, which were held several times each year in the intervals between eyres, and where, it seems likely, a lot of business of particular relevance to the peasantry was transacted.

What do these records tell us about the effects of forest law? Let us look first at access to the wood and timber within the forests. As has been already emphasized, woodcutting was an important element in the peasant economy in forest areas, and it involved many people. The records of the forest courts make this clear. We do not know, of course, what proportion of those who cut wood in the forests 'illegally' (that is, in contravention of forest law) were never caught, and who thus escape the record. In any case, the numbers presented at the eyres, though large,

---

[7] J. West, 'The Administration and Economy of the Forest of Feckenham During the Early Middle Ages' (Birmingham Univ. MA. thesis, 1964); L. M. Cantor, 'Medieval Forests and Chases of Staffordshire', *North Staffordshire Journ. of Field Studies*, viii (1968), 44 – 6.

[8] The eyres for Cannock are E 32/187 (1262), E 32/184 (1271) and E 32/188 (1286); for Wychwood, E 32/251 (1256) and E 32/137 (1272); and for Dean, E 32/28 (1258), E 32/29 (1270) and E 32/30 (1282). The figures quoted below for Cannock, Dean and Wychwood have been calculated from these eyres; the figures for Feckenham are largely extracted from West, 'The Administration'.

represent only a proportion of the total number of offenders who were detected, being confined to those whose offences were rated sufficiently seriously to be held over to the eyre, rather than summarily dealt with at one of the attachment courts. It seems reasonable to assume that these lesser offenders were fairly numerous. The offences which could be dealt with at the attachment courts were defined in 1287 as involving 'saplings under 4*d*.',[9] and the income from the attachment courts often amounted to several pounds a year, though not all of this came from woodcutting offences.[10] The more serious offenders presented at attachment courts had to provide pledges for their appearance at the next eyre, where an amercement was imposed. The lists of vert offenders (that is, illegal woodcutters) recorded in the eyre rolls are usually swollen considerably by the inclusion of pledges who were also amerced, their offence usually consisting of failure to produce the offender at the eyre at the right time. Sometimes they also appear to have had to answer for the equipment and animals — for example, the horse and cart — used by the offender in committing his offence.

Large numbers of people were involved in one capacity or another. The combined lists of vert offenders and pledges presented at eyres held in the second half of the thirteenth century regularly run into hundreds. In the case of Cannock, for example, there were over 280 presentations at the 1262 eyre, about 140 in 1271 and about 270 in 1286. In the case of Wychwood there were over 200 offenders at the eyre of 1256 and over 300 in 1272. There were about 180 offenders in Dean in 1257, a similar number in 1270 and about 350 in 1282. At Feckenham there was one single vert offender in 1260, but nearly 200 in 1270 and nearly 350 in 1280. There were long intervals between eyres at this period, but when an eyre was held a very large number of people felt its effects.

Many offenders also acted as pledges and were amerced in both capacities, but many other people were penalised for pledging offences only. The number of the latter varies considerably, but it is always significant. In the case of Cannock, for example, there were about 150 such amercements in 1262, over forty in 1271 and over ninety in 1286. In Wychwood there were over thirty simple pledge amercements in 1256 and over fifty in 1272. In Dean there were over sixty amercements for pledge defaults alone in 1258, over seventy in 1270 and about 135 in 1282. The normal practice was for two pledges to be provided, but more, sometimes several more, were occasionally required. A dozen men fined for park-breaking at Bladon in Wychwood in 1256 (not included in the vert figures recorded above) had to provide a total of forty pledges between them — that is two, four, five, and even seven, pledges each.[11] This pledging system clearly cost large numbers of people not only time and inconvenience in court attendances, but also money in amercements for defaults, and it deserves to be taken into account as one of the factors contributing to the burden and unpopularity of forest law.

The amercements imposed were variable, ranging from a minimum of 1*s*. to as high as 1 mark or even, occasionally, £1, and overall there appears to be a tendency

[9] Turner, *Select Pleas*, 63 – 4.

[10] Turner, *Select Pleas*, 47; Young, 80.

[11] It is interesting to compare these figures with those calculated for a general eyre by C. A. F. Meekings, *Crown Pleas of the Wiltshire Eyre, 1249* (Wiltshire Archaeological and Natural History Soc., Record Branch, xvi, 1961), 102 – 3.

for them to get heavier with each eyre. For example, in Cannock the amercements imposed in 1262 were mostly 1*s*., averaging about 1*s*. 3*d*.; in 1271 there were no amercements of 1*s*., but more heavier amercements, up to £1, averaging just over 4*s*. (The amercements imposed at the 1286 eyre are not recorded.) In Feckenham the amercements averaged about 1*s*. in 1270, but about 1*s*. 8*d*. in 1280. In Wychwood they averaged about 1*s*. 6*d*. in 1256, most amercements being 1*s*. or 2*s*., but they averaged about 2*s*. in 1272, with more amercements in the range of several shillings.

The amercements imposed for pledging offences alone were, in general, rather smaller than those for vert, or vert along with pledging default, but not always and not all that much so. In Wychwood, for example, when Walter son of Saloman was amerced 4*s*. at the 1256 eyre for taking an oak, his two pledges were amerced 4*s*. and 2*s*. respectively; the two pledges of William son of Stephen, amerced 2*s*. for a similar offence at the same eyre, were amerced 1*s*. each. The average amercement for vert offenders (or vert and pledging offenders) at the Wychwood eyre of 1256 was 1*s*. 10*d*., and 1*s*. 5*d*. for pledging defaults alone; in 1272 amercements averaged about 2*s*. for each group. In Dean the comparable figures were 2*s*. 5*d*. and 1*s*. 8*d*. in 1258, 2*s*. 6*d*. and 2*s*. in 1270, and 3*s*. 2*d*. and 8*d*. in 1282.

How heavy a burden was this on the people concerned? This is, of course, difficult to assess for a number of reasons. Many of those amerced had committed purely 'procedural' offences. For the rest, we often do not know the precise nature of the offence, or whether the wood was being taken for the offender's own use or for sale. The latter seems more likely to be the case with offences 'major' enough to be reserved for the eyre, rather than dealt with at the attachment court. It could be argued that an amercement of a few shillings, even though large in comparison with contemporary wages — which might be 1*d*. or 2*d*. a day for an unskilled worker — or in terms of the corn it would buy, might have been very small beer to someone operating as a woodcutter on a large scale. On the whole, however, this seems unlikely to have been the case for most of those amerced, and several indications point to the opposite conclusion. The sheer numbers involved would suggest that for individuals the activity was small-scale, and all the positive indications suggest that it was essentially a by-occupation of the peasantry. Offenders can often be identified — for example, as assarters of small pieces of arable land in the forest. Also, every list of vert offenders and their pledges includes a sprinkling of people whose amercements were excused because of their poverty. Whilst this does not necessarily mean unrelieved or abject poverty — some 'paupers' had carts and oxen — it can hardly have been applicable to prosperous operators.[12]

Some, but a minority, of offenders are presented for more than one offence; all, of course, may have committed more offences than those for which they were fined. But exceptional larger-scale activities, such as the widespread and highly organized charcoal-burning and iron-making found in the Forest of Dean at this period,[13] are normally entered separately from run-of-the-mill vert offences (and such cases have not been included in the figures quoted above). The vert offences reserved for eyres were major compared with those dealt with at attachment courts,

[12] For a recent discussion of the significance of fines excused on grounds of poverty, see M. T. Clanchy, *Civil Pleas of the Wiltshire Eyre, 1249* (Wiltshire Rec. Soc., xxvi, 1971), 18.
[13] C. E. Hart, *Royal Forest: A History of Dean's Woods as Producers of Timber* (Oxford, 1966), 43 – 9.

but they nevertheless seem in general to have been fairly minor — for example, taking a single oak or some other tree, or a 'master' branch, or a cartload of wood. Also, the amercements seem large in relation to what was taken. Where valuations of the wood 'stolen' have survived, along with the amercements imposed — for example, at the Nottingham eyre of 1334 — the latter are in general two or three times the value of the wood, which was, of course, confiscated.[14] The amercements also seem high in comparison with the ½ mark normally demanded from lords of private woods within the forest for 'waste', which often consisted of permitting assarting or felling on a scale far greater than that of typical vert offences. The amercements must have hit individuals with differing degrees of severity depending on their circumstances, but it is important to bear in mind that small sums were important to peasants operating on the edge of subsistence, and it is dangerous to dismiss even the lowest amercements, of 1s. or 2s., as either negligible or as no more than licences.

It is also worth looking at the amercements in terms of the considerable cumulative burden they could represent for forest villages. Amercements for vert offences in Cannock totalled £15 12s. 8d. in 1262 and £24 2s. 8d. in 1272. In Feckenham amercements totalled £9 18s. in 1270 and £29 12s. 8d. in 1280. In Wychwood vert amercements totalled £16 7s. 5d. in 1256 and £27 8s. 4d. in 1272. Offenders and their pledges typically came from many different forest villages, but there are clear concentrations, as if the economy of certain villages, presumably those in the more wooded parts of the forest, was more strongly forest-oriented. At the Dean eyre of 1282, for example, vert amercements totalling £5 13s. 4d. were imposed on St. Briavels (on sixteen offenders), £5 11s. 10d. on Ruardin (fifty-five offenders), £3 1s. 10d. on Lydney (thirty-two offenders), and £2 11s. 4d. on Bicknor (thirty-two offenders). In Wychwood, on men from Coombe, about forty amercements were imposed in 1256 and sixty in 1272; on men from Stonesfield, twenty-one were imposed in 1256, and thirty-four in 1272. For villages such as these the amercements imposed at each eyre amounted to a heavy tax on their woodcutting activities.

Amercements for vert offences were only part of the burden a forest eyre imposed on local communities. The second main element in forest law at this period was the protection of the deer. From the point of view of the king, this was much more profitable in cash terms. Although amercements for venison offences were far fewer in number than for vert offences, they were consistently so much higher that they added up to much more money. In Cannock, where the number of amercements levied for venison offences was never very high — fewer than thirty at each of the three late thirteenth-century eyres — the sums nevertheless amounted to about £36, £75, and the enormous sum of £364 respectively, though this last sum is inflated by two very high atypical fines. In Dean, where poaching was on a larger scale and amercements more numerous, a total of 102 amercements imposed in 1282 added up to £194. In Feckenham fifty-four offenders were amerced £157 in 1270 and 148 were amerced nearly £340 in 1280.

For our purposes, however, these figures need explanation. In the first place, the number of offenders amerced is a gross underestimate of the number of people

---

[14] H. E. Boulton, *The Sherwood Forest Book* (Thoroton Soc., Rec. Ser., xxiii, 1964), 105: see also Turner, *Select Pleas*, 67 – 8.

involved in this aspect of forest law. In the case of Cannock, for example, there were over ninety persons presented for venison offences in 1262, about 117 in 1271 and about 134 in 1286 (several of them presented for more than one offence), compared with the twenty-six, twenty-six, and twenty-eight people respectively recorded as amerced. These proportions seem not to have been at all exceptional. In Dean, the 102 amercements in 1282 came from 278 offenders. In Feckenham 258 people were presented for venison offences at the 1270 eyre and 298 in 1280, figures which dwarf the fifty-four and 148 people amerced. And as far as poaching is concerned, these are minimum numbers; men described as 'repeated' or 'habitual' offenders, of which there were many, have been counted only once, and no allowance has been made for the unidentified offenders, the *alii ignoti*, so often declared to have been guilty of offences. Nor do they allow for the unknown number of offences which either were never detected, or never reached the eyre. A large number of people were involved in poaching in one way or another. However, a high proportion of people charged with venison offences failed to attend the eyre or escaped penalties. There were many reasons for this: some of the offenders were dead, others were servants covered by amercements imposed on their masters, yet others were soldiers serving in the king's army abroad at the time of the eyre and were thus pardoned. But many others fled rather than appear at the eyre, a point to which I will return.

Also, the venison offenders, to a much greater extent than the vert offenders, were no by means typically from the peasantry. The occasional manorial lord is identifiable amongst the vert offenders, but everything suggests that they came mainly from the peasantry. Amongst the venison offenders, on the contrary, barons, bishops, parish priests and the local gentry and their households predominated.[15] The status of offenders is normally not stated explicitly, and precise figures are therefore very difficult to calculate,[16] but status can be deduced often enough for it to be clear that peasant poachers amounted to a significant minority of the total. Whatever the conventions of courtly literature, or whatever the aristocratic ethos, peasants did take deer in the royal forests, sometimes operating alone or with trusted friends or relatives, sometimes in gangs composed of poachers from one or more forest villages. They often used methods (such as snares and traps) which their social superiors scorned, and much peasant poaching was peripheral or parasitical, consisting of the spiriting-away of carcasses either lost or abandoned by other poachers, or dead of disease, or of the seizure of deer which came too close to the village. Peasants were probably responsible for the death of far fewer deer than poachers from higher up the social scale, but it is mistaken to regard their interest in the deer as negligible.

In any case, they were heavily involved, willy-nilly, in the legal procedures, through the pledging system and through the 'inquisitions of the four nearest townships', which were held when a dead deer was found — a macabre copy of the coroner's inquests held to investigate unexplained human deaths. This system was clearly being abused at this period, especially in the earlier eyres. In the first place, when inquisitions were summoned, the townships involved were almost invariably

---

[15] J. Birrell, 'Who Poached the King's Deer?', *Midland History*, vii (1982), 11–13, 17.
[16] But West, 'The Administration', 161 ff., has calculated that about half of those presented at the 1270 Feckenham eyre were poaching for social reasons, about two-thirds in 1280.

amerced for default. The expression employed, viz. 'not coming fully', may mean, as Turner assumed, a failure to provide the required information, or it may simply mean an attendance judged to be numerically insufficient. Whatever the reason, such amercements were so common as to be almost universal. Also, more than the four townships formally required to attend were regularly summoned. At the Cannock eyre of 1262, for example, as many as six, eight, or even ten townships at a time were involved with single cases, and all of them, without exception, amerced for default.

These amercements together added up to substantial sums. In 1262, for example, at the Cannock eyre, twenty-six villages were amerced a total of £7 1s., the amercements ranging from 3s. to 10s.; in 1271, twenty-four villages were amerced a total of £6, the amercements ranged from nothing — one village was excused because of poverty — to 1 mark; and in 1286 eighteen villages were amerced a total of £6 13s. 4d., the amercements ranging from 3s. 4d. to 1 mark. These figures are by no means abnormal. In Dean, between twenty-one and twenty-three villages were amerced a total of £13 7s. 4d. (an average of nearly 12s. each), £15 6s. 8d. (nearly 14s. each), and £8 10s. (8s. each) respectively in 1258, 1270 and 1282.[17] In Wychwood, twenty-three villages were amerced a total of £18 0s. 8d. (an average of nearly 16s. each), and seventeen villages £12 4s. (an average of just over 14s. each) in 1272. Whilst we are not told how these sums were levied on the villages, it seems reasonable to assume that it was their peasant inhabitants who bore the brunt. Both the financial burden and the procedures must have been disliked. As a general rule, the eyre rolls simply record the fines without comment, but hostility to the system is occasionally recorded explicitly. At the 1255 eyre for Rockingham, for example, it was said that the township of Wadenhoe had initially refused to assist the hue and cry raised by the foresters against 'evildoers' who they had spotted in the forest carrying bows and arrows; Wadenhoe had then attended the inquisition of the four nearest townships, but had refused to answer. The three other townships were also unable — or possibly unwilling — to provide information. All were duly amerced.[18]

Peasants were also involved as pledges for peasant venison offenders, both for their appearance at the eyre and then for the payment of whatever amercement was imposed, either then or for their future good conduct. Numerous pledges were often demanded, and as many as six or twelve is not uncommon. And, as with vert offences, the pledges were themselves likely to be amerced. At the 1282 Dean eyre nearly 300 pledges and mainpasts were amerced in connection with venison offences, a total of about £25. In a by no means untypical case in Cannock, Geoffrey and Richard, two men from Fradley, a hamlet on the manor of Alrewas, took a roe deer in Alrewas Hay in 1254. At this point their luck ended. They were discovered by two local under-foresters who appropriated the carcass for their own use and took 3s. as the price of their silence. The case nevertheless became known, and Geoffrey, Richard and the two foresters were all presented at the 1262 eyre. Geoffrey and Richard were imprisoned, but released on finding four pledges to pay an amercement of 1 mark. They probably also had to make an unrecorded payment to secure their release from prison, and other payments and sweeteners

[17] Bazeley, 'Forest of Dean', 254.
[18] Turner, *Select Pleas*, 27; see also 9.

were probably involved throughout.[19] In addition, ten men in Geoffrey's case and eleven in Richard's, from Fradley and Alrewas, were amerced because the two poachers had not attended on the first day of the eyre. These amercements totalled 18*s*. In addition, two of the four presenting villages, Alrewas and Kings Bromley, were amerced 10*s*. each, though this was a cumulative fine covering other defaults. So a grand total of four villages and over twenty pledges were penalised for the poaching of one roe deer, and amercements amounting to £2 11*s*. 4*d*. imposed.

As far as the peasantry are concerned, being deprived of, or restricted in access to, the deer should be seen as a significant loss, and not an irrelevance to their lives. Venison was eaten by peasants when the opportunity arose, though in what quantity it is difficult to gauge. No doubt they would have eaten more, but for forest law. After all, it constituted a very useful additional source of meat. Venison was also, perhaps, just as important for the peasantry as a potential source of cash income. Not all peasant poachers had as convenient a market as that which Bristol and other towns provided for the Forest of Dean: there was a regular illegal export of venison, as there was of wood and timber, via a series of ports along the Severn estuary.[20] But receivers appear in the records of all forests, and it seems likely that a lot of poached deer was intended for sale.

Amercements on venison offenders were assessed according to the wealth of the offender, and are so variable that average sums are not very helpful. Amercements of ½ or 1 mark are common at the lower end of the scale, with very high sums like 200 marks or £200 at the other, though these were not always paid. The tendency for amercements to increase, as Miss Bazeley noted for Dean,[21] can equally be seen in Cannock; in that forest, twelve out of twenty-six amercements were of less than 1 mark in 1262, but only two out of twenty-six in 1271, and six out of twenty-eight in 1286. Again, we must remember that amercements of ½ mark, 1 mark, or £1 represented a considerable sum, even to peasant offenders who were quite prosperous, which, clearly, many of those amerced were not. Pardons on account of poverty were not uncommon. Also, the fact that so many venison offenders fled, risking outlawry, rather than face appearance at the eyre, must be significant. The heavy fines and numerous pledges were presumably a prime cause.

Obviously, forest law affected individuals very unevenly. For some, it closed off certain opportunities but may otherwise have had relatively little impact. For others, as offenders, pledges or simply as contributors to township amercements, the burden may have been heavy. Overall, amercements levied at the eyres of the second half of the thirteenth century must cumulatively have been heavy enough to have had an adverse local impact. It is true that eyres were infrequent at this period, though we must not forget in this context the attachment courts held between one eyre and the next. We must also bear in mind that the forest eyres weighed on a peasantry facing increasing pressure from other sources. Villages were no doubt unevenly affected, but for some the eyre was comparable, in venison and vert amercements alone, with one of the contemporary lay subsidies, and affected as

---

[19] Miss Bazeley quotes payments of ½ mark and 1 mark from the mid-thirteenth century: Bazeley, 'Forest of Dean', 261–2.
[20] Hart, 41; Birrell, 'Who Poached the King's Deer?', 20.
[21] Bazeley, 'Forest of Dean', 263.

many, if not necessarily the same, people.[22] For example, Kings Bromley was a Cannock forest village where fourteen taxpayers paid a total of £2 8s. ½d. in the 1327 lay subsidy, the earliest to survive for Staffordshire.[23] Many of its inhabitants supplemented their incomes with woodcutting in the forest; fourteen were fined as vert offenders in 1262, sixteen in 1271 and eighteen in 1286. Others turned to poaching, and men from Kings Bromley were presented for this at all three of these eyres. Amercements totalling £2 13s. 8d. and £7 13s. 4d. in connection with vert and venison offences alone can be traced at the eyres of 1262 and 1271, and a reasonable estimate of amercements imposed in 1286 would be £3 4s. Alrewas, another Cannock village, also supplied both poachers and vert offenders at all three eyres; their amercements totalled at least £2 14s. in 1262, £1 15s. 4d. in 1271, and probably about £3 14s. 8d. in 1286. This compares with the £3 which the thirty taxpayers of Alrewas paid to the lay subsidy of 1327.

The third major element in the proceedings of the forest eyre was the regard, the procedure by which assarts made within the forest were recorded and charged for. It has become a commonplace that the royal forests represented the last great reserves of assartable land in England by the late thirteenth century, and assarting, under way almost from the foundation of the royal forests, was able to continue therein well into the fourteenth century. The forest dwellers were in this sense, too, lucky in the opportunities they enjoyed. However, the land did not come free. It is worth remembering in this context that lords had been prepared, from the twelfth century onwards, to pay substantial sums of money to hold their lands inside the forest 'quit of the regard' — that is, assartable, though remaining liable to other aspects of forest law, in particular the parts relating to venison. They wanted, presumably, not just freedom to assart, but freedom from the financial burden of forest law on assarts, and wanted this both on their own behalf and on that of their tenants. Permitting assarts of woodland could certainly be profitable. The bishop of Coventry and Lichfield, for example, was charging his tenants entry fines as high as 10s. an acre for new assarts in Cannock Chase, formerly part of the royal forest of Cannock, in the early fourteenth century.[24]

But not every lord had been able, like the bishop of Coventry and Lichfield, to take his manors out of the forest, and large areas remained within, and subject to, the regard. The eyres regularly record long lists of assarts with the amercements imposed for them. The lists suggest that forest assarting at this period was typically an activity of the peasantry, with the vast majority of assarts being very small, many consisting, indeed, of fractions of acres. They were often the result of collaboration between tenants, and some were communally made and held. In Cannock, for example, twenty-six acres of assart reported at the 1262 eyre lay in about thirty pieces, 186½ acres reported in 1271 in about 126 pieces, and 636 acres recorded in 1286 in about 364 pieces. These are entirely typical figures.

[22] Cf. the comments of Meekings, *Crown Pleas*, 8, with regard to the general eyres of Henry III. For the weight of taxation and other levies on the peasantry, see J. R. Maddicott, *The English Peasantry and the Demands of the Crown 1294–1341*, Past and Present Supplement 1 (1975); E. Miller, 'War, Taxation and the English Economy in the Late Thirteenth Century and Early Fourteenth Century', in *Wars and Economic Development*, ed. J. M. Winter (Cambridge, 1975), 17–18.
[23] *Staffordshire Historical Collections*, vii (1886), 197ff.
[24] J. Birrell, 'Medieval Agriculture', in *VCH Staffordshire*, vi. 36.

These assarts were not, of course, in any sense assarts of 'unclaimed' land, but of land held by some lord, or the king himself, within the bounds of the forest. It must be assumed that lords of fees within the forest had encouraged these assarts on their land or in their woods. The eyre rolls normally record not only who had made and who currently held the assart, but also who held the fee in which it was situated, though not, of course, any financial arrangements made between lord and tenant. In any case, the assarters also had to answer to the regarders. Although there was variation between forests and over time, the normal practice was for assarters to be required to pay a sum of money for making the 'illegal' assart and for permission to keep it, along with a payment for every crop so far grown on it; the former was usually equivalent to a few shillings an acre, the latter was usually 1*s.* per acre for winter sown crops, and 6*d.* per acre for spring sown crops (with no payment for years when the assarts lay fallow or otherwise uncultivated). The payments are in theory carried forward from one eyre to the next, each list recording 'old' and 'new' assarts separately. Again, practice varies, but in general, though the lists of old assarts grow longer, they do not go on growing indefinitely; some of the old assarts are 'lost'.[25] Of these, some may have been lost to cultivation (assarts in the forest were often of poorish land), others were probably just lost to forest law, and absorbed into village fields.

From the point of view of the king, assarts in the royal forests were highly lucrative. Formal arrentations of hundreds of acres of land were often initiated by royal officers, especially in the second half of the thirteenth century and in the early fourteenth, in order to raise cash. But, in any case, the normal procedures of the regard and eyre brought in useful sums. The income from the regard was often second only to amercements on venison offenders as a source of royal income from forest eyres. In the case of Cannock, for example, though only just over £3 at the 1262 eyre, income from the regard was nearly £24 in 1272 and nearly £24 in 1286. The process was profitable to the king, though it was clearly to some extent an impoverishment of the lords of estates within the forest. The peasant assarters were caught either way.

Lastly, we need to consider relations at this period between the peasantry of forest villages and the foresters, that is the officers responsible for the protection and administration of the forests on behalf of the king. Foresters have had a fairly uniformly bad press from historians, as, indeed, they had in the Middle Ages, being notorious on the one hand for their exploitation of the forests they were supposed to protect, and on the other for their harassment of local people. Abuses by foresters had always been an issue, serious enough to merit several clauses in the Forest Charter of 1217. The situation appears, however, to have been relatively little changed in the late thirteenth century, when many of the abuses supposedly checked in 1217 were still rife.

There is evidence from a variety of sources. There are, for example, general complaints about abuses, such as the long list of grievances presented by the men of the forests of Somerset, Mendip and Exmoor, dating from 1278, most of which relate to abuses by foresters.[26] Such complaints were not purely formal; there were frequent detailed accusations against specific foresters, especially at the eyres of

---

[25] The subject is discussed in J. Raftis, *Assart Data and Land Values* (Toronto, 1974), 100–9.
[26] Turner, *Select Pleas*, 125–8.

1269 – 71, when the justices seem to have made a point of enquiring into foresters' conduct. Best known, perhaps, are those made against Peter de Neville, warden of Rutland Forest, in 1269, but he was clearly not unique.[27] Caution must obviously be exercised when dealing with complaints about abuses, and they should not necessarily be taken at face value. But the persistence of the complaints seems to leave little doubt that foresters, whether hereditary or appointed, 'riding' or 'walking', were accustomed to behave in a way which was deplorable by contemporary standards. The recorded complaints tend, for obvious reasons, to come from the local gentry or above, and explicit expressions of grievances by peasants may be lacking. But there was no shortage of grounds for them. There is a sufficient degree of consistency about the complaints from different sources to suggest that certain types of abuse, of a nature likely to weigh heavily on the peasant class, were both fairly general and persistent.

The 1271 eyre for Cannock provides a good example. It records not only various foresters' improper exploitation of forest resources, in particular the wood and timber, for their own benefit (and thus to the disadvantage of the king), but also extortion and harassment of the local population. The major offender was Hugh de Evesham, riding forester for the whole of Cannock for some years in the 1260s. Some offences he was said to have committed himself; others were attributed to under-foresters he had appointed. Indeed, one of the allegations against him was that he had replaced foresters very frequently, taking large fines from each one on entry and thus encouraging them to recoup their costs at the expense of the local inhabitants. This was a familiar practice; in Rutland, Peter de Neville was accused of appointing too many foresters, more than were needed to protect the forest, which inevitably increased the burden on local inhabitants; and this was also one of the grievances of the men of Somerset.

Hugh de Evesham was also alleged to have collected and pocketed amercements for offences which should have been dealt with at the eyre, with the money received going to the king. About twenty-five of his 'victims', from whom Hugh had taken sums ranging from 3s. to 23s., were named. There is clearly an element of extortion, not just diversion of funds, here. One offender had been imprisoned for a night and a day before he paid up. This, too, is reminiscent of Peter de Neville's offences in the forest of Rutland, though he was additionally alleged to have imprisoned people in 'iron chains', and in a gaol with water at the bottom.

Hugh de Evesham and his foresters had also been levying cheminage in Cannock unjustly; that is, they had been collecting a toll on carts passing through the forest carrying goods which did not originate in the forest, and which were thus not liable. They had been taking, we are told, 4d., 1s., even 2s. per cart. Again, this was a familiar abuse. In Rutland, Peter de Neville had been levying cheminage where it was not customary, as well as for his own benefit, and abuse of cheminage figured large in the grievances of the men of Mendip and Selwood (Somerset) in 1278.

It was also alleged that Hugh and his foresters had been collecting pannage dues for pigs driven into Cannock forest but not pannaged in the demesne woods. Lastly, they had been abusing the lawing of dogs — that is, the practice whereby the paws of dogs kept in the forest had to be mutilated to prevent them from chasing the deer.

---

[27] Turner, *Select Pleas*, 44 – 53, lxviii – lxix; also Bazeley, 'Forest of Dean', 189ff.

This practice, much resented, had been limited by the Forest Charter of 1217 to those districts in which it had been customary at the accession of Henry II. It was also to be performed according to a fixed rule — that is, three toes cut from the front foot. In Cannock, as in many other forests, it seems to have been relatively unimportant by the second half of the thirteenth century, and it was hardly mentioned at either the 1262 or the 1286 eyre. But prior to 1271, we are told, Hugh de Evesham, with the assistance of a clerk whom he improperly presented as being the clerk of the justices of the forest, had been insisting on it, and had levied large sums by this method. Worse, Hugh and his clerk were not satisfied with any sort of lawing ('noluit esse contentus de aliquo modo expeditare'), but if the right back-paw was lawed said it should be the left, and vice-versa. Lawing of dogs also figures amongst the Somerset grievances.

This by no means exhausts the list of familiar late thirteenth-century abuses, and such abuses continued. Amongst the extortions alleged in 1316, for example, against one of Hugh's successors in Cannock, John de Whetales, was his extraction of 67s. from the villagers of Alrewas for permission to re-erect hedges which he had himself destroyed.[28] The lists of abuses could be extended, but to little purpose. The point is that abuses were, if not constant and universal, at least common and widespread, and of a type to make them burdensome to forest dwellers at all levels, including the peasantry. For obvious reasons, the major offenders were the more important foresters who could exercise the greatest power. Under-foresters were often local men of modest status, and their ability to oppress was accordingly restricted. However, derelictions of duty of one type or another, not necessarily at the expense of their neighbours, were by no means uncommon at this level, and the local communities could once again suffer through the pledging system. Lesser foresters were required to provide pledges for the proper performance of their duties, and these men ran the risk of being amerced for the foresters' failings. At the 1271 Cannock eyre, for example, the pledges of eight offending lesser foresters were all amerced, a total of forty-four men from sixteen forest villages. One was pardoned as a pauper, and the largest amercement was 1 mark; a total of £12 16s. 8d. was levied. The amercements of four of the foresters were also recorded, and together amounted to £2 13s. 4d.

Surviving complaints about forest law, as has been said, inevitably come from the substantial free men of the neighbourhood, and the attitude of lesser men has, for the most part, to be deduced. Attacks on foresters in connection with poaching offences are by no means uncommon, but these seem typically to be the acts of a rough element amongst the lesser gentry, out for sport and excitement, and bearing arms. A more typical response on the part of peasant poachers seems to have been to hide or flee.[29] There is, however, as indicated above, some evidence of refusal to co-operate with the procedures for catching humble venison offenders.

A quite different and very striking manifestation of hostility to foresters and forest law occurred in Cannock in 1288. In June of that year a gang of over 180 men attacked the steward of the forest, Philip de Montgomery, and two of his foresters. The sequence of events is not absolutely clear; we have only the complaint made by

---

[28] E 32/191.
[29] Birrell, 'Who Poached the King's Deer?', 15 – 16, 21; Turner, *Select Pleas*, 3, 83.

Philip in the king's court in 1289.[30] The gang, by his account, had insulted him at Alrewas, then sought out and carried off forest plea rolls in the custody of his clerk at Lichfield, where the Cannock eyres were usually held; they had also beaten, ill-treated and imprisoned two foresters. Alrewas, some four or five miles north of Lichfield, was a manor where the stewards of Cannock held land (at Fradley, a hamlet on the manor). Although the rioters are named, we are not told where they came from. They included at least a sprinkling of craftsmen: a barber and two tailors certainly, and, if we rely on surname evidence, several more, including a barker, a fuller, a couple of smiths, a butcher, a baker, a carpenter and a cooper, amongst others. There were also several chaplains and clerks, including the first two accused, Adam and William Balle. A few certainly, and probably more, came from Lichfield itself, and some of the others can be identified as tenants of episcopal manors nearby.[31] We do not, unfortunately, know exactly what it was that sparked off this particular incident, causing this particular group of people to take the dangerous step of turning on the steward of the forest, his officers and the forest records. The defendants denied culpability and Philip eventually withdrew his suit against them. No more, it appears, is heard of this particular affair.

We do know, however, that Philip offended many other people in the course of his career in Cannock. At the time of the 1286 eyre he had only recently been appointed steward, and the eyre roll records little of his doings. There is plenty of other evidence, however, of his arbitrary behaviour when steward. A series of complaints against him were made in the county court in 1293 relating to offences dating back almost a decade.[32] These ranged from consistent failure to pay to the exchequer the annual farm of 10 marks for Cannock, which he denied he owed, to various extortions of the familiar sort in the neighbourhood. In 1290, for example, he had impounded a mare found in the forest and retained both it and its new born foal, though the owner, a widow of Kings Bromley, had persistently attempted to regain it. In 1287 he had locked up a certain Henry, son of Henry of Whittington for six weeks, most of the time at Fradley, but taking him at one point to Stafford gaol 'ad modem latronis'; this was after a deer shot with arrows had wandered through a swanimote where Philip was presiding, and Henry, found lurking nearby, had been suspected. Philip's main offence, according to the plea roll, had been to have Henry taken within the bishop of Coventry and Lichfield's liberty, and therefore technically outside the forest. In 1288 Philip's brother, Roger, then apparently a forester in Cannock, had beaten up a certain Ralph Quentin of Fradley and his wife, then pregnant, breaking her arm and two ribs. Philip's various misdeeds, prominent amongst them, no doubt, his refusal to pay the farm, cost him the stewardship in 1293. He seems, however, to have been back in possession at the time of his death in 1295, a by no means unusual result for a high forest officer whose misdeeds had forced some action to be taken against him.[33]

---

[30] KB 27/118, m. 21d; printed in part in *Staffs. Hist. Colls.*, vi, part 1 (1885), 184. For other activities of Philip de Montgomery, see R. C. Palmer, *The Whilton Dispute 1264–1380* (Princeton, 1984), 116–17, 121, 122, 128, 132–45.

[31] These identifications are mostly made by comparison with the 1298 survey of the bishop's estate: Stafford Record Office, D 1734, J 2268. I am grateful to the staff of the *VCH Staffordshire* for assistance with some Lichfield identifications.

[32] *Staffs. Hist. Colls.* vi, part 1(1885), 233, 251–5.

[33] M. W. Greenslade and A. Kettle, 'Forests', in *VCH Staffordshire*, ii. 339.

For the peasantry, living in the royal forest was by no means without its advantages. The woods and pastures were a precious resource, making possible a range of activities denied to many elsewhere. Common rights to pastures and woodland were, in general, generous compared with those of areas of more intensive arable cultivation. It is significant that Edward I singled this out when being forced into recognizing disafforestations in 1305; he reminded the people of newly disafforested areas that they would lose the pasture rights within the forest that they had previously enjoyed, unless, of course, they opted to re-enter the forest to regain them — an option, it appears, no villages chose.[34] Forest law did not prevent exploitation of woodland resources, which, in the thirteenth century at least, was very far from its intention, but it presented obstacles to it. Eyres were infrequent, and the enforcement of forest law was probably very uneven in the intervening periods, depending on a range of local and national circumstances. But when eyres were held their impact was felt by large numbers of people, and more than just those who had been exploiting forest resources. The effects of the normal constraints of forest law were aggravated by the lawless and arbitrary behaviour which was widely found amongst the foresters themselves, whose large-scale exploitation of the forests on their own account cannot have made their harassment of others more palatable. The peasantry had as much reason as any in the thirteenth century to dislike, and long for, the disappearance of forest law.

[34] C. Petit-Dutaillis, 'The Forest', in id., *Studies and Notes Supplementary to Stubbs' Constitutional History*, trans. W. R. Rhodes, *et al.* (Manchester, 1908 – 29), ii. 225 – 6; Young, 141.

Edward I and the French: Rivalry and Chivalry

Malcolm Vale

The heraldic poem on the siege of Caerlaverock (1300) described the qualities expressed by Edward I's arms in terms of contrasting, but complementary, attributes of kingship. 'On his banner', wrote the poet, 'were three leopards of fine gold set on a red ground,

> '*Courant*, fierce [*feloun*], haughty and cruel [*harouge*],
> Placed there to signify that,
> Like them, towards his enemies
> The King is haughty, dreadful and proud;
> For none experience his bite
> Who are not envenomed by it.
> But he is soon revived
> With sweet good-naturedness [*débonaireté*],
> If they seek his friendship,
> And wish to come to his peace.'[1]

Edward's warlike, vindictive and pacific qualities found simultaneous expression in many aspects of his behaviour, but a dominant theme of his later years was undoubtedly conflict with France. From the peace-making and arbitration of the period before 1294 a transition to sustained warfare took place. Before that date we are presented with the image of a peace-loving ruler seeking to establish concord among the princes of Europe, moved by the interests of Holy Church and the promptings of a crusader's conscience.[2] In November 1294, as war with Philip the Fair of France loomed, Edward was seeking the prayers of the Franciscan chapter-general assembled at Assisi that 'the present tempestuous time be succeeded by a more tranquil one'.[3] Sir Maurice Powicke was emphatic in his belief that 'outside the British Isles and Gascony, Edward could do very little but try to bring his troublesome relations to come to terms with each other'.[4] In Powicke's account, Edward assumes the role of a benevolent uncle, striving, but often vainly, to

---

[1] *The Roll of Arms of the princes, barons and knights who attended King Edward I to the Siege of Caerlaverock*, ed. T. Wright (London 1864), 9. Unless otherwise stated, all manuscript references in this paper are to documents in the PRO.

[2] *CPR 1281 – 92*, 419; *Foedera*, I. ii. 815.

[3] *Foedera*, I. ii. 815 (23 Nov. 1294).

[4] F. M. Powicke, *The Thirteenth Century* (2nd edn., Oxford, 1962), 245 – 6.

165

reconcile and placate a fractious group of squabbling children. His own cosmopolitan background and pedigree placed him in an ideal position for such a task. The close relationships between the courts of England, Savoy, Bar, Champagne, Brabant, Aragon, Castile, Navarre and Provence enabled him to act upon requests to arbitrate disputes with some confidence. Powicke's analysis left no room for aggression on Edward's part — he had no wish to use his extensive continental connections against France, and he had no 'policy of encirclement', by which he sought to 'fulfil a long-treasured Plantagenet plan to stir up and organise enmity to France', either in the south-east or north-west of that kingdom.[5] This may well be true of the first decades of his reign, but it could not be said of the years after 1294.

However, there is some evidence of an increased tension before 1294 between Edward's role as diplomatic arbiter and patron of chivalry and his vassalic status as a liegeman of the French Crown. This is seen at its most obvious in the Gascon problem, to which I shall shortly return. But there is a sense in which Edward's reputation as a statesman, for want of a better word, and as the foremost representative of Western knighthood, served to challenge and threaten the position of the Capetian monarchy of France. Men sought knighthood from him, and his personal arbitration of disputes, in the years 1286–9 from his own duchy of Aquitaine — between, for example, the houses of Aragon and Anjou — hardly enhanced the status of St. Louis's heir.[6] Edward's chivalric reputation was also high at this time. In October 1279 he wrote to Philip III of France, informing him that Jean de Prie, the French king's knight, had come to England and, hearing of a tournament there, had hastened towards it 'as a knight should', although a ban on tournaments had been proclaimed by Philip.[7] A similar event took place in 1290 when Jean de Nesle, knight, participated in a tournament staged on the occasion of John, duke of Brabant's visit to England during a ban upon tourneying by Philip the Fair.[8] There was, furthermore, an expectation that Philip III and Philip IV would each behave according to the chivalric code of kingly honour in his dealings with Edward and Edward's own subjects, rather than as liegelord to vassal. In 1277, for instance, Edward requested that Philip III should so rectify matters concerning the troublesome Gaston VII of Béarn 'que ce soit a la vostre honneur . . . et a honeur de roiauté et a tous seigneurs contre leurs hommes'.[9] Edward barely concealed his assertion of equality, as king of England, with the royal house of France in some of these exchanges. One of Edmund of Lancaster's assumptions about Philip IV's behaviour in 1294 was that he would act as a 'loiaux Roy'.[10] He did not, and the easy harmony of the Anglo-French family circle, extolled by Powicke, was broken.

By the early 1290s the martial attributes and aspirations of the allegedly peace-loving Edward I were becoming more marked. If Dr. Paul Binski is right, and the Maccabean victories depicted on the walls of the Painted Chamber at Westminster date from a campaign of works undertaken between 1292 and 1297, then more attention must be paid to this 'outstanding and unique reflection of the court's

[5] Powicke, 246.
[6] *Foedera*, I. ii. 679, 690.
[7] SC 1/13, no. 12.
[8] SC 1/13, no. 38.
[9] SC 1/55, no. 6.
[10] *Foedera*, I. ii. 794.

prevalent romantic culture'.[11] The paintings were described in 1323, somewhat inaccurately, as showing 'all the warlike stories of the whole Bible', but their predominantly martial character may tell us something about the ethos of Edward's household in the 1290s.[12] A re-assertion of identification with the Plantagenet past also took place at this time. In December 1291 Edward confirmed and renewed his Plantagenet predecessors' grants of privileges to the abbey of Fontevrault, and Henry III's heart was dispatched for burial there.[13] An undated letter from the abbess to Edward, probably written at this juncture, wished him prosperity in his negotiations and reminded him that four of his ancestors were buried in the house.[14] His progress of 1286–9 through France and Gascony had been an opportunity to renew existing associations and establish new ones, and Edward's liberality towards religious houses and shrines, and the splendour of his entourage, did not pass unnoticed.[15] The otherwise robustly pro-Capetian Guillaume Guiart, in his *Branche des royaux lignages*, left his French audience in no doubt of the quality of Edward's warhorses and of the largesse which he distributed.[16] The young Philip the Fair was to some extent upstaged by Edward, as elder statesman, when the latter took the Cross during the chapter-general of the Dominicans at Bordeaux in May 1287, preoccupied all the while with the search for peace between Aragon and Anjou as a necessary condition for the crusade.[17]

Why, if Edward I consistently sought peace, did Anglo-French relations degenerate from relative harmony into outright hostility in 1294? The answer to that question lies in a series of closely inter-related problems which are difficult to disentangle. They might, crudely and artificially, be isolated under the following headings: Aragon, Gascony, Charles of Valois and Robert of Artois. Edward's dealings with the Crown of Aragon, in its rivalry with the house of Anjou for the kingdom of Sicily, should be assessed in the light of French humiliation after the disastrous 'Aragonese crusade' of 1285, when an invading French army was overwhelmingly defeated.[18] By negotiating a truce between Philip the Fair and Alfonso of Aragon at Oloron in July 1287, followed by the release of Charles of Salerno, son of Charles of Anjou, titular king of Sicily, by the Treaty of Canfran in October 1288, Edward reversed the previous roles of the French and English

[11] P. Binski, *The Painted Chamber at Westminster* (Soc. of Antiquaries of London Occasional Paper, new ser., ix, 1986), 19–21, 71–80, 82: Edward's court 'resonated as a source of new imagery, particularly the new, secular imagery of romance and chivalry'.

[12] Binski, 1, 96–103.

[13] *Foedera*, I. ii. 758.

[14] SC 1/17, no. 120; E 101/160/1, m. 2r (oblations to the house, 1303–5); J-P. Trabut-Cussac, 'Itinéraire d'Edouard Ier en France, 1286–1289', *BIHR* xxv (1952), 168, for Edward at Fontevrault on 1 Sept. 1286.

[15] Trabut-Cussac, 'Itinéraire', 168, 173–4, 175, 184 for some of Edward's oblations; also E 36/201, pp. 93–4; Guillaume Guiart, *Branche des royaux lignages*, ed. J. A. Buchon (Paris, 1828), ii. lines 3732–43.

[16] Guiart, lines 3735–7; M. G. A. Vale, 'The Gascon Nobility and the Anglo-French War, 1294–98', in *War and Government in the Middle Ages. Essays in Honour of J. O. Prestwich*, ed. J. Gillingham and J. C. Holt (Woodbridge, 1984), 144–5.

[17] Powicke, 251–2; J-P. Trabut-Cussac, *L'Administration anglaise en Gascogne sous Henry III et Edouard I de 1254 à 1307* (Geneva, Paris, 1972), 83–92.

[18] J. R. Strayer, *The Reign of Philip the Fair* (Princeton, 1980), 368–70; J. Petit, *Charles de Valois, 1270–1325* (Paris, 1900), 9–11.

monarchies in diplomatic arbitration.[19] The treaties of Oloron and Canfran were perhaps not quite the equivalent of St. Louis's Mise of Amiens (1264) or his other arbitrations, but the fact that one who was technically a vassal of the French Crown was now intervening in this manner in Philip IV's affairs could not pass unnoticed, nor unanswered, by the French. There can, furthermore, be little doubt of Edward's popularity among at least some of the Aragonese nobility. Powicke's observations that Edward was the 'hero of the troubadours of the South', and 'a bulwark against the hateful encroachments of the French', seem borne out by the eagerness of Catalan nobles to serve him in war.[20] In April 1294 one of them referred to his presence in Edward's company at Oloron in 1287 during the arbitration proceedings, and to the king's great generosity towards him on that occasion.[21] This is a theme to which I shall return.

The second area of tension was Gascony. Was Edward, as has often been argued, content to work within the limits set upon him by his father's treaty of 1259 with Louis IX? Powicke certainly thought so. Edward, he wrote, 'had no political ambitions dangerous to the continuance of peace and was punctilious in his observance of every feudal duty except the doubtful requirement to provide military service against his friends and relatives in Castile and Aragon'.[22] His evasive action in 1282 and 1285, when his military support never went to the French, was no doubt uppermost in Powicke's mind.[23] But it could be argued that Edward was striving to undo, or at least limit, the more damaging effects of a treaty which, at least initially, he had vigorously opposed. The homage which he performed to Philip IV in July 1286 was couched in a conditional form and was dependent upon French implementation of their part in the Treaty of Paris.[24] His acquisition of both the Agenais and the *comté* of Ponthieu at Amiens in 1279, and of southern Saintonge in 1286, had substantially extended his continental power base, while the marriage of his brother Edmund to Blanche of Artois in 1275 had given him a further northern French foothold in Champagne.[25] His perambulation of his French lands in the years 1286 – 9 had produced administrative reforms and ordinances for the government of Gascony.[26] The creation of a new appellate jurisdiction within the duchy of Aquitaine, which attempted to by-pass the *parlement* of Paris and the court of the French seneschal of Périgord entirely, could only have been considered as a threat by the French.[27] By June 1293, for example, two Gascon lords promised, on pain of forfeiting all their possessions, to obey his will without challenge or appeal in a case of robbery with violence.[28] There were also signs of greater friction

[19] *Foedera*, I. ii. 679, 690; Trabut-Cussac, *L'Administration anglaise*, 81 – 92.

[20] Powicke, *Henry III*, ii. 688.

[21] *Foedera*, I. ii. 797.

[22] Powicke, *Thirteenth Century*, 271.

[23] P. Chaplais, 'Le duché-pairie de Guyenne: l'hommage et les services féodaux de 1259 à 1303'; in id., *Essays in Medieval Diplomacy and Administration* (London, 1981), no. III, 20 – 3.

[24] *Foedera*, I. ii. 665; Chaplais, 'Le duché-pairie', 24 – 5.

[25] Powicke, *Thirteenth Century*, 239, 241 – 3.

[26] Trabut-Cussac, *L'Administration anglaise*, 93 – 101.

[27] Trabut-Cussac, *L'Administration anglaise*, 275 – 80; P. Chaplais, 'Les appels gascons au roi d'Angleterre sous le règne d'Edouard Ier (1272 – 1307)', in id., *Essays in Medieval Diplomacy*, no. VI, 382 – 8.

[28] *Gascon Register A (Series of 1318 – 19)*, ed. G. P. Cuttino and J-P. Trabut-Cussac (Oxford, 1975 – 6), ii. no. 193 (pp. 533 – 4).

over the question of Edward's homage to Philip the Fair for Aquitaine and Ponthieu in July 1286. Robert Burnell's speech to the French court at Paris on that occasion was in effect a warning: many of Edward's counsellors, he said, had advised him to dispute ('debatre') the terms of his homage because the treaty of 1259 had not been fulfilled, and because certain 'surprises' ('supprises') had been effected by the French in his lands. He was not yet prepared to act on that advice, awaiting Philip IV's action in remedying these abuses.[29] But the note of defiance had been sounded, and a substantial dossier of complaints could be compiled, largely from the inhabitants of lands held of Edward by the count of Armagnac and the archbishop of Auch on the eastern borders of his duchy of Aquitaine.[30]

We know with hindsight that no viable solution to the Gascon problem was to emerge until Edward III's assumption of the Crown of France broke off all feudal ties with the French in 1340. Yet the question might have been settled in the 1290s if the terms of a notorious unsealed agreement of February 1294 had been put into effect. This was the so-called 'secret treaty' between Philip IV and Edward I, negotiated through the mediation of Edward's female relatives at the French court.[31] The fact that its terms were not effected may tell us much about resistance to a settlement among at least some of Philip's entourage. The treaty was never sealed, although the original French copy in the Archives Nationales has holes for sealing cords but no clause of attestation. It bears the endorsements 'Non est ibi sigillum' and the words (in a later hand): 'Certain conventions ('convenciones') which the king of England's men requested . . . before the war, but the lord king [Philip IV] refused to consent to them'.[32] One can understand why. If implemented, the agreement would have effectively created a quasi-independent hereditary principality, or apanage, of Aquitaine, to be held by the children of a proposed marriage between Edward I and Philip's sister, Margaret of France. The thorny issue of Gascon appeals was to be settled in Edward's favour by the removal of those exemptions from ducal jurisdiction which had previously been granted to Gascon appellants. The French royal *pennonceaux*, symbolic of Capetian protection and safeguard, would no longer fly over appellants' castles, town houses or *maisons-fortes*.[33] A major cause of Anglo-French tension would be removed at a stroke. Should an appeal against Edward's or his heirs' justice succeed, there must be no dispossession of the king-duke. Should the impending marriage prove childless, all these concessions were to apply, after his father's death, to Edward, prince of Wales, as heir to Aquitaine during his lifetime.[34] By creating a new line of dukes of Aquitaine, who were to perform homage to the king of England, not France, the 'secret treaty' grasped the nettle which the peace of 1259 had sown, and effectively crushed it. Aquitaine would be held at one remove, as it were, from the reigning English monarch, whose majesty would in no way be offended or embarrassed by vassalic status or by the ceremony of homage. Anglo-French relations might thenceforward be conducted on a basis of equality.

---

[29] *Foedera*, I. ii. 665.
[30] SC 1/23, no. 114; SC 1/13, no. 17; SC 1/12, no. 38; SC 1/18, nos. 53 – 4, 55, 58; C 47/29/3.
[31] *Foedera*, I. ii. 795 – 6; Archives Nationales, J 631, no. 7.
[32] Archives Nationales, J 631, no. 7; Chaplais, *English Medieval Diplomatic Practice* (London, 1980), ii. 418 – 20.
[33] *Foedera*, I. ii. 795 – 6 (cl. xvi).
[34] *Foedera*, I. ii. 796 (cl. xxiii).

In the event, the two rulers went to war over Aquitaine at a time when a solution to the Gascon issue had actually been formulated. Historians have given primacy to Anglo-French conflict on the seas in their analysis of the outbreak of hostilities.[35] Maritime friction was not a novel problem in 1292 – 3, but historians are undeniably right in stressing the cardinal importance of a dispute between Norman and Gascon sailors and shipowners in the series of events which led to Philip IV's confiscation of Aquitaine. This conflict flared up into open war on the seas and led to the sack of La Rochelle by the men of Bayonne in 1293. Philip certainly spoke of the maritime dispute as a *casus belli* in his letter citing Edward I, as immediate lord of the Bayonnais, to reply to certain grave charges.[36] French sources spoke of a desire to recover Normandy as a motive for Anglo-Gascon aggression on the seas,[37] but Edward's concern for former Norman and Plantagenet possessions on the Continent seems confined to a somewhat vague statement, in his alliance with Adolf of Nassau in October 1294, that Philip IV and his ancestors had unjustly occupied 'our goods, lands and fiefs and those of our predecessors *a multo tempore*'.[38]

Whatever the case, the involvement of the Bayonnais in the war at sea could not be ignored by Edward. Bayonne and its shipping was vital to English interests; its fleet carried Bordeaux and other Gascon wine to England. It was to receive its own 'admiral and captain of ships and mariners' in Barrau de Sescars, knight (1295 – 7), and it formed an essential part of English maritime resources which stretched from the Bay of Biscay to the Tweed.[39] In October 1295,[40] for example, a Bayonnais ship brought a cargo of almonds, Malaga raisins and figs to England from north Africa. The Bayonnais were the carriers of the wine trade — for Bordeaux was not a great shipping port at this time — and they were important enough to be considered almost as a maritime power in their own right in mercantile treaties made by Edward with other rulers and their subjects.[41] Bayonne was a wealthy community: witness the large loans offered by its citizens to the embattled Plantagenet regime in Gascony between 1296 and 1298; it provided the king-duke with manpower as well as money, and was well placed for dealings with the Iberian kingdoms.[42] In 1287 – 8 Edward had found the loyalty of the Bayonnais especially valuable, for eight of the twenty-seven Gascon hostages whom he offered as sureties for the execution of the treaties of Oloron and Canfran with Aragon were citizens of Bayonne.[43] On their subsequent arrest by the French in 1293, Edward especially desired that his Bayonnais subjects be well treated, and not delivered to French officers (such as Jean D'Arrablaye, seneschal of Périgord, or Etienne de Beaumarchais, seneschal of Toulouse) who were known to be malevolent towards

[35] Powicke, *Thirteenth Century*, 644 – 6; Strayer, 317 – 18; C. de la Roncière, 'Le blocus continental de l'Angleterre sous Philippe le Bel', *Revue des Questions Historiques*, ix (1896), 401 – 8.
[36] *Les Olim ou Registre des Arrêts rendus par la cour du roi*, ed. A Beugnot (Paris, 1839), ii. 5 – 6.
[37] Guiart, lines 454 – 8; Petit, 27 – 8.
[38] *Treaty Rolls Preserved in the PRO, I (1234 – 1325)*, ed. P. Chaplais (London, 1956), no. 231.
[39] *Foedera*, I. ii. 795; C 47/27/3, no. 34; *Rôles Gascons*, ed. C. Bémont (Paris, 1896 – 1906), iii. nos. 3883, 4134, 4477; and p. clxxxix.
[40] *Foedera*, I. ii. 828.
[41] *CPR 1281 – 92*, 58, 59, 64; C 47/29/4, no. 26(b).
[42] Trabut-Cussac, *L'Administration anglaise*, 117 – 18; and see the numerous receipts and quittances for loans during the period 1294 – 8: E 101/152 – 5.
[43] *Foedera*, I. ii. 690.

them.[44] After the war of 1294 – 7 a loan of £50,000 from Bayonne was the only sum which Edward seems ever fully to have repaid during his lifetime.[45] Bayonne's inhabitants could never be ignored by him, nor could he afford to alienate them.

It is clear, however, that the maritime conflict formed only one link in the chain of events which led to the Anglo-French war of 1294. I hope to discuss the causes of the war in greater detail elsewhere, but suffice it to say here that complete dispossession of Edward as duke of Aquitaine appeared to be a major objective of French activity from the outset. It has been claimed by Professor Strayer that Philip IV 'began to develop a policy of his own during the early 1290s; a policy of strongly asserting royal rights against the Church and his greatest vassals, the king of England and the count of Flanders'.[46] There *is* evidence for the strenuous assertion of royal rights at this time, but Philip's own part in this policy remains unclear. French incursions into Bigorre, Saintonge, the lands of Armagnac and elsewhere in the south-west in the early 1290s culminated in the occupation of the greater part of the duchy of Aquitaine in 1294.[47] Philip IV was treating Bordeaux as *his* town by August 1294, when he annexed it to the French Crown and awarded it privileges.[48] Bayonne, if it had not held out for Edward, would undoubtedly have been treated in a similar manner. Philip had omitted, moreover, to address Edward as duke of Aquitaine in his citation before the *parlement* in October 1293 and was subsequently to refer to him merely as 'tenans ducatum Aquitanie'.[49] This makes the terms of the 'secret treaty' of February 1294 all the more puzzling. A public stance of aggressive denial of right and status was, it was claimed, masking private readiness to compromise and concede on Philip's part.[50] The personal political role of Philip the Fair has always been an historical enigma and I have no wish to enter that minefield at this point. But even if we are sceptical, with Favier and Bautier,[51] of the king's capacity and willingness to formulate and initiate policy, a pertinent question remains: who, if anyone, stood to gain from an Anglo-French war over Aquitaine in 1293 – 4? Who, if anyone, among the politically powerful in France was hostile to Edward I and his subjects?

We have, I think, at least two candidates for that honourable position, both princes of the blood, both antagonistic towards the Plantagenets. The first is Charles of Valois, Philip IV's brother; the second is Robert II, count of Artois. The English chroniclers accused Charles of Valois of stirring up hostility towards England in 1293 – 4. The annals of Dunstable claimed that 'he pursued the English with an inveterate hatred', while both Walter of Guisborough and the annals of London reported that he was the instigator of the naval battles between the Normans

---

[44] *Les Olim*, ii. 9; C 47/29/3, no. 10; *Rôles Gascons*, iii. no. 4508.

[45] M. Prestwich, *War, Politics and Finance under Edward I* (London, 1972), 213; Vale, 'Gascon Nobility', 134 – 5; SC 8/291, no. 14,538.

[46] Strayer, 49 – 50.

[47] Archives Nationales, J 631, no. 10 (Bigorre); E 101/152/6 (Armagnac); Archives Nationales J 294, no. 13 (Bigorre); Archives Départementales des Pyrénées Atlantiques, E 371, nos. 4, 8 (Bigorre).

[48] C 47/27/3, no. 7; Archives Nationales, J 631, no. 20.

[49] Chaplais, *Diplomatic Practice*, ii. 417.

[50] *Foedera*, I. ii. 794.

[51] J. Favier, *Philippe le Bel* (Paris, 1978), 2 – 5; R-H. Bautier, 'Diplomatique et histoire politique: ce que la critique diplomatique nous apprend sur la personnalité de Philippe le Bel', *Revue Historique*, dcxxv (1978), 3 – 27; cf. Strayer, x – xi, 31 – 2: 'Philip . . . had many able advisers, but he made the final decisions'.

and Anglo-Gascons.[52] The Lanercost Chronicle went so far as to allege that he desired to supplant his brother as king of France, and hated the English because Edward I supported Philip.[53] His anti-English sentiments were confirmed by the subsequent marriage of his daughter to Edward Balliol, eldest son of the king of Scotland, in October 1295.[54] Chroniclers' rumour-mongering apart, why should Charles of Valois seek to exacerbate Anglo-French tension? Strayer observes that 'it is difficult to see what Charles had to gain from the war, and he was not one of Philip's most influential councillors'.[55] Favier takes an opposing view on the latter point: 'au Conseil, le comte de Valois parle le premier, et il parle haut'.[56] His political importance was in effect sustained by the fact that he was Philip IV's sole surviving brother by Philip III's first wife, Isabella of Aragon, and thus had a special place in Philip's affections. But he had also been invested with the kingdom of Aragon by the papacy in 1283. Strayer comments that he 'had been addressed as a king when he was still in his teens and had never quite recovered from the experience'.[57] The French war with Aragon of 1284 – 5 was conducted in his name and on his behalf by his father Philip III. Moreover, his title to Aragon was not formally renounced until 20 June 1295, one year after the French occupation of Aquitaine.[58] It could be argued that any hostility that Charles felt towards Edward I stemmed from Edward's opposition to the Aragonese war, declared in February 1284, because of the marriage contracted between his daughter and Alfonso of Aragon. Edward's consequent arbitration of the Angevin-Aragonese dispute effectively deprived Charles of Valois of his Aragonese title, and the ignominious end to the war left him, as Italian chroniclers were pleased to point out, as 'Carlo senza Terra' — Charles the Landless.[59] No doubt the counties of Maine, Anjou, Alençon, and Chartres granted to him by his brother between 1290 and 1293,[60] and his place in the sun at the French court, were some compensation, but he did not wear a crown.

If Charles of Valois's claims to Aragon still held good in 1293 – 4, then he had a definite interest in the affairs of south-west France. The previous French campaign of 1284 – 5 had foundered on poor communications and supply lines, partly caused by French loss of control of the sea.[61] Gascony was an alternative point of entry into Aragon, and Bayonne might serve as a port through which supplies could be channelled via Béarn or Navarre. The Lanercost Chronicle emphasized Philip IV's action in entrusting the custody and defence of Gascony in 1295 to Charles of Valois, who led the campaign there against Anglo-Gascon resistance.[62] The French

---

[52] Petit, 27 – 8; Annals of Dunstable, in *Ann. Mon.* iii. 385; Hemingburgh, *Chronicon*, ed. H. C. Hamilton (London, 1849), ii. 42 – 5; *Chronicles of the Reigns of Edward I and II*, ed. W. Stubbs (RS, London, 1882 – 3), ii. 101.

[53] *Chronicon de Lanercost*, ed. J. Stevenson (Edinburgh, 1839), 150 – 1.

[54] *Foedera*, I. ii. 831.

[55] Strayer, 318.

[56] Favier, 14.

[57] Strayer, 369.

[58] Petit, 22; J. N. Hillgarth, *The Spanish Kingdoms, 1250 – 1516* (Oxford, 1976), i. 264.

[59] Petit, 23; *Foedera*, I. ii. 227 – 8.

[60] Petit, 19, 24 – 5.

[61] J. R. Strayer, 'The Crusade against Aragon', in *Medieval Statecraft and the Perspectives of History: Essays by Joseph R. Strayer*, ed. J. F. Benton and T. N. Bisson (Princeton, 1971), 107 – 22.

[62] *Chron. de Lanercost*, 156; Petit, 28 – 31; Archives Nationales, J 164b, no. 58 bis.

were still very nervous about Aragon in the early 1300s, charging Bernard Saisset, bishop of Pamiers, with attempting to arrange a marriage in 1295 – 6 between Roger-Bernard, son of the count of Foix, and a daughter of the king of Aragon, against French interests in the Languedoc.[63] With Bayonne firmly holding out for Edward I, and his army stricken in May – June 1295 with an epidemic while besieging St. Sever — the key to the southernmost reaches of the duchy —, Charles's ambitions were once again thwarted.[64] But he had come within a short distance of realizing one of his aims.

There was clearly an anti-Plantagenet group or faction within the council of Philip IV. This may have been dominant in the early 1290s. How far Philip was able, or indeed willing, to control that faction remains unclear. The evidence of Edmund of Lancaster's letter to Edward I in 1294 suggests that he was not.[65] Like Philip VI of Valois in the early 1330s, Philip IV's control of his own counsellors may have been tenuous, and the statement by Edmund of Lancaster that the surrender of Aquitaine by Edward's officers was to be countermanded by Philip 'when some of his counsellors had departed' is revealing.[66] To whom did this refer? The finger points towards Charles of Valois, and towards royal lawyers such as Pierre Flote, who was also known for his anti-English sentiments. Flote had been active in the annexation of Bigorre by the French in 1293 – 4, in the proclamation of Philip's citation to Edward in the duchy of Aquitaine, and in preparing for war in Saintonge and northern Aquitaine.[67] He had been overseeing the garrisoning and repair of castles at Mauretain, Pons, Saintes and Blaye on the eve of Philip's confiscation of the duchy.[68] With Raoul de Nesle, constable of France, Flote, Charles of Valois and, as we shall see, Robert of Artois, all opposed to a settlement with Edward, the royal will was in a decidedly weak position — if, that is, Philip ever really intended to implement the 'secret treaty'. If Charles of Valois had the upper hand in French policy at this date, some puzzling aspects of Anglo-French affairs are perhaps resolved. In a contemporary poem on the treason of Thomas Turberville (an English knight captured, with others, by Charles of Valois at Rions in Gascony on 7 April 1295) there are constant references to a 'messire Charles', 'le bon chevalier', as if he were king of France.[69] Sir Goronwy Edwards was perplexed by the fact that the poem's author did not seem to know that Philip IV was on the French throne. Such allusions would be rendered comprehensible if in fact they referred not to Philip but to his brother Charles. The intercepted letter written by Turberville to Guillaume de Hangest, *prévôt* of Paris, in (August?) 1295, giving classified information to the French about Edward I's plans and movements,

[63] P. Dupuy, *Histoire du differénd d'entre le pape Boniface VIII et Philippe le Bel* (Paris, 1655), 632 – 3, 634, 646, 653 – 6.
[64] Petit, 29 – 31.
[65] *Foedera*, I. ii. 794 – 5.
[66] *Foedera*, I. ii. 795.
[67] *Comptes Royaux, 1285 – 1314*, ed. R. Fawtier and F. Maillard (Paris, 1953 – 6), i. 9989; 7681, 7699 – 700, 7731, 7732, 7959, 10,064; *Les Olim*, ii. 13, 21.
[68] *Comptes Royaux*, i. 7982 – 7, 7972 – 82, 8064. See also J. G. Black, 'Edward I and Gascony in 1300', *EHR* xvii (1902), 523 for Flote's reported remarks to Boniface VIII on the dispossession of Edward by the French of his continental lands.
[69] *Chron. Lanercost*, 484 – 7.

speaks of 'le haut seigneur'.[70] Historians have normally assumed that this refers to Philip IV, but Turberville was Charles of Valois's prisoner, and his anxiety about the welfare of his sons, held hostage in France while he spied in England, might make more sense if Charles was his, and their, captor.[71] Charles's brutal treatment of the Gascon members of the garrison at Rions, whom he executed, did not bode well for the safety of Turberville's children.[72]

Active intervention in Anglo-French issues by supporters of Valois interests at the court of France could only lead to war. Charles of Valois was probably responsible for provoking that war, and the accusation levelled by the French against certain Gascon subjects of Edward I rings true: they were alleged to have killed some Normans and French customs collectors in the duchy 'to spite the king of France and his brother Charles'.[73] French infiltration into Aquitaine and on its frontiers — at Blaye, Bourg and Fronsac in the north, and in Bigorre and the *pays d'Armagnac* to the south — had already begun before the outbreak of war in 1294.[74] It was not the result of accident or the fortuitous ebb and flow of events. Some Catalan nobles professed themselves disappointed that war had not broken out between Philip IV and Edward by December 1293, as they had anticipated.[75] The strong anti-French sentiments of the count of Urgel, of Artoldus of Alagone, and of other Aragonese nobles were no doubt fuelled by memories of the French invasion of 1284 – 5, and Edward received at least thirteen offers of service from them, with men-at-arms and foot serjeants, in March and April 1294.[76] One of them said he would serve Edward against the French 'to the death', while others appear to have been offering simultaneous service in the French war or a crusade under Edward's leadership.[77] Events in the *pays d'Armagnac* and the Agenais during 1293 had evidently led to rumours of an Anglo-French war as Edward's lieutenant, Sir John St. John, mobilized forces, bribed the count of Armagnac and resisted all French efforts to exercise any form of sovereignty over Aquitaine.[78] There were many other issues at stake besides the maritime conflict which were to precipitate Anglo-French war. It could be argued that Edward I's *de facto* sovereignty over Aquitaine was a standing provocation in the eyes of an influential party within the French royal council, especially when it stood in the way of Valois ambitions. As

[70] J. G. Edwards, 'The Treason of Thomas Turberville, 1295', in *Studies in Medieval History Presented to F. M. Powicke*, ed. R. W. Hunt, W. A. Pantin and R. W. Southern (Oxford, 1948), 296 – 309, esp. 296, n. 4. The letter is printed on pp. 298 – 9 from Bartholomew Cotton, *Historia Anglicana*, ed. H. Luard (RS, 1850), 304 – 6. For Guillaume de Hangest as *prévôt* of Paris, in 1295, see Archives Départmentales de Pas-de-Calais, A 38, no. 12b.

[71] Edwards, 'Treason of Thomas Turberville', 299, 300.

[72] Petit, 28, 29.

[73] *Les Olim*, ii. 7, 15, 19 – 20; cf. SC 8/291, no. 14,521 for a different story from the Anglo-Gascon side.

[74] See above, n. 47; *Comptes Royaux*, i. 8056.

[75] *Foedera*, I. ii. 707 – 8, 807.

[76] SC 1/14, no. 147; SC 1/16, nos. 17 – 19; SC 1/20, no. 5; *Foedera*, I. ii. 797 – 8.

[77] *Foedera*, I. ii. 797; he would serve Edward 'usque ad mortem'; and see ibid. 787, 793, 798 for offers of service on crusade. For payments of war wages to these Aragonese nobles for militaray service against the French in 1295 – 8, see E 101/152/8, no. 36; E 101/153/1, no. 23; *Rôles Gascons*, iii. clxxxiv – clxxxv, clxxxviii, nos. 4478, 4479, 4486.

[78] Trabut-Cussac, *L'Administration anglaise*, 109; E 101/152/6, nos. 1, 2, 4; E 101/208/1, nos. B 1, A 8. See also Archives Nationales, J 631, nos. 10(1) and (2), for a French summons to the count of Armagnac to perform homage at Paris (Dec. 1293).

subsequent events were to show, there were also strong acquisitive instincts at work among the vassals, clients, allies and dependants of French magnates which were met by the grant to them of lands, rents and offices in Aquitaine during the occupation of 1294 – 1303.[79]

The history of that occupation is largely unwritten. A central figure in the French campaigns and their aftermath, however, was Robert II, count of Artois. Suspicious of Edward I's intentions since about 1275, hostile to the extension of Plantagenet interests in France, and especially vulnerable to English aggression on the seas through his possession of Calais and St. Omer, Robert replaced Charles of Valois as Philip IV's lieutenant in the south-west in 1296.[80] Yet his part in the preliminaries to war cannot be overlooked. The volume of expenditure which he incurred on the Calais garrison between August 1293 and March 1294 was unusual, and it suggests that the garrison had already been put on a war footing.[81] On 29 June 1294 payments are already found in the Artois accounts for war service at Calais against Edward, 'segneur des Engles'.[82] Edward had renounced his homage to Philip IV in letters dated 20 June.[83] Early in 1294 Robert of Artois had received most of the French court at Hesdin and Creil, where the future Charles IV was baptised.[84] Charles of Valois was there, and we might speculate whether the plan to deceive Edmund of Lancaster and dispossess Edward I of Aquitaine was conceived on that occasion. The unsealed 'secret treaty' was drawn up in February 1294, immediately after the visit of Charles of Valois and other counsellors to Robert of Artois. We know that Robert held an influential place among Philip IV's advisers. In November 1294, the *Grandes Chroniques* report, the French reply to Edward I's ally, Adolf of Nassau, took the form of a blank parchment on which were written two words: 'Troup Alemant'. This, it was said, was the work of Robert of Artois, as contemptuous of a German princeling as he was hostile to a Plantagenet rival for the sovereignty of France.[85]

The Anglo-French war marked something of a watershed in relations between the two powers. Although the family relationship between the ruling houses was maintained, harmony and stability were never fully regained. The aftermath of Edward I's involvement as an impartial arbiter in Angevin-Aragonese affairs proved destructive of Anglo-French peace. Great magnates around the throne of France pursued their particularist ambitions to the detriment of Anglo-French relations. Although French marriages were arranged for both Edward and his son, these did not lead to a full and complete reconciliation after 1303. The note of

[79] *Rôles Gascons*, iii. clxv – clxxxii, cxc; Archives Nationales, J 78, fos. 12v – 13v for confiscations and valuations of land in Gascony by the French (1297 – 1300).
[80] Powicke, *Thirteenth Century*, 239; Archives Départementales de Pas-de-Calais, A 41, nos. 12 – 18 for Philip IV's letters appointing him to the lieutenancy of Gascony and the duchy of Aquitaine (15 – 16 Apr. 1296).
[81] Archives Départementales de Pas-de-Calais, A 38, nos. 72, 74, 78; A 40, no. 23; A 136, nos. 162 – 4 (Aug. 1293 – Mar. 1294).
[82] Ibid. A 39, no. 28.
[83] *Foedera*, I. ii. 807; Chaplais, *Diplomatic Practice*, ii. 418.
[84] Archives Départementales de Pas-de-Calais, A 134, no. 19; A 135, nos. 18 – 20; Petit, 26.
[85] R. Fawtier, 'Un incident diplomatique franco-allemand au temps de Philippe le Bel', *Annuaire-Bulletin de la Société de l'Histoire de France* (1946 – 7), 27 – 38. The reply is very reminiscent of Louis VI of France's retort to the emperor — 'Tpwrut Aleman' as reported by Walter Map, *De Nugis Curialium*, ed. M. R. James (Oxford, 1914), 228 – 9.

impatience and irritation found in Edward's letter of 16 September 1302 to Henry Lacy, earl of Lincoln, and to Amadeus, count of Savoy, his envoys to France, is striking.[86] The king of France, he said, had already put off the day of agreement to terms of peace 'seven or eight times', and Edward can wait no longer. He has summoned parliament and cannot tolerate any further delays in their deliberations at Hesdin. With Scottish affairs still in the melting pot an *entente* with France was unlikely to prove lasting. It was the election of Clement V as pope in 1305 which was, perhaps, in part responsible for the notable fact that there was no Anglo-French war until 1324. Mediation by Gascon popes from Avignon succeeded where Celestine V and Boniface VIII had failed. Robert of Artois and Pierre Flote met their deaths in the carnage at the battle of Courtrai in July 1302, while Charles of Valois sought a crown in Italy and the Empire, without success. Philip the Fair's attention turned towards religiosity, Flanders and the destruction of the Templars. The passing of the *dramatis personae* of the early 1290s may have helped to guarantee some measure of peace between England and France. Former rivalries remained, but they were far less envenomed by antipathy between individuals, stemming from the pursuit of self-interest. Yet the origins of Valois hostility to England, and of the rival claims of Plantagenet and Valois to the French Crown, may be sought between 1285 and 1307. The French occupation of the duchy of Aquitaine between 1294 and 1303 left a tenurial disarray that was never properly resolved and which contributed to Anglo-French tensions. It has recently been argued that the so-called Hundred Years War lasted until the reign of Henry VIII. We might also, I suggest, question traditional interpretations, which seek its origins in the Treaty of Paris of 1259. In that process of revision, the reign of Edward I, and especially its latter part, is worthy of closer attention.

[86] SC 1/13, no. 109.